ALSO BY RICHARD THOMPSON FORD

Racial Culture: A Critique

THE RACE CARD

THE RACE CARD

HOW BLUFFING ABOUT BIAS MAKES RACE RELATIONS WORSE

RICHARD THOMPSON FORD

FARRAR, STRAUS AND GIROUX ■ NEW YORK

Farrar, Straus and Giroux
18 West 18th Street, New York 10011

Distributed in Canada by Douglas & McIntyre, Ltd.
Printed in the United States of America
First edition, 2008

Grateful acknowledgment is made for permission to reprint the following material: Selection from *When Work Disappears* by William Julius Wilson, copyright © 1996 by William Julius Wilson, used by permission of Alfred A. Knopf, a division of Random House, Inc. Excerpts from *Radical Chic & Mau-Mauing the Flak Catchers* by Tom Wolfe, copyright © 1970, renewed 1999 by Tom Wolfe. Reprinted by permission of Farrar, Straus and Giroux, LLC.

Library of Congress Cataloging-in-Publication Data
Ford, Richard T. (Richard Thompson)
    The race card : how bluffing about bias makes race relations worse / Richard
    Thompson
Ford. — 1st ed.
      p.   cm.
    ISBN-13: 978-0-374-24575-7 (hardcover : alk. paper)
    ISBN-10: 0-374-24575-4 (hardcover : alk. paper)
    1. African Americans—Social conditions.   2. Racism—United States.   3. United
States—Race relations.   4. Malicious accusation—United States.   I. Title.

EL85.86.F65 2008
305.896'073—dc22   2007021443

Designed by Debbie Glasserman

www.fsgbooks.com

10   9   8   7   6   5   4   3   2   1

In memory of Richard Donald Ford

■ CONTENTS

THE RACE CARD

■ INTRODUCTION
PLAYING THE RACE CARD

In November 1987, a deputy sheriff was dispatched to an apartment building in Dutchess County, upstate New York. There a resident of the building led him to a large plastic garbage bag that contained a seemingly unconscious Tawana Brawley. Brawley's body was smeared with feces, her clothes were torn, the crotch burned away from her jeans, and she was not wearing a bra or underwear. An ambulance was dispatched, and Brawley was taken to the hospital. When her clothes were removed, the markings were stark and unambiguous: the words "nigger," "bitch," and "KKK" were scrawled on Brawley's torso in black charcoal.[1]

The sheriff's office, sensing that they were in over their heads, called the FBI to report a likely civil rights violation. Doctors examined Brawley for injuries and evidence of rape. They found neither. Brawley could not—or refused to—speak to hospital staff and detectives about what had happened. Eventually, communicating by nodding and shaking her head, she indicated that she had been raped by several men. Then came the bombshell. When asked if she could identify the attackers, the silent Brawley scrawled two words on a piece of paper: "white cop."

When Brawley was released from the hospital, her family thought a warm bed and an interview with a New York City television station might help her to rest and recover. Against the advice of the hospital social worker, her mother and aunt publicized the horrifying story. They did so, they said, out of fear that the incident would be covered up by a racist law enforcement establishment.

The last thing they needed to worry about was too *little* publicity. The family enlisted (or was conscripted by) lawyers Alton Maddox and C. Vernon Mason and the Reverend Al Sharpton. Thereafter, "Brawley's story" (she never told her own story publicly, which gave her representatives plenty of, let's say, interpretive license) was the featured topic of discussion on innumerable news and current events programs, including the archetype of talk TV, *The Phil Donahue Show*, and its downmarket competitor, *The Morton Downey Jr. Show*. Sharpton—not Brawley—named names, accusing a local police officer, who later committed suicide, and assistant district attorney Steven Pagones, who later successfully sued Sharpton for defamation. Sharpton—not Brawley—spun a conspiracy theory worthy of its own X File, implicating the Irish Republican Army, the Cosa Nostra, New York governor Mario Cuomo, and a mysterious man with a missing finger.[2] (Could Dr. Richard Kimble's one-armed man have been out of the loop?)

Something was badly awry. Even without Sharpton's embellishments, Brawley's story—to the extent that she told one—didn't jibe. Witnesses saw her climb into the garbage bag herself after looking around furtively. All of the materials necessary to stage the assault were found in her old apartment. She was seen at a party shortly before she was discovered by police. When examined at the hospital, she showed no signs of exposure despite subfreezing temperatures, suggesting that she hadn't been outside for long. Brawley never had the chance to explain these discrepancies, and she never *had* to explain them: on the advice of her lawyers, she refused to cooperate with police and prosecutors, so she never gave a detailed account of events. She was spirited away to undisclosed locations while her handlers gave incendiary interviews to the press and spun race-baiting conspiracy theories. Sharpton, in a heartwarming display of sensitivity, said that asking Brawley to meet with New York's Jewish attorney general would be like asking a Holocaust survivor "to sit down with Mr. Hitler."[3]

A grand jury found no evidence of wrongdoing and concluded that the whole affair was probably a hoax. To this day we cannot know whether Brawley was assaulted by someone—named or unnamed, known to her or unknown—whether she was cajoled or pressured into playing a role in an elaborately orchestrated hoax, or whether she just made the whole thing up. Owing in large part to the exploitation of the case by her lawyers and handlers, any truth is so intermeshed with a tissue of lies that there's no separating the two. As a result, "Brawley's story" is still available for charlatans and demagogues to cite as evidence of an elaborate white racist conspiracy. For such people and those who believe them, the Tawana Brawley incident is a reason to resist law enforcement, to distrust the criminal justice system, and to secede from mainstream society into black separatist cults such as Louis Farrakhan's Nation of Islam. (Farrakhan has vowed vengeance on Brawley's attackers: "You raped my daughter, and I will kill you and dismember your body and feed it to the fowl of the air," he frothed.[4]) But for most people, whatever else it was, the Tawana Brawley debacle was a prime example of the damage done—to lives, to reputations, to careers, and most of all to the truth—by playing the race card.

Almost all Americans agree that racism is wrong. Many believe that it remains a serious problem that affects many people on a regular basis. But a lot of people also worry that the charge of racism can be abused. We can all think of examples: Tawana Brawley's claimed assault seemed to have been a staged hoax. Michael Jackson—a musician who enjoyed the most lucrative career in the history of recorded music—teamed up with Brawley's former handler, Al Sharpton, to accuse his recording label, Sony Music, of a "racist conspiracy" to undermine his popularity after sales of his disappointing latest album are, well, disappointing. The multimillionaire—who, through untold plastic surgeries, has achieved the Aryan phenotype of Snow White—declared fearlessly, "When you fight for me, you're fighting for all black people, dead and alive." (That rumbling you hear is the sound of thousands of former slaves, sharecroppers, and victims of Jim Crow turning in their graves.) Prince, a musician whose contract was not quite as good as Michael Jackson's but still extraordinarily generous, complained that he was a "slave" to his record label (years later Prince made a deal with Jackson's old label, Sony, apparently unafraid of the racist conspiracy). Clarence Thomas, when charges of sex harassment surfaced during his confirmation hearings for the Supreme Court of the United States, compared his critics to a lynch mob. And of course there's O. J. Simpson. We all know what happened with O. J. Simpson (don't we?).

The Race Card will examine the prevalence of dubious and questionable accusations of racism and other types of bias. I will argue that the social and legal meaning of "racism" is in a state of crisis: the term now has no single clear and agreed-upon meaning. As a result, it is available to describe an increasingly wide range of disparate policies, attitudes, decisions, and social phenomena. This leads to disagreement and confusion. Self-serving individuals, rabble-rousers, and political hacks use accusations of racism, sexism, homophobia, and other types of "bias" tactically, in order to advance their own ends. And people of goodwill may make sincere claims that strike others as obviously wrongheaded.

In a sense, the Tawana Brawley incident was a classic example of playing the race card: Brawley and/or her handlers used a claim of racial bias in order to gain something they didn't deserve—notoriety, attention, money, public support for their controversial racial politics. But in another sense the incident was atypical. Playing the race card typically involves jumping to a conclusion not compelled by the facts; Michael Jackson's album sales were disappointing—that's a fact—but it's far from obvious that they were disappointing *because Jackson was the victim of racism.* By contrast, it appears that Brawley or her handlers actually fabricated the injuries, as well as disingenuously claiming that racism was to blame for them. The Brawley incident didn't involve jumping to a conclusion that the facts didn't

support; it involved making up facts that would support the de-
sired conclusion.

Still, this unusual case demonstrates something about playing
the race card more generally: false or exaggerated claims of bias
piggyback on real instances of victimization. They "work" because there are enough similar verified cases for the lies and ex-
aggerations to seem plausible. Brawley's story was plausible to
many people because they knew of similar incidents that actually happened. There are racist police, and they sometimes abuse
black people. When asked many years later whether he would
apologize for his role in the incident, Reverend Sharpton defended his conduct: "Apologize for what? For believing a young
lady?"[5] People who believed Brawley did so because they gave
her, rather than the police, the benefit of the doubt. They began with the presumption that black people often suffer from
racism and police often lie. People who began with the opposite
presumption—that blacks rarely suffer from racism and police
are usually truthful—never believed her. In the Brawley case,
the latter presumption yielded the correct conclusion. But that
doesn't make it a superior presumption in general. It would have
yielded the wrong conclusion in many other cases, such as when
New York police did indeed sexually abuse a black man—Abner
Louima—and lied about it in an unsuccessful cover-up attempt.

The cases of Brawley and Louima involved objective facts
that people could observe and verify. But many claims of racism
don't involve such hard facts; they involve prejudice or bias—a
state of mind we can't observe directly. Consider the following
high-stakes struggle, where many people think the winner played
the race card.

.   .   .

The year 1991 marked the end of an era in American civil rights. Thurgood Marshall—the first black Supreme Court justice, the lead attorney for the NAACP in the historic racial desegregation case *Brown v. Board of Education*—announced his intention to retire from the bench. Immediately the speculation and maneuvering concerning Marshall's replacement began. It was widely expected that another African American would be—indeed, *would have to* be—appointed. Liberals and civil rights groups began a predictable campaign directed at the Republican president—George H. W. Bush—who would nominate Marshall's successor. It was crucial, they insisted, that the nation's highest court include a person of color. The Bush administration would demonstrate the racial insensitivity—indeed bigotry—that its enemies had long suspected if it appointed a white person to fill this vacancy. Partisan politics and ideological litmus tests surely should be put aside in this instance. Marshall's vacancy should be filled by a person who could understand and express the unique experience of racial minorities in this country.

If it had its druthers, the Bush administration would certainly appoint a conservative. And the most prominent conservative judges were white. But Republicans couldn't afford to ignore the race issue. Part of the GOP's long-term strategy involved improving its dismal level of support among minorities. But the party couldn't shake its reputation as racially insensitive or downright racist. Its long-lived "Southern strategy" relied on race-baiting to deliver white votes to GOP candidates. Bush had been elected, in part, on the strength of a notorious ad campaign that many felt exploited racial bigotry. The ad pilloried Democratic candidate Michael Dukakis for supporting a program that allowed prison inmates to take "furloughs" from incarceration. The ad informed the public that a convicted murderer, Willie Horton, beat a man and raped his fiancée after failing to return from furlough. The ad prominently featured Horton's menacing black face, complete with shaggy Black Panther Afro and beard. Bush's campaign manager, Lee Atwater, crowed, "By the time this election is over, Willie Horton will be a household name." Atwater did not exaggerate. By the end of the campaign, one might have thought Horton was Dukakis's running mate. The ad may have helped Bush win the election, but it didn't help Bush or the Republicans improve their standing with African Americans.

Bush faced a dilemma. If he nominated a white conservative to the Supreme Court, it would reinforce the perception that he and the Republicans were insensitive to racial injustice, hostile to civil rights, even closet racists. But the black judges with the stature and experience for the position were civil rights liberals.

Beltway conservatives must have bristled at this bind. The liberals were using a blatant racial quota—something conservatives vehemently opposed on principle—to push the president to a more liberal nominee. Many of the "New Right" became conservatives in reaction to this kind of identity politics. They had seen their neighborhood schools forcibly integrated through racial busing imposed by liberal judges. They felt that their cherished family alma maters had succumbled to the cheap thrills of radical chic and caved in to the pressures of black nationalist mau-mauing and feminist hectoring. "Disadvantaged minorities" displaced their sons in the entering classes of Ivy League universities; militant feminists demanded integration, disrupting the comfortable esprit de corps of campus men's clubs. The traditional liberal arts curriculum had been watered down with overtly political ethnic and feminist authors, a concession to a misguided and trendy pluralism. The grande dame of classical education—Western Civilization—had been raped by radicals and begat such bastardizations as "World Civilizations" and "Cultures, Ideas, and Values." In the newly hyper-liberal colleges, they had been forced to sit through what they felt were self-righteous screeds about "white male oppression," and they were browbeaten by pious professors and students alike, each competing to be more sensitive and tolerant than thou.

And were the people who got into college through race and gender quotas grateful to be there? Hardly. Instead, they harangued and harassed, complained and cajoled for ethnic studies, feminist studies, special theme houses, "sensitivity" days, mandatory tolerance workshops. They held marches, sit-ins, and rallies for every conceivable left-wing cause.

And it wasn't enough for them to have their special self-segregated programs (the rationale of *integration* was conveniently forgotten once they had bullied their way in). They also wanted to piss on everyone else's fun. The only silver lining in all this cloudy "social progress" was that the introduction of large numbers of women made it easier to get lucky. But the feminists were quick to put a stop to that: they pressed for sex harassment codes, turned dorm counselors into antisex police, and proposed fraternization rules so strict that you had to get a signed and notarized consent form before you could so much as ask a coed out on a date. They bullied the universities—successfully in many cases—to kill off the Greek system just because a party or two got a little bit out of hand.

When graduation finally came, these same malcontents followed the conservatives right into government and private industry, making the same demands there. So everyone had to sit through race and gender "sensitivity training" at work. There were new rules everywhere to make sure no one's delicate sensibilities were ever "offended." And now they were doing it again, playing the race card to force the president of the United States to choose a left-wing affirmative action nominee for the Supreme Court.

But conservatives had an ace up their sleeves. A black conservative with just enough experience to be a plausible candidate but not so much as to have left a long paper trail of controversial published opinions. One can imagine the number of champagne corks that popped the night someone—maybe a young, up-and-coming member of the Federalist Society—made his career in conservative politics with the suggestion "Clarence Thomas." Imagine the strategy meeting of some unknown conservative think tank. The jowly old guard grumbling; the fresh-faced Young Turks scowling. Marshall's getting up in years; what to do if he retires while our team is in the White House? How do we deal with the race issue? Then someone says it: "Clarence Thomas." It was racial politics jujitsu: use the enemy's strength against him. *We have to pick a black nominee? Fine. We'll give you a black nominee so conservative he makes Edmund Burke look like Che Guevara. So what that he's just barely been appointed to the federal bench? Are the quota-crazy affirmative action liberals going to say that a black candidate is unqualified?*

Clarence Thomas hit the liberals right between the eyes. Liberals had pressed so forcefully, so righteously, so sincerely on the importance of racial diversity on the Court. They had carefully honed all of the moves in support of affirmative action. They had perfected the subtle and not so subtle insinuation that anyone who suggested that an affirmative action candidate wasn't qualified was a closet racist. Now all of these finely tuned arguments would be redeployed in support of the most conservative jurist since Hammurabi. The liberals would have to swallow hard and accept Thomas or confront their own best arguments and the charge of hypocrisy to boot.

Liberals were suddenly on the run. They had defeated other ultraconservative candidates, such as Ronald Reagan's nominee Robert Bork, focusing on their published opinions, public statements, and scholarship to demonstrate that the nominees' views on hot-button issues such as abortion and civil rights were outside the political mainstream. They tried to do the same with Thomas. Prominent black law professors testified, expressing concern about Thomas's hostility to school desegregation and affirmative action, but Thomas had no scholarly career and hence no scholarship. He had made few public statements and, since he had served as a judge for only two years, had published few controversial opinions. When asked about his views on abortion, Thomas stonewalled, insisting that he had not considered one of the few legal issues about which almost everyone—lawyer, Beltway warrior, and civilian alike—had an opinion. The Harvard Law School professor Christopher Edley pointed out that "when applied to fundamental matters, this [answer] is almost disqualifying. A well-qualified nominee should at least be able to suggest . . . the framework for his or her analysis. How else can you discern someone's constitutional vision, which is the key question before you?"[6] But Edley's plea for a tough look at Thomas's qualifications fell on deaf ears. Because his race subtly but effectively insulated him from criticism about his qualifications, Thomas's inexperience was proving to be an advantage. He didn't need to impress the Senate; he just had to avoid giving them ammunition against him. Thomas was able to deflect hard questions by demurring.

Conservatives were buying confetti and chilling bottles of Krug when Anita Hill turned up in the District. Hill was a prim young black woman who had worked with Thomas on the Equal Employment Opportunity Commission (EEOC). She claimed that Thomas had sexually harassed her, following a classic pattern: he asked her out, she declined, he started hassling her with off-color jokes and references to porn. Hill was a believable accuser, in large part because it was hard to imagine that this proper woman could have invented a story that included a porn star named Long Dong Silver and references to pubic hair on a can of Diet Coke. *Someone* had to have exposed her to these ideas. Not that Thomas was an obvious suspect, this tightly wound man, impeccably sexless in Beltway-standard gray flannel and blue serge. But look closely enough and you could almost see it: the leer, the gleam in the eyes, the licking of the lips. Could he be Willie Horton's kith and kin after all—a sexual predator dressed up for Court?

The Senate confirmation hearings began as a duller than average legal theory symposium involving issues such as "fidelity to the Constitution" and the meaning of "penumbral rights." After Hill's accusations they morphed into a *Jerry Springer* episode that had put on airs. The nation witnessed a parade of disgruntled former coworkers, jilted ex-lovers, and other "character witnesses" testifying to the integrity or duplicity of Thomas and Hill. *The Clarence 'n Anita Show* offered the viewing public that most comfortable scene of American pop theater, wherein the vain and cocky black man gets taken down a notch or two by the headstrong black woman. Hill played a demure Sapphire

Stevens to Thomas's somber Amos Jones, with EEOC colleague and Thomas supporter John Doggett making a cameo as King-fish Stevens.

The daytime drama came to a head when a beleaguered Thomas described the hearings as a "high-tech lynching for uppity blacks." Although race had thus far served as a silent inoculation against critique, here it was deployed openly as a full-strength antibiotic. Thomas sought to link his struggle to sit on the highest Court in the United States to the struggles of African Americans to avoid physical mutilation, torture, and death. He implicitly evoked the experience of blacks such as Emmett Till, a young black man from Chicago who was tortured and killed by whites after teasing a white woman in Mississippi. He compared milquetoast Democrats on the Senate Judiciary Committee to an angry mob armed with firearms and strong rope.

No one dared openly scoff, but many found the analogy harder to swallow than a diet cola of dubious purity. The irony of the moment was striking, even in this, a political drama that Oscar Wilde could have written: Thomas—a corrosive skeptic of accusations of racism during his tenure at the EEOC—cried racism the moment his nomination was in real jeopardy. When the chips were down and the stakes were high, this staunch defender of color blindness shamelessly played the race card.

Irony notwithstanding, it's possible that race *did* play a role in validating Hill's accusations. Clarence Thomas was about to enjoy the highest honor the legal profession can bestow—an appointment to the Supreme Court of the United States—when Democrats introduced the nation to Anita Hill. At the very moment when Thomas should have been basking in the admiration of his peers, he was forced to address charges of a most embarrassing and sordid nature. Nothing could be less consistent with the esteem in which members of the federal judiciary were typically held. Nothing could have more effectively undermined the judge's persona of cool rationality, objectivity, and cerebral detachment than the image of the sex fiend so enslaved to bodily passions that he abused his authority and preyed on his employees. Thomas must have been furious. *Attack me for my record, for my reasoning, for my ideology if you must. But this? This is (literally) hitting below the belt.*

Worse yet, these charges had an ugly racial overtone, intended or not: the black man as sexual predator. That's how many of Thomas's colleagues and much of the nation would receive them. The people who advanced the charges and pressed the issue had to have known this. These charges were probably more believable to many people and certainly much more damaging psychologically to Thomas because of his race. In this light, the claim that the hearings were a "high-tech lynching" isn't quite so far-fetched. Even those disinclined to support Thomas on his merits might worry that the stereotype of the oversexed black man colored, so to speak, the proceedings, making the charges seem more plausible. Veteran antiracists, well acquainted with theories of illicit and unconscious racism, might doubt that it was mere coincidence that the first Supreme Court nominee to face such resistance—based not on his record or his competence, but on his *sexual* predilections—was a black man.

"I believe Anita Hill" became a slogan of left liberals during the confirmation hearings. But like most slogans, it stood for more and less than its literal denotation. It stood for a feminist conviction that sex harassment demanded attention and condemnation. It stood for opposition to Thomas and his ideological views generally. It stood for solidarity with a brave woman who faced the full brunt of the right-wing public opinion machine. It stood for all of these things, almost to the exclusion of a sober and objective evaluation of her story and its plausibility. Mightn't an embattled Thomas reasonably have suspected that part of the reason so many believed her and not him, part of the reason her story, tarnished by the passage of time, gained the luster of plausibility and for many the gleam of Truth, was that her account confirmed one of the most pernicious of racial stereotypes?

WHAT IS THE RACE CARD?

In 1903 the black sociologist W.E.B. Du Bois opined that "the problem of the twentieth century is the color line." In the twenty-first century, will the problem be that everyone talks a good line about color?

Playing the race card is not new. Tom Wolfe called it "mau-mauing" back in 1970. Ever since the civil rights movement convinced the majority of Americans that racial prejudice is petty and contemptible, people have complained of racism loud and long, for good reasons and, sometimes, for bad ones. But when Wolfe coined the term, mau-mauing was the exclusive tactic of underprivileged minorities: people with legitimate complaints of discrimination, if occasionally excessive modes of expressing those complaints. Today the rhetoric of racism is a national patois, spoken fluently by ghetto hustlers and Wall Street stockbrokers, civil rights agitators and Republican Party hacks, criminal defense attorneys and Supreme Court nominees. Lawyers and judges and parishioners and priests have mastered the sleight of hand required to play the race card.

Superstar entertainers complain of racism when negotiating, renewing, or breaching their multimillion-dollar contracts; liberal and conservative politicians alike play subtle race politics to win elections or secure the confirmation of nominees: wealth and privilege are no impediments to deploying the race card. Nor, for that matter, is race. Upper-class WASPs complain of "reverse racism"—a melodramatic description of integrationist policies that no one believes are motivated by racial animus or bigotry. And if race isn't directly involved, you can always insist that whatever's eating you is like racism. Opponents of same-sex marriage aren't just narrow-minded religious zealots; they're the moral equivalent of the KKK. A rule that requires obese passengers to buy the number of seats they occupy—which in crowded coach class may be *two*—isn't a way to ensure that other customers get their share of scarce elbow room; it's like making Rosa Parks stand in the back of the bus. A dress code against tattoos, body piercings, funky haircuts, or cutoff shorts isn't just uptight; it's a new Jim Crow. Smoking bans consign nicotine addicts to "ghettos" or "concentration camps." Gripes are as common as face cards in a pinochle deck. The race card may turn yours into a winning hand.

Playing the race card is wrong and troubling for several reasons. Most obviously, it's dishonest. When people transgress or just screw up, they should take their lumps—not try to wriggle out of them with tactics of distraction or blame shifting. When people face disappointments, they should forbear graciously, not try to wheedle a more favorable outcome through false accusation. Playing the race card is also dangerous and shortsighted. Like the boy who cried wolf, people who too frequently cry racism are unlikely to be taken seriously when a predator actually emerges from the woods. Playing the race card places all claims of racism—valid and phony—under a cloud of suspicion. Finally, playing the race card is mean-spirited. Racism is a serious charge—it ruins careers and destroys reputations. When warranted, it should. But when trumped up, the charge of racism is a particularly vicious slander.

But the race card is not a simple matter of opportunism and deception. It is a by-product of deep ideological conflict in our society over how to describe and deal with questions of social justice. When bigotry was openly tolerated, people often announced it or did nothing to conceal it. Therefore, many of the earliest struggles for civil rights aimed at some conspicuous targets: Jim Crow laws, blatantly discriminatory practices, out-and-out race-based exclusion. But today most people try to hide their prejudices. As a result, a lot of time and energy must be spent just trying to determine whether bigotry is in play or not. Everyone involved—accuser and accused alike—has an incentive to lie and dissemble, to downplay or to exaggerate. And as overt prejudice has receded, we've developed new theories of prejudice designed to tease out hidden or repressed motivations and to identify inadvertent forms of wrongful discrimination.

This has given rise to a great deal of conflict over how to define bigotry and how to decide whether it's at work. Some of this conflict is necessary and healthy. We should refine and revisit our understanding of wrongful discrimination as part of an ongoing struggle for social justice. And we should debate and argue over civil rights, which reflect some of our society's most profound moral commitments. If no one ever pressed novel or controversial civil rights claims, we could never expand our conception of justice.

But there are also costs to more ambitious applications of civil rights. The extraordinary social and legal condemnation of racism and other social prejudices encourages people to recast what are basically run-of-the-mill social conflicts as cases of bigotry. Overuse and abuse of the claim of bias is bad for society and bad for social justice. When a conflict really does involve hatred or deep-seated irrational prejudice, dialogue is pointless and condemnation is appropriate. But the emotionally charged accusation of bigotry is counterproductive when a conflict involves questions on which reasonable people can differ. Playing the race card makes it too easy to dismiss rather than address the legitimate concerns of others. And the accusation of bigotry inevitably provokes defensiveness and resentment rather than thoughtful reaction. The resulting interactions usually don't qualify as speech, much less dialogue. They're generally closer to mud wrestling. No one gets away clean.

When does a grievance deserve the special and unequivocal condemnation reserved for racism? Despite more than a century of litigation under the Constitution and federal civil rights laws, we still don't have a straightforward answer to that question. In fact, in some ways the answer is getting more convoluted and confusing, and the resulting conflicts more numerous and frustrating.

Some people are convinced that most accusations of bias are disingenuous. There are plenty of pundits, politicians, and bloggers ready to dismiss any accusation of bias as calculating and self-serving. One Internet blog posted this parody: "Is the society not giving you what you think it owes you? Then it's time to get yourself the Race Card . . . It's like a 'Get Out of Jail Free' card, but much, much more. Losing an argument in a debate? Throw down your Race Card and quickly hush your opponent . . ." Clever, but this perspective suffers from a toxic cynicism and a blissed-out naïveté all at once. On the one hand, it implies that racism is not a real social problem, that less than a generation after federal troops were required to integrate schools and court orders were needed to integrate lunch counters, there's no racial bias left. Anyone who suggests otherwise is playing the race card. On the other hand, it presumes that racial minorities are so devious as to consistently make claims they know to be false, and that many people are credulous enough to believe them, despite the fact that racism has long since gone the way of wooden shoes.

At the same time, many people—and not only the credulous and the opportunistic—believe such accusations as Clarence Thomas's shrill complaint of a high-tech lynching and Brawley/Sharpton's apparently staged and obviously managed racial assault, and they rally to the causes of some unlikely victims. Major black organizations such as the Los Angeles branch of the NAACP rallied to Clarence Thomas after his notorious exclamation. Law professor Patricia Williams, one of academia's more nuanced and astute commentators on issues of race and gender, struggled to find in Tawana Brawley's story evidence of her victimization rather than her duplicity: "Even if she did it to herself . . . Her condition was . . . the expression of some crime against her, some tremendous violence, some great violation that challenges comprehension."[7]

Indeed, some people object to the idea that anyone might ever "play the race card." For instance, Professor Michael Eric Dyson argues, "There's no such thing as a race card being played by black people not already dealing with the race deck that white America has put on the table."[8] This is true enough as far as it goes. Playing the race card is an effective tactic because accusations of racism are plausible, and they're plausible because there are in fact a lot of instances of racism. But don't some people take advantage of this real social evil for unearned advantage? And don't people, even with good intentions, occasionally misapprehend their plight, complaining of prejudice when other factors are to blame? What accounts for such disagreements? Why do some reasonable people see evidence of racism where others see only the smirking one-eyed jack of the race card?

POST-RACISM

In the summer of 2006, *The Economist* magazine informed the hoi polloi that "serious champagne drinkers sip only the prestige cuvées produced by a handful of winemakers." The article quoted Jean-Claude Rouzaud, the former manager of the Louis Roederer house, who opined that a three-hundred-dollar bottle of Roederer's Cristal Champagne was intended for "that 3–5% of consumers who really know wine, and who take the time to taste it correctly." Under the subheading "Unwelcome Attention" (the editor's phrase, not Rouzaud's), the article went on to note what any moderately attentive student of American pop culture already knows: the most conspicuous consumers of high-end champagne—Cristal in particular—are not oenophiles of highly refined sensibilities, but rather "rap artists, whose taste for swigging bubbly in clubs is less a sign of a refined palate than a passion for a 'bling-bling' lifestyle that includes ten-carat diamond studs, chunky gold jewelry, pimped up Caddies and sensuous women." When asked how the venerable house of Roederer feels about this, the new director, Frédéric Rouzaud, took the bait: "What can we do? We can't forbid people from buying it. I'm sure Dom Pérignon or Krug would be delighted to have their business."[9]

Days after the publication of the article, hip-hop artist Jay-Z announced a boycott: "It has come to my attention that the managing director of Cristal . . . views the 'hip-hop' culture as 'unwelcome attention.' I view his comments as racist and will no longer support any of his products."[10]

What are we to make of a boycott—the time-honored tactic of the struggle for basic civil rights—of prestige cuvée champagne? Why, when black unemployment, poverty, rates of incarceration, and life expectancy remain severe and unaddressed problems, did anyone pay a moment's attention to the offhand comment of the representative of a vintner with roots in prerevolutionary France? Jay-Z talked the line of a scrappy civil rights activist, but with the inflections of a jilted socialite: "Jay-Z . . . will now be serving only Krug and Dom Pérignon," sniffed the press release. When a young, black, self-described "hustler" from Brooklyn seems as precious as a Park Avenue debutante, we've turned some sort of corner in race relations. But where are we headed?

Is M. Rouzaud's wary, though not overtly hostile or contemptuous, reaction to hip-hop—an art form that often explicitly extols a life of violence and crime—racist, as Jay-Z insists? Rouzaud's comments *might* have reflected racism—*we don't want blacks drinking our wine*—but they might have reflected concern over the association of the brand with an ostentatious subculture that extols violence and crime. Do we think the reaction would have been much different had, say, the notorious British punk band the Sex Pistols embraced Cristal Champagne during the band's heyday in the 1970s? (Unlikely, I admit.) It would have been fair enough for Jay-Z to boycott Cristal because Rouzaud insulted the *hip-hop* culture, of which he is a part, but that wouldn't have made headlines or garnered much sympathy. After all, a lot of people, including some prominent blacks, have disparaging things to say about hip-hop. By contrast, *racism* from the director of a well-known international company *is* news, and it guarantees the instinctive condemnation of millions of people. Because Rouzaud's statement was subject to multiple interpretations, one had a choice as to whether to frame the insult narrowly, in terms of hip-hop, or broadly, in terms of race. It's not surprising that the personally affronted Jay-Z chose the latter.

Having done so, he triggered a chain of predictable—indeed, reflexive—reactions. Contemporary racial politics make it a virtue to assume the worst when confronted with such ambiguous circumstances. The person who assumes the best of others and offers plausible alternatives to the verdict of racism is typically dismissed as naïve or even complicit in racial injustice. This presumption of guilt leads people to play the race card, and it effectively silences those who would call their bluff.

At the same time, presuming the worst is understandable in a society in which racism persists but is rarely expressed openly. If Rouzaud is a racist, he certainly wouldn't announce it. But he might inadvertently reveal his prejudice in the context of an interview about a bunch of black nouveaux riches who guzzle his finest cuvée as if it were cheap malt liquor. People who are regularly at risk of suffering from concealed racism can't afford to take Pollyanna's perspective. A marked man had better always look for hidden assassins; a black person—marked by race for social contempt—had better always look for hidden bigotry.

A 2006 article in the arts and culture magazine *Black Book* announced the rise of a "post-racist" culture. The term is too clever by half, but still evocative and compelling. Like "postmodern" or "postcolonial," the prefix in post-racist doesn't suggest the demise of what it modifies—in this case racism. Instead, "post" suggests a sort of supernova late stage of racism in which its contradictions and excesses both cancel out and amplify its original functions.

The post-racist has absorbed the values of the civil rights movement—she is perfectly comfortable with black authority figures, black classmates, black neighbors. He thinks it's unremarkable that the secretary of state is a black woman. She says that she doesn't really think of her black friends as "black," and she means it. She also freely indulges in the black stereotypes our culture has on offer: hip-hop's image of the black thug, the black pimp, the black drug dealer, the black crack whore, the black hustler. The post-racist is free to be explicitly and crudely bigoted because he does so with tongue planted firmly in cheek. The post-racist parodies racism, but she doesn't exactly repudiate it. Instead, she revels in its excesses with almost a kind of nostalgia, just as the film *Austin Powers: International Man of Mystery* archly mocks the 1960s spy movies and swinging London but also yearns for them with an almost heartbreaking sincerity.

One of the intriguing characteristics of post-racism is that it is practiced by all races on an almost egalitarian basis. A black bartender quoted in the *Black Book* article quipped, "This is the best time in history to be a black man in America because it's easier than ever to sleep with white women." This crass assessment of racial justice is characteristically post-racist. It manages to say something profoundly humanist (it's a better world today because erotic attachments no longer need observe the color line), but at the same time vaguely racist (black men so obsessively long for sex with white women that they define their quality of life largely by the availability of such opportunities).

Perhaps Jay-Z's exquisitely constructed public image and Rouzaud's reaction to it are examples of post-racism. Jay-Z's image would be incomprehensible without a shared backdrop of racial stereotypes. The hip-hop persona is both a reaction to racist stereotypes and also—let's face it—a performance of them. Given this, Rouzaud's ill-considered comments are all the more ambiguous. Was his apparent distaste for hip-hop culture a reflection of a racist distaste for *blacks* or a less-objectionable distaste for the antisocial behavior stereotypically attributed to blacks by racists? When we're dealing with such ambiguities, one person's righteous accusation of prejudice will look to another like a cheap shot at playing the race card.

The civil rights reforms of the 1960s codified a remarkable transformation in social attitudes and norms. In less than a generation, racial bias was demoted from legally enforced common sense to legally prohibited nonsense. Racism became unlawful, immoral, and, perhaps more important, déclassé. In 1942 only 32 percent of whites believed that the races should attend the same schools; 68 percent favored segregation. By 1964 those figures had almost flipped: 63 percent favored integrated schools while 37 percent preferred segregation. In 1944, 55 percent of whites believed the best jobs should be reserved for whites; by 1970, only 12 percent did.[11]

Today antiracism has been incorporated into the dominant institutions of society. Schools once accepted racial integration only under court order, the armed forces only under executive order, private enterprise only under congressional mandate. Now universities, the military, and private business combine forces to defend integration and race-conscious affirmative action. Officially sanctioned racist propaganda has been replaced by multicultural sensitivity training. Once antiestablishment, antiracism is now part of the establishment. This change in social norms, as much as the legal liability attached to racial discrimination in housing, employment, and public accommodation, is the invaluable legacy of the civil rights movement. Civil rights legislation and the change in social attitudes that accompanied it have dramatically reduced the severity and extent of deliberate and overt race discrimination. Racism persists, but contrary to the claims of some racial demagogues, it hasn't simply changed form or become subtler. It is also not as prevalent or as severe as it was in the era of Jim Crow.

The black civil rights movement is now as much a part of American nationalist lore as the Boston Tea Party or Paul Revere's midnight ride. Like the colonists who tipped the East India Company's heavily taxed orange pekoe into Boston Harbor, the soon-to-be leaders of the civil rights movement were long-suffering solid citizens, pushed to rebellion by manifest oppression. Popular history (after a scant forty years already slipping into legend and cliché) has it that Rosa Parks refused to yield her

seat on a Montgomery, Alabama, public bus simply because she
was tired. No political activist she: just a simple workingwoman
who had had enough (in fact, Parks *was* a committed civil rights
activist). According to legends informed by poetry and song, the
tea boycott in New England and the bus boycott in the Old
South both involved reluctant revolutionaries, ordinary people
inspired to extraordinary actions by a reflexive hostility to injustice. They were people who wanted to tend their own gardens
but got fed up with being treated like manure. Once they were
roused to action, these reluctant revolutionaries were fierce partisans. They faced the bayonets and rifles of the world's strongest
and most disciplined army. They faced fire hoses, firebombings,
billy clubs, and rottweilers. They risked injury, imprisonment,
and even death. They exhibited the classical American virtues of
proud courage and grim determination—true grit.

They prevailed because of their commitment, but also because of their savvy. The minutemen combined the modern
weapons of Europe with the supple tactics of the Native American warrior. They used the terrain to their advantage. Clothed
to blend in with the landscape, they attacked the conspicuous
files of redcoats from behind the cover of brush. They mounted
perhaps the world's first guerrilla war against an imperial
regime. The freedom riders combined the nonviolence of
Gandhi with the oratory charisma of Winston Churchill and
the media sense of Edward R. Murrow. They knew they
couldn't win by force, and they didn't try. Instead they prevailed
through persuasion and moral example. They understood that
they needed to convince not Bull Connor and George Wallace,
but Hubert Humphrey and Lyndon Johnson. Both the freedom
fighters and the freedom riders had a gift for practical problem
solving, an outsider's disdain for conventions, a maverick's abil-

ity to think outside the box—the paradigmatic Yankee virtues of pragmatism and ingenuity.

And perhaps most important, both revolutions are stories of progress, examples of American idealism and industriousness shaping a society where continual improvement can almost be taken for granted. American history is, from this popular perspective, a story of uninterrupted technological, economic, and moral progress. At least since the Jacksonians advanced the doctrine of Manifest Destiny, Americans have taken comfort in the belief that our position in the world and in history is preordained. An indispensable part of this confidence is the belief that we as a nation are getting not only stronger but also better: wiser, nobler, more beneficent, and more just. Our institutions and customs are superior, not only because they contain timeless principles and reflect unshakable truths, but also because they possess the capacity to adapt and improve. Just as the cotton gin replaced manual cleaning of the raw crop, so too American moral ingenuity eventually developed superior replacements for slavery, sharecropping, and Jim Crow segregation. The civil rights movement—once a marginal and suspect political radicalism—has been neatly woven into this tale of inexorable national progress. Now racial justice is among the most touted achievements of American society. Like assembly-line production, the tungsten filament, and jazz, it is a source of national pride and a valuable international export. It builds morale at home and helps in the symbolic balance of trade abroad.

As a result, the accusation of bias—racial bias and any other kind of bias analogous to it—is a potent weapon. Racism is not only unfair and irrational, it is unpatriotic and anti-American. And, according to this story, racism is also deviant: deviant in the literal sense that it is rare, and deviant in the colloquial and pejorative sense that it is twisted, sick, and repellent. Here nationalism meets popular psychology. The racist is a fossil of an ancien régime of blood privilege and also a pathetic and potentially dangerous psychopath; a fetishist of skin, hair, and lips; a moral pervert.

Obviously there's a lot to like here. Antiracist causes acquire authority as a result of their conscription into the vanguard of nationalistic pride, and they enjoy legitimacy as a result of their induction into the popular cult of psychotherapy. But along with these advantages come the characteristic drawbacks of patriotic nationalism and pop psychology: on the one hand, jingoism and fanaticism; on the other, sentimentalism and magical thinking. Like patriotic movements generally, antiracism now attracts yahoos and opportunists: "It's a Black Thing; you wouldn't understand" is as insipid and dangerous a slogan as "My country right or wrong." Just as hack politicians wrap themselves in the flag, they now also seek cover in the mantle of racial justice. And like the formulaic 12-step programs of dime-store psychotherapy, antiracism has spawned an industry where the narcissistic confessional substitutes for introspection, cheap theatricality stands in for valuable insight, and simplistic dogma masquerades as analysis.

Playing the race card is a symptom of this crisis of partial success. In dealing with overt racism, the antiracist has the full coercive power of government and the weight of popular consensus behind her. This access to power and influence attracts the unscrupulous opportunist along with the sincere victim and the honest petitioner. And as in any exclusive club, there's not only the problem of gate-crashers, there's also that of inappropriate demeanor. For most of American history, antiracism was a movement of resistance and critique. Antiracists fought against the dominant institutions of society, seeking reform or fomenting rebellion. Because obvious racial injustices persist—and simply out of custom and habit—antiracist rhetoric retains the belligerent, confrontational tone appropriate to a marginal protest movement. But today's antiracists often must defend, enforce, and strengthen dominant norms, using the influence of large and powerful bureaucracies and the coercive power of government. The fiery style of the revolutionary mixes badly with the cool professional technique of an authoritative bureaucracy. Speaking truth to power is an anachronism when the person speaking also has the power. So as charlatans cry "racism" to finagle undeserved advantages, the bad fit between rhetoric and reality, between adopted pose and social position can make even sensible claims sound like grandstanding.

The Race Card will examine such disagreements and seek to address the question that underlies them: When are complaints of prejudice valid and appropriate and when are they are exaggerated, paranoid, or simply dishonest? I'll try to take an unsentimental look at such claims, defending those that deserve sympathy, scrutinizing those that deserve suspicion, and ridiculing those that deserve contempt. In this book I'll examine four reasons people seem to play the race card.

1. When people complain of racism, it is typical to assume that there must be a blameworthy racist who should be made to pay. But many of today's racial injustices are not caused by simple prejudice; instead, they are the legacies of the racial caste system of our recent past, entrenched by the inertia of class hierarchy and reinforced by the unforgiving competition of capitalist markets. As a result, many

people have legitimate grievances, but no racist to blame for them. The victims of the injustices will correctly blame racism, but too often they will incorrectly try to find someone to label a racist. Skeptical observers who see no racists will conclude that the complaint is unreasonable and perhaps dishonest. I call this the problem of *racism without racists.*

Chapter One will examine the phenomenon of racism without racists. In pursuit of this idea, I'll go to storm-damaged parishes of the Big Easy, the mean streets of New York, and the fashionable boutiques of Paris's *rive droite.* Was Hurricane Katrina a racial justice issue? When a Yellow Cab ignores a black man's hail, is it racism? If a store clerk is surly to a black customer, can we conclude that she's a bigot?

2. The success of the civil rights movement inspired many others to frame their struggles in similar terms. Feminists, gays and lesbians, the disabled, and the elderly are just a few of the groups who have successfully made explicit analogies to the cause of racial justice. Conservatives attack affirmative action as reverse racism. Multiculturalism redefined racism as discrimination based not only on skin color or heredity, but also on "culture." And a host of interest groups, such as dog owners, the obese, and cigarette smokers, have implausibly but insistently compared their causes to the struggle against racism. At best, these claims seek to extend the principles underlying civil rights to new situations. But at worst, these claims seem to define "bigotry" so broadly that the losing side of almost any social or political

conflict can claim to be the victims of racelike bias. Today almost anyone can play the race card by making claims of what
I'll call *racism by analogy.*

Chapter Two looks at the explosion of racism-by-
analogy claims. These claims take to the skies in lawsuits
against airlines; they hit the ground running in aerobics stu-
dios, check in to chic San Francisco hotels, and lay about in
Santa Cruz cafés. Is discrimination on the basis of culture,
weight, or appearance as bad as discrimination on the basis
of race? Should the law prohibit these, as well as a growing
list of arguably analogous biases? How can we distinguish
those types of discrimination that demand legal sanction
from reasonable distinctions, defensible preferences, and
sensible generalizations? Because the law often offers little
or no redress for garden-variety unfairness, many people
are tempted to recast their grievances in terms that the law
will recognize: in other words, to play the race card.

3. Although there is widespread agreement that racism and
analogous prejudices are wrong, there is no agreement as
to what counts as racism. The success of the civil rights
movement encouraged more ambitious claims, and the
phenomenon of racism without racists led activists to apply
the civil rights model to subtler forms of racial injustice.
Today, there is greater disagreement as to what counts as
racism. There are several reasonable definitions available,
each of which will yield a different conclusion given the
same set of facts. The difficulty in figuring out who is and is
not a racist begins with the problem of *defining discrimination.*

In Chapter Three, I'll show you why the definition of

discrimination is malleable and contested, using controversies from the underground of rock music and from the skyscrapers of corporate America. I'll examine scientific experiments that seek to probe the unconscious mind. Scientists now claim to discover biases you didn't even know you had, repressed in the recesses of the subconscious. Should their findings be used in court to back up claims of discrimination? I'll give you the history of discrimination in the law. Sometimes the law offers a valuable alternative to the jumble of ideas about discrimination used by social critics and social scientists; sometimes it just adds to the confusion. Is it racism if an employer adopts a policy that incidentally excludes a disproportionate percentage of minorities, or is it so only if he adopts it *because* it excludes them? Is it sex discrimination if a company fires a female employee for a combination of good reasons and sex stereotypes? Is racial profiling always a form of racism—even when the profile is accurate and used in good faith? Can a police department round up every black man in town as a part of a manhunt for a criminal at large? Is affirmative action really "reverse racism"? The law has answers to these questions—some that may surprise or even anger you.

4. The practical goals of civil rights are contested. During the Jim Crow era, antiracists agreed that the goal was to dismantle explicitly discriminatory practices and formal segregation. But it wasn't clear whether the ultimate goal was formal legal equality, or economic equality, or whether there was a substantive commitment to social integration. With blatant discrimination on the wane, it has become

obvious that antiracists don't agree on the ultimate goal: mainstream liberals favor social integration, but black nationalists and some multiculturalists reject integration in favor of racial solidarity and cultural autonomy. When the ultimate goal is contested, it can be hard to tell what furthers racial justice and what hinders it. For instance, affirmative action is inconsistent with formal equality, but it furthers economic equality and integration; separate ethnic and racial organizations and clubs promote solidarity and cultural autonomy but violate norms of equality and hinder social integration. This can produce a catch-22, where any course of action will be "racist" according to someone. I call this problem the *clash of ends.*

Chapter Four will look at conflict over the ultimate goals of the civil rights movement. Should we still strive for integration, or can we now conclude that segregation is a result of innocent preferences for solidarity and community? We'll examine America's racially segregated ghettos and scientifically designed housing projects to find out why, despite the efforts of some of our best minds, racial segregation can be as bad today as in the era of Jim Crow. And we'll visit Ivy League universities to see why some people think we should give up on integration and instead try to make real the old solecism of separate but equal.

We can do better. In Chapter Five, I'll argue that we can and should refine the legal and cultural definition of discrimination to make it more precise and less subject to abuse. Although no simple definition of "racism" is available, an understanding of the history of American racial injustice—and of the potential and the limits of legal intervention—suggests practical and intuitively compelling limits to the law's application.

Not only can we do better; we must. Ever since the acquittal of O. J. Simpson, the idea that race is a "card" to be played for selfish advantage has become commonplace. The Simpson trial and the popular reactions to it are prime examples of the risks playing the race card poses to racial harmony and social justice. The race card threatens to undermine public support for civil rights and other policies that promote social justice. It breeds and exacerbates distrust between the races, making genuine claims of racism less credible. It helps to fracture society into mutually suspicious and antagonistic social groups, eroding the political solidarity that could underwrite social harmony and egalitarianism. And it distracts attention from the real issues involved in conflicts that are mislabeled as instances of bigotry. The unforgiving social and economic conditions that remain unaddressed, in part as a result of playing the race card, entrench the social disadvantage of the most vulnerable—disproportionately racial minorities—and thereby fuel another round of increasingly desperate uses of the race card.

■ ONE
RACISM WITHOUT RACISTS

We all saw the footage of the looters: thugs rioting through Wal-Mart and sporting goods stores, grabbing fancy basketball shoes, jewelry, plasma televisions. *Plasma televisions for chrisssake! Where are they going to plug them in? The whole damn city is underwater and these jokers are stealing flat screen plasma televisions. No wonder they didn't have the sense to get out before the storm hit.*

Professor Boyce Watkins, author of *What if George Bush Were a Black Man?*, is the guest on Fox News.[1] And the Fox News anchor wants to know what the professor has to say about these black hooligans helping themselves to Wal-Mart's plasma TVs, taking advantage of a national tragedy for selfish gain: "Let's talk about this issue of looting . . . If you're going to go and take water or food to feed your family, I see that very differently than taking a plasma *television*. Do you see those those are two very different things, Professor?"

Professor Watkins starts with the sociological context—or what the Fox News audience might call the usual liberal excuses: poverty, failing schools, unemployment. The anchor is having none of it: "What about taking televisions? What about taking things that you can't even plug them in?"

Professor Watkins blusters, in response, "Well, if you define looting as going into someone else's territory and taking something that doesn't belong to you, you can argue that we're looting in Iraq right now." *Iraq! He has to reach all the way to Mesopotamia to avoid the issue! Liberating a country from a genocidal dictator is the same as stealing a plasma TV? These liberals will say anything.*

The anchor stays on message: *"Is it okay to take a plasma television?"*

"When you are struggling to help your family, whether it's to get whatever they need or whatever the case may be, the fact is that the line between legality and morality suddenly changes."

Or whatever the case may be? C'mon professor, the case was that they were stealing television sets. "I'm talking about the line between necessities and luxury items," insists the anchor.

"Luxury items? I think that if you're going to focus on the problems of society, you want to focus on the big looters . . . I don't see any point in picking on the poor and downtrodden." And so it goes.

The second Fox News anchor chimes in—they're double-teaming him now. *A black looter told an Associated Press reporter that*

*looting was a way of getting back at society. Does the professor agree
with that?*

"Yes, absolutely."

*So as a leader of the black community, you defend the stealing of tele-
vision sets?*

He's flailing now: "But there are looters in Iraq . . . looters at
Enron. Why not focus on them?" *Because a hurricane just destroyed New Orleans two days ago and now a bunch of thugs are using
the opportunity to loot and steal, remember, Professor?*

No one talked about race at first. After the levees failed, it took
a day or two for the shock to wear off. At first, all anyone could
talk about was the sheer scope of the catastrophe, the biblical, Ce-
cil B. DeMille proportions of the destruction. An entire city sub-
merged. A hurricane big enough to drown a city (who could deny
the effects of global warming now?). Then the sharper eyes began
to regain their focus. It wasn't the *entire* city. Most of the French
Quarter—what everyone who doesn't live there thinks of as
"New Orleans" anyway—was spared. And it wasn't the storm that
flooded the city; it was the lake and the Mississippi River. What
was really astounding was that it didn't happen sooner. Much of
the city was basically a lake bed, with the Mississippi River on one
side and Lake Pontchartrain on the other, each suspended several
feet above the city by one of the largest levee systems in the world.

After senses and sensibilities recovered, it was hard not to notice that almost all of the stranded victims of Katrina were
black. Black people huddled in the Convention Center and the
Superdome after their houses and apartments were destroyed.
Black people on buses to Houston, Atlanta, and Albuquerque,

where they would wait for the recovery or, more likely, stay and start afresh. Black people on rooftops and in the upper floors of apartments, stubbornly refusing to leave their homes behind or desperately waiting for help in escaping the aftermath of a storm they had gambled wouldn't be so bad. Black people "stealing" loaves of bread, fresh water, baby formula. Black people happening upon plasma TVs and platinum watches in abandoned stores. Black people as far as the eye could see.

The footage looked like some third world country, some UNESCO famine relief commercial. The sheer scope of the devastation, the inadequacy of the relief efforts, the violence filling the void left by the absence of effective law enforcement, the scale of human suffering. It couldn't be the United States. *We* have a government that works and can help people in need, but here it was two, three days, even a week after the flood, and the government, like some banana republic, still hadn't gotten fresh water, food, and medical supplies—*the basics*—to many of the victims. There were reports, later repudiated, of cannibalism among the victims. Was this urban fable a subliminal reference to the Donner Party of the American frontier, a reflection, however bizarre, of some sense of national identification with the victims as archetypically American survivors? Or was its inspiration the stereotypical bone-through-the-nose savages of the Dark Continent?

Then came the photo captions. There couldn't have been much time even to fact-check those captions, much less vet them for political correctness. But there they were, two pictures, two captions, on the same day no less: August 30, 2005, the day after the levees broke. Both front and center on Yahoo News.

One shows a black man wading through the water carrying a sack: "A young man walks through chest-deep floodwater after looting a grocery store in New Orleans on Tuesday." The other one shows a white couple wading through the water; the woman is carrying a sack: "Two residents wade through chest-deep water after finding bread and soda from a local grocery store . . ."

The black guy is a looter, a gangbanger, a stone-cold Crip out for an easy score. *Isn't that a boom box in his hand? Oh, wait, it's a pack of diapers.* The white couple: Jeannie and Jean Valjean, driven by adversity to take a loaf of bread, no doubt to feed their small children who are, unfortunately, just outside the frame. *I bet they even left their names and telephone numbers and a note apologizing.*

It's all over the Internet later that day. Post-Katrina racism. Yahoo News was just a dramatic symbol for a much larger issue. People started asking questions that were barely veiled accusations. Why was the federal response so slow and inadequate? Why did President Bush stay in Texas *on vacation* two days into the catastrophe? If those victims had been white Floridians rather than black Louisianans, would Bush have cut his vacation short? People thought they knew the answer, because a year earlier a hurricane struck white communities in south Florida. The response was rapid and, by one account "generous to the point of profligacy."[2] Bush delivered relief checks personally. Local officials praised the generosity and efficiency of the Federal Emergency Management Agency.

Katrina hit the Gulf Coast on Monday; the levees failed on Tuesday. By Saturday, on national television, rapper Kanye West called the president of the United States a racist. West was a host for a benefit concert for the Red Cross—one of those heartwarming yet wrenching events in which celebrities do their part to help, soliciting donations, singing appropriately inspirational songs, and reading prepared scripts in front of monitors that run footage of the disaster and its unfortunate victims. West was paired with Mike Myers, the comedian best known for his role in *Austin Powers: International Man of Mystery.* Myers didn't yuck it up that Saturday. The atmosphere was grave and earnest. He stuck to his script: "The landscape of the city has changed dramatically, tragically, and perhaps irreversibly. There is now over twenty-five feet of water where there was once city streets and thriving neighborhoods."

West was equally earnest, but he spoke extemporaneously: "I hate the way they portray us in the media. You see a black family, it says, 'They're looting.' You see a white family, it says, 'They're looking for food.' And, you *know*, it's been five days because most of the people are black . . . with the way America is set up to help the poor, the black people, the less well-off, as slow as possible . . ."

Myers looked like a deer caught in the headlights of a speeding bus. He stammered through the next part of the prepared script: "The destruction of the spirit of the people of southern Louisiana and Mississippi may end up being the most tragic loss of all . . ." He trailed off, looking pale and shaken, perhaps by the plight of the Katrina victims, but more likely by West's unexpected political commentary.

West grabbed the opening to offer a parting observation: "George Bush doesn't care about black people!"

Doctor Brown, I hope you will tell President Bush how much we appreciated . . . to know that our federal government will step in and give us the kind of assistance we need,"[3] enthused Louisiana governor Kathleen Blanco on Monday, August 28, 2005, the day before the levees broke. "We are indeed fortunate to have an able and experienced director of FEMA," added Louisiana senator Mary Landrieu. Things were going well for Michael Brown, the director of the Federal Emergency Management Agency. Brown was experienced, but as it turned out, not at disaster relief. He was a politically connected Beltway lawyer. His deputy chief of staff had been a campaign strategist for Bush. When Brown was appointed to run FEMA, some complained that "seasoned staff members are being pushed aside to make room for inexperienced novices," but the critics were being proved wrong. The eye of the storm missed major population centers, and like the Gulf Coast itself, FEMA had weathered the storm. Brown basked in the praise: "What I've seen here today is a team that is very tight-knit, working closely together . . . and in my humble opinion, making the right calls."

Then the levees gave way. Suddenly the tight-knit, right-calls Katrina relief efforts were plagued by mishap, incompetence, and carelessness at every level. Federal, state, and local officials failed to coordinate their efforts and clashed over control. Supplies ordered and anxiously awaited by one group of officials were turned away as unneeded by another. Some victims received multiple payments for the same losses while other waited weeks for relief. Waste and graft were the rule, efficiency and fair dealing the exceptions. Now no one was claiming that FEMA had made the right calls.

Thousands of people—the sick and elderly along with the young and predatory—were evacuated to the nearby "refuges of last resort": the Superdome and the Convention Center. Storm winds ripped the roof off of the Superdome, leaving the twenty-four thousand evacuees without electricity—meaning without light or air-conditioning in a windowless dome. Temperatures inside the Superdome rose to over 100 degrees. Conditions were no better in the Convention Center. There, too, power and plumbing failed, leaving the building a stifling cavern of darkness, the air heavy with the stench of sweat, human waste, and fear. The Louisiana National Guard was stretched thin because of deployments overseas and flooded barracks. Without a military presence to keep order, police found themselves overwhelmed. Asked to venture into a fetid void, illuminated only by the regular flash of gunpowder, several officers quit on the spot.[4]

The state scrambled to assemble buses to evacuate the people who had not yet left the city, but the rumors of mayhem and chaos—looting, robbery, and even rape—had started to spread. Local bus drivers refused to go to New Orleans. FEMA was supposed to step in to provide transportation, but "the logistics of wrangling up enough buses to get the people out . . . took . . . three days," according to the Louisiana Office of Homeland Security and Emergency Preparedness.

Less than a week after the governor and senator praised FEMA's team spirit and professionalism, Aaron Broussard, the president of Jefferson Parish—which includes suburban New Orleans—appeared on national television, excoriating FEMA's high-handed incompetence. Not only wasn't FEMA helping, he said, but their incompetent intermeddling was hindering local relief efforts. He had arranged for Wal-Mart to send desperately needed drinking water to the parish, but FEMA turned the trucks back. The Coast Guard had promised to provide diesel fuel; FEMA ordered them not to release it. To dramatize the plight of his parish, Broussard told a poignant story involving the parish's director of emergency services: "His mother was trapped . . . and every day, she called him and said, 'Are you coming, son? Is somebody coming?' And he said, 'Yeah, Mama, somebody's coming to get you. Somebody's coming to get you on Tuesday. Somebody's coming to get you on Wednesday. Somebody's coming to get you on Thursday. Somebody's coming to get you on Friday.' And she drowned Friday night. Nobody's coming to get us . . ."[5] It was a devastating interview. The story illustrated everything that was wrong with the Katrina relief efforts: the helplessness of local government faced with a disaster of such proportions, the incompetence and callousness of federal officials, the endless waiting, the human suffering. There was only one problem. It wasn't true. The director's mother had drowned, but the rest of the story, Broussard's staff later clarified, was based on a "misunderstanding."

Katrina was, if not a perfect storm, a perfect catastrophe. When the levees broke, help was thin on the ground. The volunteer military was stretched dangerously thin. Worse than fighting a war on two fronts, the United States military was fighting *two separate wars*. In Iraq, American forces easily toppled the government in Baghdad, but Saddam Hussein's supporters had dispersed into the countryside to mount an increasingly vicious guerrilla campaign. American forces were also engaged in Afghanistan. For years during the 1980s Afghan warlords had held the world's other superpower, the Soviet Union, at bay, miring their forces in the nation's notoriously difficult terrain with a ruthless guerrilla campaign. They were now threatening to do the same to the United States. The Bush administration called up thousands of reserve troops and deployed members of the National Guard to support the foreign occupations. Those troops weren't available to help the victims of Katrina, and the relief effort suffered as a result.

Many said the demise of New Orleans was a testament to modern hubris, a symbol of the limitations of technology, an "iceberg-proof" *Titanic* for the new millennium. But the truth was more prosaic: the tragedy of New Orleans was not the arrogance of modern science, but rather the inertia of postmodern bureaucracy. The levees failed because they were improperly maintained and never designed to withstand a Katrina-size storm. Their engineers were *not* overconfident—they had insisted for years that the New Orleans levee system would not survive a major hurricane. The White House had cut budget requests from the Army Corps of Engineers for levee maintenance. Lack of political will—not lack of foresight—doomed New Orleans.

George Bush doesn't care about black people. Somehow Kanye West's closing thought didn't make the West Coast rebroadcast. But the sentiment found its way around the world. Polls taken several weeks after the disaster show that 85 percent of blacks thought the Bush administration was negligent in handling the relief efforts.[6] I. V. Hilliard, a New Orleans minister, alluded to the deployment of American forces overseas, complaining, "Are you telling me we can coordinate a relief effort on the other side of the world and we can't do it here? I'm not saying they didn't care. I'm saying they didn't care enough. I can't help but think race has something to do with it."[7] Meanwhile, in the Middle East, Iranian television featured politicians and pundits commenting with concern on America's racial divide. The influential news outlet Al Jazeera ran stories about the hurricane and American racism. One article editorialized: "Poor black Americans . . . are now suffering third world conditions in the most advanced nation in the world. It's not as though the Bush administration couldn't have done more . . . they chose not to . . . [Given what they've done in the Middle East] it's not so surprising to see this administration rape their own people and leave them stranded."[8] Congresswoman Cynthia McKinney insisted, "The world saw American-style racism in the drama . . . [of] the Katrina survivors."[9] Katrina was proving to be an international public relations disaster as well as a natural catastrophe.

"No one is going to tell me it wasn't a race issue," said one of the evacuees. "When the city had been pretty much evacuated, the people that were left there were mostly black."[10] During a congressional hearing several months after the disaster, Republicans were desperate to defend the performance of the Republican administration, FEMA, and its top brass. They struggled to respond to victims diplomatically but still rebut charges of racism. "I don't want to be offensive when you've gone through such incredible challenges," Representative Christopher Shays began warily, before telling a Katrina survivor that he didn't believe her account of police brutality. "You believe what you want," the survivor snapped angrily. Earlier, the Reverend Jesse Jackson had compared the temporary shelters in the New Orleans Superdome to the hull of a slave ship. Victims at the hearing compared the conditions in temporary shelters to Nazi concentration camps. The best response Republicans could muster was that no one in New Orleans had been marched into a gas chamber. "They died from abject neglect," shot back a community activist.

Slate's senior political editor, Jacob Weisberg, suggested, "Because they don't see blacks as a . . . constituency, Bush and his fellow Republicans do not respond out of the instinct of self-interest when dealing with their concerns . . . Had the residents of New Orleans been white Republicans in a state that mattered politically, instead of poor blacks in a city that didn't, Bush's response surely would have been different."[11] This is as compelling a case of post-Katrina racism as anyone has made. But, as Weisberg was careful to note, this doesn't really suggest that Bush is a racist. It suggests that he is calculating, callous, and moved to action only by self-interest, generous to those who can help him, and indifferent to those who can't: in other words, a politician. Blacks in New Orleans happen to be among the unfortunate people this president doesn't count as allies. If President Bush doesn't care about black people, as Kanye West would have it, perhaps he doesn't care about Democrats or New Yorkers either. Indeed, many have complained that similar political calculations have diverted needed antiterrorism funds from likely targets in blue states like New York and California to relatively unthreatened red states. But try explaining this nuanced distinction to someone who spent a long, hot week in the Superdome without fresh water.

Racial conflict didn't end with the initial relief and evacuation efforts. The reconstruction of New Orleans quickly shaped up to be as much about race and racism as the reconstruction of the former Confederate states after the Civil War. Politicians promised to rebuild, to reclaim the city's former "glory." A handful of critics pointed out that this wasn't aiming very high: other than the small historic core, pre-Katrina New Orleans was an impoverished urban dystopia. More than a quarter of the city's population eked out their lives below the poverty line. The city's schools were underfunded, poorly performing, and some of the most segregated in the nation: 93 percent black.

Crime was rampant. Police were often corrupt, and law-abiding residents were either too intimidated by thugs or too distrustful of police to report crime or testify against criminals. And most of the city had been built on land that was geographically ill suited for development: "New Orleans naturally wants to be a lake," a geologist told *Time* magazine a week after the disaster. The damage was so complete that some politicians and economists seriously proposed abandoning the city for good. When asked about rebuilding New Orleans, Republican speaker of the House of Representatives Dennis Hastert said, "[It's] seven feet under the sea level . . . that doesn't make sense to me . . . it looks like a lot of that place could be bulldozed."[12] Harvard economist Edward Glaeser also argued against rebuilding New Orleans: "There's some small core of the city that should be there, but the city itself has been in decline for fifty years . . . surely some of the residents are better off by being given checks and being allowed to move elsewhere."[13] Of the people displaced by Katrina and housed in the Houston Astrodome, First Mother Barbara Bush said, "What I'm hearing, *which is sort of scary,* is they all want to stay in Texas . . . and so many of the people in the arena here, you know, were underprivileged anyway, so this is working very well for them."[14]

For many, the very suggestion that the displaced New Orleanians might as well not come home smacked of racism. The parts of New Orleans that escaped flooding were the oldest parts of the city—the historical French Quarter and neighborhoods nearby. These were the most desirable neighborhoods in the city and, not surprisingly, overwhelmingly white. The poorer black population lived in the outlying areas, which were heavily damaged by the post-Katrina flooding. When people proposed "bulldozing" the city, naturally they were talking about the neighborhoods most damaged by the flooding—the black neighborhoods. When people talked of saving only a "small core" of the city, as Harvard's Glaeser and others did, they meant the French Quarter and neighborhoods nearby— the white neighborhoods. From an economic or environmental point of view this made sense. The older city was built before the elaborate levee system on relatively high ground; the outlying development was built on what would have been watershed—or permanently underwater—but for the levees. But from the perspective of the city's black residents, as well as many blacks nationwide, it sounded like a proposal to whitewash the city.

And this wasn't just any city. New Orleans occupies a special place in the hearts of black Americans. It is the birthplace of ragtime and jazz, a city with a distinctive French- and Spanish-influenced black culture—Creole—and lifestyle not found elsewhere. Historically, race relations in New Orleans were distinctive and in many ways less oppressive than in much of the American South. Had this been Atlanta or Houston, perhaps the offer of a check and a bus ticket to a new home might have been more favorably received. But there's a reason the song is called "Do You Know What It Means to Miss New Orleans?" Clearly, the politicians, geologists, and academics who wanted to leave it underwater didn't.

Some saw rebuilding as a chance to improve the troubled city, but this too had menacing implications. A New Orleans labor activist told *The Nation* magazine, "For white tourists and businesspeople, New Orleans' reputation is 'a great place to have a vacation but don't leave the French Quarter or you'll get shot.' Now the developers have their big chance to disperse the obstacle to gentrification—poor people."[15] Many black people in many American cities had heard proposals to "improve" their neighborhoods before. At first it was candidly called slum clearance. The rationale was blunt: Dirty, overcrowded, ramshackle slum neighborhoods are blights on a city. They breed disease and social dysfunction. We should tear them down and replace them with modern, well-planned neighborhoods. Wide, multilane, traffic-friendly treelined boulevards will replace the dim alleys and narrow gridlocked streets of the concrete jungle. Bright, spacious, and sanitary modern apartment blocks designed in the International style will rise in place of the squalid tenements and subdivided row houses of a Jacob Riis photograph or an Upton Sinclair novel.

Slum clearance had an old and varied pedigree. The most famous and dramatic example was the reconstruction of Paris in the nineteenth century by the urban planner Baron Georges-Eugène Haussmann. He simply bulldozed much of the medieval labyrinth of the old city to make way for the wide modern boulevards and uniform architecture of the modern City of Light. It helps, when carrying off such a large-scale redevelopment project, to have the support of an emperor. Haussmann was hardly universally beloved—indeed, he was widely reviled—but the people who didn't care for his plans were not in a position to resist them. In the United States during the twentieth century, slum clearance required more delicacy. By the 1950s, politicians had come up with a new, more progressive-sounding name for it: urban renewal. The name suggested that the goal was not to raze the slums (and rid the city of their residents). Nor was it to radically remake the city, as it was for Haussmann. The goal was more modest, backward-looking, and pragmatic—to renew, to restore, to return the city to its (often imagined) former glory.

Older black residents of San Francisco still talk wistfully about the Fillmore District. During the 1950s and '60s, the Fillmore was the heart of West Coast jazz, the Harlem of the West. The Fillmore was targeted for urban renewal over the protest of many of its residents. Sixty-four city blocks were condemned for redevelopment projects that included the Japan Trade Center, an elevated boulevard along Geary Street, and various private businesses. By the 1970s the land was cleared and twenty thousand residents were displaced. But the proposed redevelopment stalled. Geary was elevated and the Japan Center was built, but much of the private development never materialized. No one was interested in investing in a ghost town surrounded by black slums (and after "redevelopment," they really were slums, having lost their economic and cultural heart). Large parcels remained vacant for almost two decades.

Nationwide, black neighborhood after black neighborhood fell to urban renewal. During the 1950s, more than eighty thousand people were forced from their homes in two hundred American cities under urban renewal. Hundreds of thousands more lost their homes to federal highway projects when planners took the opportunity to clear slums when condemning land for the interstates. Some displaced residents were relocated; many weren't. Vibrant, if not posh, neighborhoods were destroyed under the rubric of urban renewal. This happened in city after city: Boston's West End, Chicago's South Side, Pittsburgh, Philadelphia, Atlanta, New Haven, Kansas City, St. Louis, San Francisco. Not every displaced neighborhood was home to blacks: Boston's West End, for instance, was an Italian neighborhood. But by the mid-1960s, the pattern was clear enough to inspire the gallows witticism: Urban renewal is Negro removal.

"I don't care what people are saying Uptown or wherever they are!" exclaimed New Orleans mayor Ray Nagin. "This city will be chocolate at the end of the day. This city will be a majority African-American city. It's the way God wants it to be."[16] This appeal to racial anxiety made national news and gave the misleading impression that Nagin was a black nationalist ideologue, some sort of Creole Eldridge Cleaver. In fact, Nagin was a moderate Democrat, the preferred mayoral candidate of the New Orleans white upper class and business community in the 2002 election. Nagin's "chocolate city" speech obscured his support for a redevelopment plan premised on a downsized, wealthier, and whiter New Orleans. Bring Back New Orleans— the local civic organization for redevelopment in the city— envisioned converting large tracts of formerly developed land into greenbelts to protect against future flooding.[17] One prominent local developer told the Associated Press, "As a practical matter, these poor folks don't have the resources to go back to our city, just like they didn't have the resources to get out of our city." But many people thought that the slow pace of redevelopment made this a self-fulfilling prophecy: as Representative Barney Frank put it, "a policy of ethnic cleansing by inaction."[18]

Truth mingled freely with urban legend, established fact with conjecture, in the murky swamp of post-Katrina New Orleans. It was a fact that the overwhelming majority of people stuck in New Orleans right after the flood were black. There was no doubt that relief efforts were hampered by miscommunication and lack of foresight. Everyone acknowledged that police were overtaxed and law and order had broken down. And post-Katrina New Orleans will almost certainly be whiter (and richer) than the pre-Katrina city. But were the disaster relief efforts themselves a disaster because of contempt or indifference toward the predominantly black victims? Were overtaxed police officers aggressive toward evacuees because of their race? Was Bring Back New Orleans part of a deliberate plot to whitewash the Big Easy?

STACKED DECK: "STRUCTURAL RACISM"

It's no secret that blacks are disproportionately poor, drastically overrepresented in the nation's jails and prisons, and almost as underrepresented in our colleges and universities. No one has to ask whether our cities are racially divided. Ask any ten-year-old where to find the black neighborhood in her city, and—if there is one—she'll be able to tell you. Consider this description of a major American city:

> Locals call the street the "Berlin Wall," or the "barrier, " or the "Mason-Dixon Line." It divides the suburban Grosse Pointe communities, which are among the most genteel towns anywhere, from the East Side of Detroit, which is poor and mostly black. The Detroit side is studded with abandoned cars, graffiti-covered schools, and burned out buildings. Two blocks away, within view, are neatly-clipped hedges and immaculate houses—a world of servants and charity balls, two car garages and expensive clothes. On the one side, says John Kelly, a Democratic state senator whose district awkwardly straddles both neighborhoods, is "West Beirut," on the other side, "Disneyland."[19]

Detroit's racial segregation is extreme, but not unrepresentative. One could write something similar comparing East Oakland with the city's posh Montclair district, comparing San Francisco's Western Addition with the nearby yuppie paradise of Pacific Heights, comparing Spanish Harlem with the old-moneyed Upper East Side several blocks south, or comparing the South Side of Chicago with Hyde Park, as urban sociologist William Julius Wilson did in several important studies of the effects of black segregation. One could have written something similar comparing the predominantly white French Quarter and Garden District of New Orleans with its predominantly black neighborhoods to the north and east. But those black neighborhoods have been flooded.

Racism didn't flood the black neighborhoods of New Orleans, but racism established and enforced the residential patterns that made those neighborhoods black. Residential segregation took hold of our nation's cities generations ago, when no one denies that overt racism was the norm. Some of the nation's earliest race riots were sparked by white residents who used violence to drive black families from their neighborhoods. Many American cities were segregated by force of law until the Supreme Court invalidated racial zoning in 1917. Those cities and many others replaced racial zoning with an almost equally effective private substitute—racially restrictive real estate covenants—until those too were invalidated in 1948. Banks, real estate agents, residents, and in some cases the federal government conspired to enforce segregation informally until Congress prohibited housing discrimination in 1968. And civil rights legislation was no silver bullet. Even today, studies and audits continue to find illegal discrimination in the sale and rental of housing. Some landlords lie and claim no vacancies when blacks ask to rent an apartment but offer white applicants several vacancies on the same day. Some real estate agents "steer" black applicants to black neighborhoods and refuse to show them available properties in white neighborhoods.

Today's segregated neighborhoods were marked out in the pre–civil rights era. We've inherited the racist urban planning of past generations just as surely as we've inherited the gridiron streets of Manhattan, the freeways of Los Angeles, and the cable cars of San Francisco. So when the victims of Katrina insist that it's no accident that so many of the victims of the disaster are black, they are right. It is no accident that black neighborhoods developed in the less desirable parts of the city—the parts of most cities that were available when blacks were excluded from white neighborhoods. It is no accident that blacks continue to live in historically black neighborhoods. Poverty leaves many blacks few other options. The entrée provided by friends and relatives leads others to settle with their own race. And the fear of lingering racism deters many who do have the means from moving into white neighborhoods. In this sense, Katrina was both a natural disaster and a racial justice issue.

But is there a group of living racists who are directly responsible for the injuries suffered by the Katrina victims? Contrary to Kanye West's assertion, there is little evidence that George Bush cares less about poor black people than about poor whites. The conservative Bush administration was ideologically predisposed to be contemptuous of social programs and the agencies that administered them. That included FEMA, which the administration staffed with political hacks rather than experienced professionals and placed under the Department of Homeland Security, where its disaster relief mandate was diluted by the counterterrorism agenda. These were, in retrospect, very bad decisions, but they weren't racist. FEMA mismanagement could as easily have left white San Franciscans huddled in inadequate shelters for days after a major earthquake.

Katrina is a prime example of a racial injury without racists. Like most American cities, New Orleans is racially segregated. Its black residents are disproportionately poor, and they live in the least desirable, most dangerous areas of the city, so they suffered the most in the wake of Katrina. Their homes were disproportionately located in the areas that flooded. They were disproportionately without cars to move themselves and their belongings to higher ground, and therefore they were disproportionately among those unable to leave town before the storm hit. New Orleans's black residents suffered as a result of racism—the racism that established black segregation and a crippling cycle of poverty. They also suffered because of the shortsightedness, neglect, and government incompetence that made the aftermath of Katrina worse than it had to be. It's natural to want to hold the available blameworthy parties responsible for *all* of these evils. But most of the racists responsible for the distinctly *racial* cast of the Katrina disaster are dead and gone.

Some racial problems are as bad as or worse than they were in the Jim Crow era. Black segregation and ghetto crime rates have lingered and, in some cities, actually worsened. These problems—the direct result of historical racism—create new racial injustices by leading otherwise fair-minded people to accept racial stereotypes as fact and, tragically, by making race an accurate, if crude, proxy for some types of antisocial behavior. But ongoing racial bigotry and animus don't bear most of the blame for these depressing social conditions. Instead, they are the legacy left by past generations. These racial problems are embarrassing and distressing to many people today. But no one knows exactly what to do about them. Our tools for describing, analyzing, and righting racial injustice assume that racial injustices are the work of racists. When there's no one to blame, we find ourselves without relevant ideas and awkwardly unsure of what our commitments entail.

This type of racism—or, more precisely, racial injury *without* racists—accounts for a large and growing share of the racial injustice in our society. The overt and vicious racial contempt of the recent past poisons interracial relations today, transforming what might otherwise have been minor inconveniences into severe traumas and making unintentional slights seem like deliberate snubs. If we are to enjoy either racial justice or social harmony, we must correct these problems. But in a growing number of cases it's both counterproductive and unfair to look for racists to condemn. These are social problems that demand social solutions—not individual misdeeds that demand excoriation and individual reparation.

As civil rights laws eliminated some of the most blatant forms of bias, activists and policy makers began to identify more subtle types of racial disadvantage. This inevitably led them to attempt to use the language of civil rights—"racism," "discrimination," "bias," "bigotry"—to address complex social problems with multiple causes, such as inner-city poverty, disproportionate arrest and incarceration rates, and neighborhood segregation. But these problems were not as easily analyzed and condemned as Southern lynch mobs and Jim Crow laws. And they were much more widespread than Jim Crow segregation. The more subtle and complex problems didn't look like "racism" to a lot of people.

And the new claims pointed an accusing finger at much larger group of people. Suddenly it wasn't just Southern rednecks who were racists. It was also Yankee suburbanites who fled the central cities, leaving poor black ghettos in their wake. It was white ethnics, Jews, and later Asians who owned businesses in black neighborhoods and were accused of racial exploitation. It was working- and middle-class people who opposed busing and supported tougher law enforcement in their troubled neighborhoods. Many of these people, at some personal risk, had actively opposed racism in the early struggles. They considered themselves exempt from charges of racism. These new claims of racism provoked skepticism and resentment, not just from people who opposed antiracist reform all along, but also from many who actively supported the first wave of civil rights reform. To the skeptics, the people making the new claims were just playing the race card.

HAILING TROUBLE

In the fall of 1999 a tall and striking black man traveled from California to visit his daughter, a student at Columbia University. He was spending the day with his daughter and her roommate, and the small group stood on an uptown street corner to hail a taxi. Most black New Yorkers could predict what happened next. They waited. They waited as at least five empty cabs ignored the man's outstretched hand and drove past. Later the same day, they needed a taxi again. Again the ordeal. When the man finally succeeded in getting a cab, he asked to sit in the front seat, where he could stretch out his long, tired legs. The driver refused the request. It was the last straw. The man had had enough of New York City taxis.

Most black New Yorkers put up with surly and possibly big-oted cabdrivers. They complain to their friends and family, but that's it. What're you gonna do? File a complaint? No one thought the Taxi and Limousine Commission took such complaints se-riously. Racist taxi drivers are a fact of life in New York, as much a feature of the city as big cockroaches and small cocktails. But this man wasn't a New Yorker. He thought something should be done.

So Danny Glover decided to do something about it. He hired a lawyer and filed a complaint with the New York City Taxi and Limousine Commission. Then he held a press conference. Mo-tivated by the glare of celebrity, the newspapers ran front-page stories about a problem as familiar to New Yorkers as the Chrysler Building. Glover's complaint was merely an echo of a very old gripe, amplified by the power of celebrity. Long before Danny Glover was told to move to the back of the cab, racial bias among taxi drivers had become a stock example of modern racial in-justice. For instance, literary critic and Afro-American studies professor Henry Louis Gates, Jr., used taxi racism to demon-strate the risks of postmodern theories of racial identity:

> To declare that race is a trope [a literary figure, an effect of
> language] is not to deny its palpable force in the life of every
> African-American who tries to function every day in a still
> very racist America. In the face of . . . [any] critique of . . .
> "black essentialism," Houston Baker demands that we re-
> member what we might characterize as the "taxi fallacy."
> Houston, Anthony and I attempt . . . to hail a taxi to return
> to the Yale Club. With the taxis shooting by us as if we did
> not exist, Anthony and I cry out in perplexity, "But sir, it's
> only a trope."[20]

Similarly, philosopher and social critic Cornel West recounts his taxi encounter (or to be precise, the lack thereof):

> This September my wife, Elleni, and I made our biweekly trek to New York City from Princeton . . . I left my car—a rather elegant one—in a safe parking lot and stood on the corner of 60th Street and Park Avenue to catch a taxi. I felt quite relaxed since I had an hour until my next engagement. At 5:00 p.m. I had to meet a photographer . . . in East Harlem . . . I waited and waited and waited. After the ninth taxi refused me, my blood began to boil . . . Needless to say these incidents are dwarfed by those like Rodney King's beating or the abuse of black targets of the FBI's COINTELPRO effort in the 1960s and 1970s. Yet the memories cut like a merciless knife at my soul as I waited on that godforsaken corner.[21]

Glover was angry but not vindictive: he simply wanted to publicize the problem and prompt modest reform. Glover, the mellow northern Californian, proposed to counter the pernicious influence of racial stereotypes with sensitivity training for taxi drivers. Sensitivity training? That might cut ice in San Francisco, but in New York City sensitivity training went down about as easily as a wheatgrass martini. Glover had unleashed forces beyond his own control. Right on cue, two days after the unluckiest cabbie in Manhattan refused to let Danny Glover ride shotgun, Reverend Al Sharpton jumped out of Pandora's box and threatened a race discrimination lawsuit against the Taxi and Limousine Commission.

Three days after Sharpton threatened to sue the TLC, Mayor Rudy Giuliani announced Operation Refusal, an undercover sting designed to smoke out biased cabbies. Operation Refusal used a time-honored technique for proving bias: the matched-pair audit. Two plainclothes agents—one white and one black—hit the streets and stood a few yards from each other. They were positioned so that approaching traffic would reach the black agent first. Both tried to hail a taxi. If a driver passed the black agent and pulled over for the white agent, the driver was cited for discrimination. A related sting was designed to root out refusals based on neighborhood. When the agent was picked up, he or she would ask to be taken to an address in Harlem, a rough part of Brooklyn, or the South Bronx. If the driver refused, he would be cited. Similar stings involved apparently disabled passengers or women with infants and strollers.

As a general rule, black community activists and civil rights leaders didn't much care for Giuliani and his law-and-order approach to governing. Giuliani—a former district attorney—actually did the kinds of things that many average New Yorkers said *they'd* do if they were in charge. Before Giuliani, it was widely believed that New York City was "ungovernable." Graffiti-covered subways, urine-soaked alleyways, gridlock traffic, petty (and serious) crime, aggressive panhandling, homeless "squeegee men" who'd spit on your windshield and smear the dirt around and then demand a tip, racist taxi drivers—these were all just unavoidable downsides of living in the nation's greatest, grittiest metropolis. Giuliani was having none of that attitude. He knew what he'd do with those punks who painted their names all over the N train. He knew how to stop people from taking a leak on the sidewalk. He knew how to handle the pimps and perverts who took over Times Square after dark. He knew how to deal with the scum who made life tough for decent, hard-working New Yorkers.

Giuliani subscribed to the "broken windows" theory of criminal behavior authored by criminologists James Wilson and George Kelling. Wilson and Kelling argued that petty offenses left unchecked led inexorably to more serious crimes. Broken windows sent a message to the criminally inclined: this is a place where law and order have taken a hiatus. "If the neighborhood cannot keep a bothersome panhandler from annoying passersby, the thief may reason, it is even less likely to call the police . . . or to interfere if the mugging actually takes place."[22] "Quality-of-life" offenses were more than just a hassle for the average citizen. They were gateways to general lawlessness. So no offense was too trivial to attack.

Giuliani worked with the Metropolitan Transit Authority to stop graffiti and catch people who jumped the turnstile and beat the fare. He dispatched police to patrol the subways and deter criminals before they got any big ideas. He busted vandals and shakedown artists for petty crimes because petty crime and vandalism are magnets for more serious offenses. He enforced vagrancy laws and put the squeegee men out of business. He went after the smut trade, pushing pornography as close to the city limits as the First Amendment would allow and busting hookers and johns alike. Giuliani painted a line on the street and dared motorists to cross it. A long-standing but under-enforced policy—the "Don't Block the Box" program—made gridlocking a law enforcement priority. With scofflaw motorists on notice, he turned to errant pedestrians, instituting a crackdown on jaywalking.

"Broken windows" is one of the most controversial theories in modern sociology. The hypothesis has attracted a steady and thick stream of critical responses, some of which challenged the causal link between petty crime and serious crime and others of which resisted quality-of-life policing on predictable civil liberties grounds. But "broken windows" makes intuitive sense: everyone *feels* less safe in a dirty, chaotic neighborhood than in a neat and orderly one. And Giuliani's "broken windows" approach to law enforcement worked—or at least it seemed to work—much more so than any of his critics and many of his supporters could have imagined. Crime plummeted to its lowest levels in decades. Critics were quick to point out that crime plummeted nationwide during the same period—maybe national trends such as the waning of the crack trade or the aging of the population were to be credited rather than Giuliani. But these critics missed the point. The genius of "broken windows" is that it doesn't really matter whether cracking down on petty crime reduces violent crime or not; it reduces petty crime. And petty crime is what most people suffer in day-to-day life. Violent crime is scary, but very few people are victims of a mugging or a rape. By contrast, it was the rare New Yorker who hadn't been hassled by a mentally ill street person or accidentally stepped into a puddle of urine, and no one in the five boroughs could avoid the visual blight of graffiti and derelict buildings.

Under Giuliani's watch, the wild city became almost Swiss in its cleanliness and order. Times Square, once ground zero for vice and smut, became a site of family-friendly entertainment, endorsed by no less fastidious a groundskeeper than the Disney Corporation. Graffiti vanished from subway car and street corner alike. Before Giuliani, the romance of New York City was that of a gritty concrete jungle, home to a scrappy bohemianism and an aggressive and callous materialism. After Giuliani it was credibly portrayed as a frothy urban playmate stuffed with haute cuisine and candy-colored cocktails, clad to its freshly highlighted tips in haute couture from chic boutiques. The city still never slept, but before, it was up late because of constant fear and agitation; now it stayed awake to hit the latest posh nightspot or exclusive gallery opening. The city's public face had morphed from Bernhard Goetz into Carrie Bradshaw.

But if one stumbling block could break the mayor's stride, it was race relations. Giuliani's tough law enforcement approach fell with predictably disproportionate force on minority communities. In 1997 police officers tortured and raped a black man named Abner Louima, who was in their custody. Al Sharpton became an adviser to Louima in the publicity surrounding his lawsuit against the city, leading a series of demonstrations in which the mayor's name figured prominently. When Louima described his ordeal at the hands of New York's Finest, he claimed that one officer taunted him: "Dinkins is out. Now it's Giuliani time!" (He recanted the "Giuliani time" claim, but the phrase stuck, later becoming the title of a critical documentary.) In early 1999 police shot and killed an unarmed black man— Amadou Diallo—after he reached for what turned out to be his wallet, apparently to show the officers identification. The officers fired more than forty shots, of which nineteen found their mark. Reverend Sharpton became an adviser to Diallo's surviving relatives and led a series of demonstrations linking police racism to Giuliani's leadership. In the wake of the Diallo shooting, another prominent minister remarked that under Giuliani, "New York City has become the Mississippi of 1964."

Giuliani's response to taxi racism was both predictable and surprising. He was as tough on racism as he was on any other quality-of-life offense. The city's Taxi and Limousine Commission made it clear that the tough new initiative was motivated by the same commitment to enforce civility through legal sanctions that had motivated all of Giuliani's quality-of-life reforms: "Refusal is against the law. And this is the Giuliani administration's attempt to ratchet that up so people understand. If the cabdrivers can't see decency on a human level, they will understand it on an economic level." Operation Refusal had actually been in place several years before the Glover incident made taxi bias front-page news, but after the Glover publicity it was given additional teeth. The new Operation Refusal was classic Giuliani: the iron fist inside the iron glove. Now the offending driver was not just cited. The new Operation Refusal empowered police to suspend the cited driver's hack license and impound his taxi on the spot.

Operation Refusal put liberal civil rights activists in an awkward position. They had made careers out of bashing the Giuliani administration's aggressive law enforcement tactics *and* its insensitivity to racial bias. Now the target of aggressive law enforcement was racism. To his credit, Giuliani went after racial discrimination with the same zeal he had exhibited in his pursuit of gangbangers, panhandlers, hookers, gridlockers, and jaywalkers. Like him or not, he was consistent: if there was a crime problem, you could count on Giuliani to take a flamethrower to it.

But there were at least two problems with Operation Refusal from the perspective of civil rights liberals. Most obviously, it was summary justice. The police would impound the taxi and suspend the hack license *before* the hearing that determined whether or not the driver was guilty. Norman Siegel of the ACLU complained, "They are punishing drivers before giving them a chance to explain their side of the story . . . you can't just hang people first and then give them the trial afterward."[23] The second problem was slightly more subtle. The overwhelming majority of New York City cabbies were and are racial and ethnic minorities themselves. In 2000, 82 percent of New York cabbies were foreign-born.[24] The antibias crackdown on overwhelmingly non-native and nonwhite cabdrivers itself had the potential to look like xenophobic bias, motivated by stereotypes about foreign cabdrivers with funny accents, exotic names, and outdated prejudices. And enough of the alleged racial discrimination involved black cabdrivers discriminating against black customers to raise doubts about the accusations and about the crackdown generally. One commentator offered this account of Operation Refusal in 2001:

> Howard Green is black. He lives on 132nd St. . . . On Dec. 21, he was cruising up the middle of 1st Ave. in Manhattan. At 5th St. he was hailed by Officer Kenneth Padilla, working undercover. Surrounded as he was by traffic, there was no way that Green could have pulled over to make the pickup without causing an accident. He had his license grabbed, four days before Christmas. They set his hearing date in May.
>
> This guy's been driving for 25 years. It's all he knows. So the upshot of Danny Glover's showboating is that a hard-working black man who lives with his mother in Harlem gets thrown out of work four days before Christmas.[25]

Black-on-black discrimination is far from unheard of, but it did cast the problem in a somewhat different light. It suggested that the problem may not have been that cabdrivers refused potential passengers "solely because of the color of their skin" as Mayor Giuliani claimed when discussing Operation Refusal.[26] Instead, it may have involved something more complex and morally ambiguous: the high crime rate in many minority neighborhoods. The same commentator put it bluntly:

Here's what Danny Glover doesn't know: like most drivers, I'll pick up anybody up and take him anywhere he wants to go . . . And middle-aged black people are the best tippers of all. But I won't pick anybody at all up in certain neighborhoods, I don't care what color they are. I don't cruise neighborhoods where the street is dominated by drug dealers or gangster types. I wouldn't pick Tony Randall up if he was trying to hail me at 163rd and Amsterdam . . . It's not who you are or what you look like so much as where you're standing . . . This is not about racism, it's about discrimination. Racism is wrong, discrimination is not . . . Trouble comes in all shapes and sizes, and when you're on your own, you have to be discriminating for the sake of your own well being.

We'd all have it be otherwise, but some neighborhoods are more dangerous than others. Should we demand that cabdrivers ignore this unfortunate fact?

This focus on neighborhoods soft-pedals the central problem of taxi discrimination: *race* is a convenient proxy for neighborhood. It's hard to believe that the cabdriver who won't willingly go north of Columbia University will "pick up anybody and take him anywhere he wants to go." If it's okay to refuse to stop for anyone north of 115th Street, as the cabdriver suggests, then isn't it also okay to refuse to stop for anyone likely to ask to go north of 115th? And if the proposition is that it's okay to refuse people likely to ask to go to dangerous neighborhoods, then let's be honest about who those people are. The same fear, justified or not, that leads a taxi driver to discriminate based on neighborhood—where you're standing—will lead him to discriminate *based on race*.

But when the taxi fails to stop, is it racism? Let's look at a Professor West's taxi experience—offered as an unambiguous example of modern racism—and ask what it really tells us. One hates to cross-examine, but a few details stand out immediately in West's account. He left his "elegant car" in a "safe lot" at Sixtieth and Park. Doesn't this suggest that West himself fears that parking in Harlem would not be safe? Isn't this exactly the kind of fear—fear of crime—that might lead a non-racist but risk-averse cab-driver to avoid the same neighborhood? West won't risk his no-doubt-insured car; the cabbie must risk his livelihood, maybe even his life?

Of course there is plenty of "rational" discrimination that we should prohibit. Lunch counters in the Jim Crow South argued that excluding black customers made good business sense, given the attitudes of their white customers. Had the courts accepted this excuse, they would have made the Civil Rights Act impotent. Law professor Richard Epstein argues that race discrimination might make economic sense when race is a good proxy for cultural difference. Employees with similar cultural backgrounds, he speculates, may get along better at work, lessening the number of time-consuming and inefficient workplace conflicts.[27] The Civil Rights Act, thankfully, does not countenance an exception for such efficient racial homogeneity.

When discrimination is rational, deciding whether or not we should prohibit it requires a cost-benefit analysis. Let's contrast a classic example of Jim Crow discrimination with the taxicab problem. One could say that white bigots suffered a type of injury by being forced to mingle with blacks in settings that were previously segregated. But this "injury" was entirely a function of their own correctable prejudices. Indeed, many such people came to revise their views in the light of the racially integrated experiences the civil rights laws made possible. Those who stubbornly retained racist preferences dwindle in numbers as the years pass, and thanks to civil rights legislation and changing social mores, much of their bigotry will die with them. Integrated public spaces and workplaces are a central goal of modern civil rights legislation, in part precisely because they are among the most important sites of adult socialization. Integration helps people of different backgrounds assimilate to a common culture of the marketplace—and ultimately to a common civic culture as well. Even if Epstein is right to suggest that homogeneity may be easier and more efficient in the short run, the law appropriately takes a longer view.

Contrast taxi racism. Cabdrivers who avoid high-crime neighborhoods are not acting on their own prejudice, nor as agents of someone else's prejudices, as lunch counter owners who cited their customers' preferences for racial segregation were. They are acting on understandable concerns about crime. And unlike the short-run costs of correctable bigotry or cultural misunderstandings, crime will not diminish as a result of civil rights enforcement. Here we face an unambiguous distributive question: Should we force taxi drivers to take risks in order to ensure that minority race customers have equal access to taxis?

Maybe. Cabdrivers benefit from legal restrictions on competition—you can't just paint your car yellow and start picking up passengers. In return, they're supposed to accept all comers on an equal basis. But it's common knowledge that this rule is honored in the breach—try getting a cab to Kennedy Airport at 4:00 p.m. Even with the legal barriers to entering the profession, it's hard to make the case that cabdrivers are among the privileged members of society who should be expected to shoulder redistributive burdens. At any rate, no one has even tried to make the case in those terms. No one got their hackles up over an infraction of taxi regulations—they did so over *racism*.

If the real problem isn't simple racism but rather racial segregation and crime, an alternative analysis suggests itself. Ironically, a cause of race discrimination by taxi drivers is the rule that prohibits drivers from discriminating on the basis of neighborhood. A driver wouldn't be tempted to use race as a proxy for a person likely to request a dangerous neighborhood if he could simply select passengers on the basis of destination. This alone would eliminate much of the problem of *race* discrimination, strictly defined: Danny Glover on his way downtown to dinner probably would have gotten a cab much sooner under such a modified rule.

But of course this would fix the problem of race discrimination by exacerbating the problem of neighborhood discrimination, which itself falls with disproportionate severity on racial minorities. How could we fix this problem? An obvious market-based solution would be to allow cabdrivers to vary their fare with the destination of the passenger. If licensed cabs could do so, presumably they would set the fare to compensate for the risk of crime, and some might be as willing to go to high-crime neighborhoods as to any other.

Some readers will probably object that this market-based solution would increase the cost of transportation for the poor residents of high-crime neighborhoods. This is true. But the analysis does demonstrate that the problem we face is *distributive*: Who should bear the costs associated with high-crime neighborhoods? If we thought the distributive consequence of partial deregulation unacceptable, we could reverse it directly by subsidizing the fares to high-crime neighborhoods with public revenues—perhaps with the proceeds of a tax imposed on fares to more desirable destinations. My point here is not to insist that partial deregulation and subsidy through tax and transfer is the only—or even the best—solution to the problem. It's to point out that we can't even see this as a potential solution as long as we think of the problem as one of "racist" cabdrivers.

No doubt some cabdrivers are old-school bigots. But the larger racial injustice is that blacks are disproportionately stuck in high-crime neighborhoods where reasonable people are afraid to park their cars, much less pick up strangers. Many of the residents of these neighborhoods would avoid them too if they could. It *is* racism that makes this so—not only the blatant and legally enforced racism of the past, but also the racism of some landlords, banks, and real estate agents today. Every black person who needs a cab in New York City is an indirect victim of this racism. As it happens, so are the cabdrivers caught between the risk of crime and the accusation of racism. Operation Refusal does not simply or even primarily punish bigots. Its real effect is to shift some of the costs of neighborhood segregation and racially disproportionate poverty from minority race taxi customers of all income levels onto working-class taxi drivers of all races. There may be a good justification for this particular redistribution, but none of Operation Refusal's many proponents has offered it. Rather than deal honestly with the real and pervasive costs of our society's unresolved racial divide, hard-nosed politicians, pointy-headed academics, pencil-pushing bureaucrats, and rabble-rousing activists alike have dealt the card.

AN AMERICAN IN PARIS

The upscale shops along the rue de Faubourg Saint-Honoré are vaguely intimidating in the way that only the French—to be precise, only the Parisians—can be vaguely intimidating. Parisians are at times warm and ingratiating, at others chilly and intimidating. They are without equal in the English-speaking world in both modes. A resident of any of the twenty arrondissements has the ability to make an American feel crude, clumsy, and unsophisticated with only the slightest effort. Parisians are especially likely to deploy this impressive talent in reaction to some characteristically crass American habit, like requesting beef well-done, demanding Coca-Cola when the meal demands Bordeaux, or failing to respect the appointed times for coffee breaks, lunch hour, or closing.

So it's no surprise that when a middle-aged black woman born in rural Mississippi presented herself at the venerable and exclusive leather goods house of Hermès at 24 Faubourg Saint-Honoré on June 14, 2005, fifteen minutes *after* the appointed closing hour, and asked to make a quick purchase, she did not leave with a trademark orange Hermès shopping bag or with a good impression of Gallic hospitality. Indeed, she left feeling humiliated. But this was worse than the humiliation American tourists in Paris have come to expect. She was convinced that her request had been rebuffed because of her race.

When Oprah Gail Winfrey returned home, she didn't let the matter drop. Before her jet lag had worn off, the Internet was humming with the story of Oprah's encounter with Parisian *racisme*. According to varied accounts, Oprah was kicked out of the store while white customers continued to shop; Oprah arrived after the store was closed and was denied entry; Oprah was told to her face that she wasn't welcome, because Hermès had had trouble with North Africans; Oprah was politely asked to return during normal business hours, and North Africans were not mentioned; the clerk didn't recognize Oprah without her makeup; the store manager greeted "Madame Winfrey" by name and offered her calling card before turning her away. Within a week, the major news outlets had picked up the story; reporters reported, opinion leaders opined, pundits blew hot air. A spokeswoman for Oprah described the incident—*sans ironie*—as Oprah's "*Crash* moment," referring to a popular film that depicts racially motivated police harassment in Los Angeles.[28] An editor for *Vibe* magazine remarked, "What flashes through my mind are images of water fountains that say 'whites only.'"[29]

We'll never know for certain whether one of the world's most influential women was turned away from Hermès because of her race or simply because the store was closed and could not accommodate her. Hermès firmly denies the accusation of racial bias, but of course, they would. The bare facts of the account do not support an inference of racism (both Hermès and Ms. Winfrey have denied that the clerk referred to "North Africans"). But Oprah Winfrey is a celebrity and businesswoman who is accustomed to exceptional service. Celebrities regularly arrange to shop after hours in order to avoid crowds. Arranging for the store to open at midnight especially for you is a tangible symbol of elite status. In these days of instant credit and overnight millionaires, a status-conscious salary man can afford luxuries that once distinguished the elite. But the upstart social climber can't talk an already exclusive retailer into an after-hours browse that excludes the regular clientele. And the common poseur with a platinum American Express card can't cajole Hermès to stay open after closing time just so he can pop in to pick up a bauble or two. In the retail competition that Gilded Age sociologist Thorstein Veblen called "conspicuous consumption," what separates the alpha men from the beta boys is no longer the toys themselves, but how they are acquired. Did you get that Rolex on eBay or did you buy it at the end of the personal tour of the watchmaker's factory in Geneva? Did you queue up for your Hermès "Kelly" bag with the rest of the petite bourgeoisie, or did you receive yours the way Princess Grace herself undoubtedly did: surrounded by antiques from the ancien régime in the couturier's private room, while sipping a flute of complimentary Veuve Clicquot?

More was at stake than a silk scarf or a leather wallet. Oprah Winfrey's status as a celebrity shopper, as a VIP purchaser, as the grande dame of conspicuous consumers, was also on the line. This is a woman who sings the praises of her preferred brands on the most popular television talk show in the history of the medium. Oprah hosts a legendary once-a-year show wherein she distributes fantasy gift bags of high-end products to every member of the audience: getting a seat in the studio audience for "Oprah's Favorite Things" is a grown-up's equivalent of finding a golden ticket to Willy Wonka's chocolate factory. Oprah's persona—an unlikely but winning combination of girl next door and super-elite cognoscente—is too convincing to be an act. It's a safe bet that her sincere sense of self, like that of so many of her loyal viewers and fellow citizens, is underwritten by the charisma of the brand name, the mystique of the exclusive commodity. That's why getting turned away from Hermès was more than just disappointing; it was psychologically devastating. It was, in the words of Oprah's close friend who accompanied her on the unfortunate shopping excursion, "one of the most humiliating moments of her life."[30]

Marxists call it commodity fetishism. Through commodities we replace human social relations—for Marx, productive labor; for our purposes here, social status and esteem—with the exchange of goods and services. For Marx, commodity fetishism meant that the money value of manufactured goods stands in for the alienated relationship between human laborer and human consumer. For Hermès and its customers (and wannabe customers), luxury goods stand in for the relationship between the hoi polloi and the social elite. The right watch, suit, or handbag acquired in the right way establishes one's position in the leisure class much as does *Forbes* magazine's list of the most influential celebrities (of which Oprah Winfrey was first among unequals in 2005, the year of her Hermès humiliation). The luxury brand name is not just a sign of status, it *is* status, status made tangible. That's why being denied access to the commodity is, as Oprah's friend complained, *humiliating*: it is a withholding or denial of status.

Although ultra-luxury retailers were not on the traditional civil rights agenda, the question of status and humiliation was of central concern during the civil rights movement. The movement's most dramatic intervention was in the area of public accommodations: hotels, restaurants, theaters, and retail stores. It was here that Jim Crow segregation imposed the most socially visible stigma. Black customers were made to enter and exit through service doors and sit in the back of buses (when they were allowed to sit at all). They were quarantined in inferior sections of restaurants and shunted off into the nosebleed seats at the theater. They were assigned separate drinking fountains and served (if at all) on paper plates so as not to contaminate the dishes whites would use.

Practical hardships compounded this daily symbolic humiliation. Many hotels and restaurants didn't have segregated sections for blacks. These establishments just refused blacks altogether. A black family traveling couldn't plan to simply stop at a motel when they were tired or grab a meal at a restaurant when they were hungry. They needed to know exactly where they were going to stay and exactly where their meals would come from. The spontaneous road trip could end with a night spent in the car parked on the side of the road; the unexpected call of nature might have to be answered indiscreetly, behind a tree or a bush.

It's hard to avoid the conclusion that these petty humiliations were a big part of the appeal of Jim Crow segregation to its apologists. It wasn't only that whites wanted to avoid competition from blacks for jobs, housing, and lunch counter seats. They also wanted to experience the expensive pleasures of social superiority. Jim Crow's come-on wasn't only the promise that the good seats were reserved for you, but also the necessary implication of that promise: other people were confined to the lousy seats. Jim Crow offered whites a shorter line for the bathroom at the next rest stop. And it also gave a gleeful poke in the ribs and a nod in the direction of the black man or woman trying to retain their dignity as they squatted behind a tree. Jim Crow created a society saturated with status hierarchy. Jim Crow wasn't simply unjust. It was sadistic.

Civil rights legislation readily eliminated these practices in public accommodations. As law professor Randall Kennedy points out, "Compliance with the [antidiscrimination] law in the South was relatively prompt and extensive . . . [and] the ethos of the law has helped to change hearts and minds and conduct in a fashion beyond what many sit-in protesters could ever have imagined."[31] Racial justice in housing and employment markets continues to elude the most talented and tenacious minds in the legal profession, but today it is rare that anyone suffers racial discrimination when eating at a restaurant, going to the movies, or checking in to a hotel. It does happen. For instance, in 1991 black patrons—and only black patrons—were required to pay for their meals in advance at a San Jose, California, Denny's; in 1993 black Secret Service agents waited more than an hour for their Grand Slam Breakfasts at an Annapolis, Maryland, Denny's, while white customers seated at the same time enjoyed after-meal refills of coffee. But these incidents were unusual. They made news, resulted in lawsuits, and created a toxic spill of bad press for corporate management. Today Denny's is known as a model of diversity in the restaurant industry.

Racial justice in public accommodations came more readily than in housing and employment for two reasons. One, discrimination in public accommodations is easier to spot. When someone is denied a job or an apartment, there may be a lot of legitimate reasons—bad references, bad credit, a bad interview. People have to qualify for jobs and apartments. No one expects the employer or landlord to take the first comer—they're entitled to be selective. Because many of the legitimate criteria of selection are imprecise and subjective, it's often hard to tell whether or not illegitimate criteria, like race, also weighed in the balance. By contrast, in most public accommodations the typical rule is "first come, first served." Slightly more selective establishments may enforce the norm "no shoes, no shirt, no service," while only the most fastidious demand that "gentlemen wear jackets and ties" (and even in such rarefied settings the tie requirement is increasingly honored in the breach). You don't need to qualify to eat a meal at a restaurant or get a drink at a bar. Any adult who pays the bill and doesn't start a fistfight is usually welcome. So if a paying customer is treated badly or turned away, she's entitled to know why. Sometimes it's not hard to narrow it down to racism.

The second reason is that discrimination in public accommodations cuts against the economic interests of proprietors. It's bad business to turn away or discourage customers that you could accommodate at a profit. Businesses in the Jim Crow South *had* to enforce segregation—law and custom demanded it. The proprietor who defied Jim Crow would wind up subject to a white boycott at best, in jail at worst. Civil rights laws gave non-racist proprietors an excuse to do what they—as business people—must have wanted to do anyway: admit any customer who could pay the bill. Civil rights legislation was all upside in terms of profits. The businesses got new customers without the expense of maintaining and policing separate areas. And they ran little risk of losing white customers. After all, to whom would they lose them? *Every* business was now required to accept blacks on a nondiscriminatory basis; white racists could boycott integration only by staying home.

It's telling that whites did not stay home in droves. This suggests that Jim Crow was not motivated by a deep-seated aversion to intermingling with blacks, but rather by a desire for regular contact with blacks *on an unequal basis*. White supremacy and its institutions of exclusion or hierarchy require other races as the object of their contempt. What good is a pedestal if there's no crowd to look up with longing and envy? What's the point of a velvet rope if it's not keeping out an unwashed mob? Had blacks not existed, the Old South would have had to invent them.

Federal antidiscrimination laws made these depraved pleasures of blood privilege unavailable. A blow to the flaccid self-esteem of white supremacists, no doubt. Still, for all but the most committed racial sadists, what remained on offer after the Civil Rights Act—a hotel room, dinner and a movie, a night on the town—was still worth the price of admission. True, things weren't what they used to be. The meal was the same, but the dinner show featuring the ritual humiliation of other human beings had ended its run for good. Pity, but one still had to eat.

Oprah Winfrey brought this social baggage with her to Hermès. Exclusion from public places was one of the most flamboyant gestures of contempt during America's long interregnum between the abolition of black slavery and the establishment of formal racial equality. Now let's imagine a black woman from rural Mississippi old enough to have directly experienced this contempt as a child. Turned away while others perused the exclusive boutique's fineries at their leisure, of course she would reflexively feel the shame that Jim Crow had conditioned her to feel.

Columbia University law professor, *Nation* magazine columnist, and MacArthur fellow Patricia Williams also didn't need to ask why she was not admitted to SoHo's Benetton one December afternoon in 1986, an experience that inspired the following:

> I pressed my round brown face to the window and my finger to the buzzer, seeking admittance. A narrow-eyed, white teenager wearing running shoes and feasting on bubble gum glared out, evaluating me for signs that pit me against the limits of his social understanding. After about five seconds, he mouthed "We're closed," and blew pink rubber at me. It was two Saturdays before Christmas, at one o'clock in the afternoon; there were several white people in the store who appeared to be shopping . . . I was enraged . . . I was willing to boycott Benetton's, random white-owned businesses, and anyone who ever blew bubble gum in my face again.[32]

Benetton was a pioneer of multicultural chic, the first major fashion retailer to aggressively feature multiracial models in its advertising. In the 1980s it was still surprising—and I have to say, refreshing—to see people of many races together in a fashion spread. Short, swarthy Central Americans; gray-eyed and freckled Scandinavians; lanky, blue-black sub-Saharan Africans; lithe, tanned Southeast Asians, all juxtaposed in hip, funny, and suggestive poses, a visual manifesto for social if not sexual mis-

cegenation: the United Colors of Benetton. The physically striking and professionally successful Patricia Williams could have
been one of Benetton's models. This irony was not lost on
Williams herself, who deftly juxtaposed Benetton's advertised
ambition—to "wrap . . . every one of the world's people in its
cottons and woolens"—with its employee's inability to "let someone like me into the realm of his reality."[33] South of Houston
isn't the right bank of the Seine, and Benetton isn't Hermès;
still, it's hard to avoid a feeling of déjà vu.

Several months after her tête-à-tête with the Hermès shop clerk,
following all the inconsistent stories circulated in major newspapers, on television, talk radio, and Internet blogs, Oprah discussed the incident on the season premiere of her own talk show.
Oprah did not—as anticipated, if not really expected—recount
her personal experience with color prejudice to a teary-eyed audience live in the studio and in millions of living rooms and
kitchens nationwide. She did not spark the national conversation
about race that former President Clinton promised but could not
deliver. She did not call for a global boycott of Hermès and sym-
bolically burn an offending handbag on national television.

Instead, the CEO of Hermès U.S.A. joined Oprah and her live
studio audience of breathless American women. The fix was in:
this was to be a strategic reconciliation, scripted in advance by
diplomats, reviewed by lawyers, and vetted by public relations
consultants. The Hermès chief executive expressed deep regret
that Oprah had encountered a "very rigid" employee, but he insisted that although customers were still inside, the store was
closed when Oprah arrived, and the staff was under instructions
to finish transactions and show customers to the door as quickly

as possible. Oprah, wounded but proud, said that she knew "the difference between the store being closed and the store being closed *to me.*" She insisted that the employee was not only "rigid" but also "rude," but she stopped short of "racist." Instead she sought common cause with "everybody who's ever been snubbed because you were not chic enough or the right class or the right color or whatever—I don't know what it was." Ambiguity firmly established, the terms of détente could be settled. Hermès apologized and announced sensitivity training for its employees; Oprah quashed boycott rumblings, offering her invaluable blessing, if not her encouragement, to Hermès shoppers.

Like any détente, this one was possible because both sides had something to lose from continued hostilities. Hermès, like most exclusive retailers, walks a thin line between acceptable elitism and odious snobbery. It could not afford to confirm the nagging suspicion that the modern hierarchy of merit and money symbolized by its stores hides an aristocracy of blood and inherited privilege. Oprah's persona is no less delicate: part hometown girlfriend, part jet-setting elite, the epitome of a local girl made good, her charisma depends on living the stardust aspirations of her audience as an approachable surrogate. Oprah has to be aristocrat and ordinary girl, elite and average. The popular reaction to her Hermès story was dangerously mixed. Some expressed sympathy and solidarity, but many were incredulous. Luxury boutiques are notoriously snotty; what else is new? Who can afford to shop at Hermès anyway? The store was closed. Did she want them to open up after hours just for her? Did Oprah expect star treatment?

Even if race was the reason Oprah was denied the sedan chair and fan of palm fronds customary for celebrities, the accusation was treacherous for her: *Because of my racial status, I didn't get the advantages of my celebrity status.* There's something Orwellian about an egalitarian demand for one's rightful position as VIP—a civil rights claim to a color-blind hierarchy of the rich and famous (all customers should be treated equally, but some more equally than others). It's hard to muster up a lot of outrage when someone is complaining not of being treated badly, but of being treated—*quelle horreur!*—*just like everyone else.* There's a wonderful scene in the play *How to Succeed in Business Without Really Trying*: the firm's new management announces that from then on, there will no more special favors or nepotism. Everyone will be on an equal footing and evaluated according to merit and productivity. On hearing this, the boss's nephew—a longtime beneficiary of nepotism—cries, "But that's not fair!" Oprah may have felt like a mistreated subaltern, but to many she sounded like the boss's nephew.

As is so often the case with accusations of bias, the whole truth may never out. The terms of the informal détente between the two multinationals, Oprah and Hermès, clearly require citizen Oprah Winfrey to refrain from making accusations of racism. And Oprah's image as down-home celebrity with a predominantly white fan base makes the race card a risky play. Middle America dislikes black radical agitators and malcontents as much as it dislikes racism: Oprah could morph from victim to villain during the commercial break. Given the pressures, both domestic and geopolitical, we're entitled to treat Oprah's account of events as a negotiated formal statement.

When a black person suffers a slight or indignity, it's often plausible that racism was behind it. Like the black New Yorker trying to hail a taxi, even if we can't know the motivations involved in each individual case, we can be sure that some of the slights that racial minorities suffer involve racism. It's a good bet that Oprah believed she was turned away from Hermès because of her race (her carefully worded official account doesn't rule this out). She said she knew the difference between the store being closed and it being closed *to her*. She insists that the clerk was rude. She's a black woman, and she knows what racist contempt feels like. And regardless of what the clerk was thinking when she closed the door in Oprah's face, the effect on Oprah was the same. If the reason for Oprah's humiliation was that the incident at Hermès triggered memories of her past experiences with racism, then Oprah's race was the reason she felt humiliated. In this sense, Oprah was humiliated *because of her race*.

But none of this proves that the clerk intended a racial slight. Hermès's alibi is consistent with the facts. Oprah arrived after the store's posted closing hours. The door was unlocked because stragglers remained inside, but staff was desperately trying to get them to leave as quickly as possible. Hermès customers are used to being handled with kid gloves as well as buying them: the staff couldn't unceremoniously eject people. But they needed to prepare for an after-hours event; they had to complete open transactions and move customers toward the exit. And they needed to make sure no one else came in and started browsing. In explaining her frustration, Oprah contrasted the rough treatment she received with the courtesy others enjoyed, mimicking the staff's polite salutations: *"Bonsoir, Madame." "Bonsoir, Mademoiselle." "Adieu. Bonsoir."* But what Oprah heard as solicitous banter between staff and customers may have been the frazzled staff's attempt to politely but firmly usher stragglers out. Likewise, perhaps what Oprah took for rudeness was really stress ("Oh, no, not another customer *now*").

Or perhaps it *was* rudeness. After a full day of customer service, the staff was ready to call it a day. And this was Paris after all, where workers strike over lesser offenses than unscheduled overtime. Or suppose, worse yet, it was rudeness *intended* to exclude and humiliate. Even then it's possible that the salesperson was not a racist, but an equal opportunity snob. Exclusivity is a big part of what Hermès sells (and what its customers want to buy). Luxury boutique sales staff shift effortlessly between sycophantic attentiveness to attract the right class of paying customer and withering contempt to repel the hoi polloi. This is part of the ritual that transforms a leather bag from a receptacle for your stuff into a status symbol and a fetish object. It's possible that our hapless Parisian shopgirl made a practice of snubbing dressed-down Americans and mistook Oprah for one of the middle-class tourists—of every race—who she routinely made feel unwelcome.

The Lawyers' Committee for Civil Rights in San Francisco has launched a "retail discrimination" project to confront social injustices in our nation's temples of commerce. The project's first publicized case involved a blatant snub. According to the plaintiff's complaint, the store manager at a San Francisco women's clothing store rejected a return from a black customer with the observation, "I know you wore it, because that is what you people do." Few cases will be this blatant; most objectionable encounters will be more like Oprah's at Hermès. Given the inevitable ambiguities of retail discrimination and the relatively trivial nature of the injuries, is litigation the appropriate response? In a society where racism still destroys careers, threatens liberty, ruins and even ends lives, can we afford to make a federal case of being snubbed at the mall?

In our racially charged society, a minor snub or simple lapse of etiquette may be misinterpreted as a racial insult. The deliberately intimidating environments cultivated by high-end retailers are especially prone to trigger this type of racial injury by proxy.

But is the larger problem racism? Or could it be the cutthroat competition for esteem and status that mars not only the world of work but even our supposedly free time? As the social critic Christopher Lasch observes, "Pleasure, once it is defined as an end in itself, takes on the qualities of work . . . Play is now measured by standards of achievement previously applicable only to work . . . Personal life . . . has become as anarchical, as warlike, and as full of stress as the marketplace itself. The cocktail party reduces sociability to social combat."[34] In some social circles, one must vacation in the right places at the right times and be seen doing the right things, even if one would prefer to be somewhere else. One must not only follow fashion, but chase and keep up with it, changing entire wardrobes seasonally and engaging in a restless pursuit of the latest "it" item. One must go to the hottest restaurants and nightclubs at the time of night when they are at their most smoldering and gain access despite the crowd of hopefuls being turned away. Like jobs and wealth in economic theory, the frenzied pursuit of elite status trickles down to non-elites, who engage in their own equally ruthless, if less rarefied, forms of one-upmanship. Middle-class high school girls obsess over finding the perfect pair of two-hundred-dollar designer blue jeans, unintentionally mocking the proletarian garb of past generations. Across town, inner-city young men line up to buy three-hundred-dollar tennis shoes that they will keep pristine in their boxes for fear of soiling them (or of inviting assault from an envious peer).

These conditions invite dignitary harms of all kinds, including those based on race. It is easy to mistake an equal opportunity slight for a racial one, because the same libidinal desire for status and social dominance that motivated Jim Crow racism also creates the modern social Darwinism of work, leisure, and consumption. In a society where hierarchies are everywhere and almost everyone is snubbed on some occasion, perhaps it is unrealistic to expect widespread outrage for ambiguous racial slights. A climate that breeds status envy and nurtures unattainable desires is a perfect incubator for thoughtless racial bigotry, for the unfounded perception of racial injury, and for the defensive and retaliatory use of the race card.

HOW THE RACE CARD CAN CREATE RACIAL INJURY

During a trip to New York many years ago I complained to a friend (who generously agreed to put me up for the night) that I had missed my flight waiting forty-five minutes for a cab. As a Californian used to transportation that responds with scrupulous color blindness to a key in the ignition, I was unprepared for this commonplace Manhattan insult. "Some of them even switched on the off-duty signs when they saw me with my hand up," I groused. The implication was clear enough. My friend, a lifelong Manhattanite, replied with bemusement, "You tried to hail a cab with a bunch of luggage at four o'clock? *Everybody* knows five o'clock is the shift change. No one wants a fare to the airport at four o'clock. They'll be late turning the cab over to the night driver. *Maybe* the cabs didn't stop because you're black, but I bet it was the luggage."

I was annoyed to have my righteous indignation so deftly pierced. But I was also strangely relieved. Of course the cabdrivers who avoided me were "wrong," in the sense that the law requires them to take customers anywhere in the city of New York. That's why they turned on the off-duty sign when they saw me—they were willing to take a short fare, but not one to the airport. They were *discriminating* against me. But not because of my race. White people suffer this type of discrimination too. They get stranded on the sidewalk with two suitcases an hour before their flight is supposed to leave, and they learn to leave early or arrange for a hired car when they have a five-thirty flight. It wasn't just schadenfreude that made me happier when I discovered this. It was also the realization that what I had assumed was racism was really a more universal human problem. It's still a hassle of course, but not necessarily a symptom of my debased social status.

It's a commonplace belief that the victim of racial stigma will benefit from "naming" her injury and blaming the guilty parties. By these lights, questioning or downplaying the severity of the stigma will deprive the victim of the catharsis that can come only from facing the horrible truth of her injuries and having others acknowledge her pain. But this truth-and-reconciliation approach can do more harm than good when bigotry is ambiguous. If no deliberate racial slight took place, no stigma should result. In uncertain circumstances, insisting that race or racism played a role may itself be the cause of stigma and injury. When I missed my flight that afternoon in New York, I was not only annoyed, I was also ashamed and humiliated, thinking I had been shunned because of my race. After my friend explained that the cabs may have refused me because of my luggage and not because of my race, I wasn't ashamed and humiliated anymore. I was relieved. I could look at the incident as a learning experience (hire a car next time) and as an initiation into the club of savvy travelers. Standing on that godforsaken corner no longer marked me as a member of a stigmatized caste. It joined me to millions of other people of all races and backgrounds who doubtless had to learn the same lesson in the same way. The stigma was gone.

This leads me to consider another interpretation of Oprah Winfrey's reaction to her encounter at Hermès. Suppose her first reaction to being refused entry to Hermès was—as mine was at being passed up by those taxis—to experience it as a racial slight and suffer all of the humiliation that such a slight necessarily entails. But by the time the television show aired, she had considered other interpretations of events. Perhaps she decided not to assume the worst: the shop clerk could just have been a snob. And so, although she was still angry at having received rough treatment from a shop clerk, she had shed the unique stigma that accompanies a racial slight. This has to be a healthier approach than insisting on a racial insult that may not have been intended.

I imagine some readers will see this as an apology for naïveté and denial. But one needn't turn a blind eye to unpleasant truths in order to look at ambiguous facts from all possible perspectives. If both racism and a more innocent or more complex explanation are plausible causes of an incident, it's just as wrong to insist on racism and refuse to consider the other possibility as it would be to deny the possibility of racism. In terms of psychological ailments, blissful denial and depressive paranoia are about on par. We shouldn't adopt Pollyanna's worldview and assume bigotry away unless there's irrefutable proof, but if circumstances are ambiguous, the resulting experience of stigma should also be correspondingly muted.

A mantra of the modern feminist movement insists that "the personal is political." While this was apt in the limited circumstances in which early feminists applied it—gender relations where love and loyalty served to obscure power and privilege— few ideas have been as misleading and counterproductive when applied broadly. But today this sentiment informs many of the identity movements of the New Left. Early social justice movements attacked material disadvantage, political disenfranchisement, and violent repression. But as the long, hot summers of the 1960s and 1970s passed into history and cliché, social movements for women, gays and lesbians, the disabled, and racial groups have become as likely to advance claims based on symbolic suffering and purely psychological injury.

Playing the race card lets the victim of personal humiliation give back as good as he got. In retaliation for the racial insult, the victim can deploy the accusation of racial bias. Sometimes part of the appeal of the race card is the thrill of the vendetta. After impotently suffering a lifetime's worth of racial injustices— some profound and others petty, some intentional and others the result of callous disregard, some as blatant as a Las Vegas billboard and others as subtle and refined as haiku, some from people whose wealth and power protect them from retribution and others from people too poor and pathetic to extract redress from—now, *finally*, a chance to make the bigots pay. The race card is a lousy way of achieving any tangible social change, but what it lacks in lasting effect it makes up for in instant gratification. Here's what Tom Wolfe wrote about this aspect of the racial "confrontation":

> It wasn't just that you registered your protest and showed the white man that you meant business and weakened his resolve to keep up the walls of oppression . . . There was something

sweet that happened right there on the spot. You made the white man quake. You brought fear into his face . . . So for the black man, mau-mauing was a beautiful trip. It not only stood to bring you certain practical gains . . . It energized your batteries. It recharged your masculinity . . . This was the difference between a confrontation and a demonstration. A demonstration, like the civil rights march on Washington in 1963, could frighten the white leadership, but it was a general fear, an external fear, like being afraid of a hurricane. But in a confrontation, in mau-mauing, the idea was to frighten white men personally, face to face . . . "You—yes you right there on the platform—we're not talking about the government, we're not talking about the Office of Economic Opportunity—we're talking about *you*, you up there with your hands shaking in your pile of papers."[35]

Because racism is now often diffuse, ambiguous, and implicit, it can be hard to know who—if anyone—is to blame. But if one is to make the accusation of racism personal, one needs a specific target. If one takes racial issues personally, to respond in kind requires a personal accusation. This leads some to attack individuals who are not themselves blameworthy, like the low-level poverty services bureaucrat in Wolfe's account, like a cab-driver trying to make an honest buck, or like a harried shop clerk trying to close for the night.

Attacking innocent bystanders isn't only unfair, it's counterproductive. It undermines a thoughtful analysis of the real underlying social injustices that prompted outrage in the first place. Playing the race card has little to do with legitimate grievances or responsible social protest. The race card may provide a temporary advantage, but in the long run the house still comes out ahead. Wolfe on mau-mauing is instructive:

> And then later on you think about it and you say, "What really happened that day? Well, another flak catcher lost his manhood, that's what happened." Hmmmmmmmm . . . like maybe the bureaucracy isn't so dumb after all . . . All they did was sacrifice one flak catcher, and they got hundreds, thousands . . . They've got replaceable parts. They threw this sacrifice to you, and you went away pleased with yourself. And even the Flak Catcher himself wasn't losing much. He wasn't losing his manhood. He gave that up a long time ago . . . Just who is fucking over who . . . You did your number and he did his number, and they didn't even have to stop the music . . . The band played on.[36]

Taking every racial issue personally can blind us to the many racial injustices for which no one is to blame. If every racial injustice entitles its victims to lambaste the person nearest to hand, then when there is no racist to blame, it follows that there must be no injustice. As racial politics increasingly focuses on trivial slights, innocent slips of the tongue, and even well-intentioned if controversial decisions, the most severe injustices—such as the isolation of a largely black underclass in hopeless ghettos or even more hopeless prisons—receive comparatively little attention because we can't find a bigot to paste to the dartboard.

■ TWO
WILD CARD: RACISM BY ANALOGY

People for the Ethical Treatment of Animals (PETA) calls for "Animal Liberation" on its website. PETA champions all of the usual causes of animal welfare. It admonishes the concerned citizen to adopt abandoned dogs and cats from shelters, to neuter and spay pets, and to report abuse of animals to the authorities. But PETA goes a good deal further than this. It bills itself as "The Animal *Rights* Organization," and the designation is more than nominal. PETA's brief manifesto is that "animals are not ours to eat, wear, experiment on, or use for entertainment." The organization opposes all testing of pharmaceuticals or cosmetics on animals and the use of animals in medical research. Instead, PETA advocates "human studies": it would prefer that potentially dangerous drug testing and medical experiments be conducted on human volunteers willing to run the risk (or so desperate they'll do it for the money?) rather than on animals, who are unable to refuse. They believe that the consumption of meat or animal products is immoral (to wit, the radical vegan slogan "Meat is murder"). They would ban the use of poisons or traps to eliminate infestations of vermin, in-migration of pigeons, swarms of mosquitoes, or plagues of frogs and locusts.

By their own account, the members of PETA are not simply more aggressive animal welfare advocates: they explicitly reject animal "welfare" in favor of animal *rights*—and by this they mean more or less the same rights that Homo sapiens enjoys in a handful of wealthy liberal societies. In its agenda as well as in its affect PETA is as different from, say, the Humane Society as the Black Panthers were from the NAACP. Famous for provocation and agitprop, PETA has organized demonstrations in which members throw red paint—symbolizing blood—on the mink coats of passersby. It sponsored a series of advertisements in which models such as *Baywatch* actresses Pamela Anderson and Traci Bingham posed nude over the tagline "I'd rather go naked than wear fur"—to the delight of red paint–wielding activists and red-blooded young men and to the chagrin of feminists and fur wearers.

In 2005 the latest provocation in PETA's campaign for animal rights included a website slide show comparing animal husbandry to human slavery, racist lynching, and genocide. Under the heading "Sold Off," a photo of a cattle auction is paired with an etching of a slave auction. Under "Hanging," a steer dangles from a chain in a slaughterhouse in one frame and the adjacent image depicts two black men lynched from a tree. "Beaten" compares a hunter clubbing a seal to a white mob kicking a black man doubled over in pain. "Branded" equates the branding of cattle and of African slaves.

The website, at the risk of flogging a dead horse, augments the visuals with text:

> Will future generations look back at ours with the same shame and horror we feel when we read about ships crammed with slaves or about the forced winter march of American Indians away from their homelands? An objective look reveals that our generation still operates in the same way. The only difference is that yesterday's victims—used and abused because they were "different" and powerless—are now of other species.

PETA's "Animal Liberation" website irritated more than a few members of the planet's dominant species. Civil rights groups issued sharp denunciations. For instance, Mark Potok of the Southern Poverty Law Center snapped, "Black people have had quite enough of being compared to animals without PETA joining in."

And then there was the "Holocaust on Your Plate" media campaign, which compared what most people consider part of a balanced diet to—yes, I'm afraid so—the gas chambers at Auschwitz. After months of protest from Holocaust survivors and Jewish organizations, PETA issued what it called an apology. Apparently reviving the archaic meaning of the term—a formal defense or justification—PETA's apology unapologetically asserted:

> the logic and methods employed in factory farms and slaughterhouses are analogous to those used in concentration camps. We understand both systems to be based on a moral equation

indicating that "might makes right" and premised on a con-
cept of other cultures or other species as deficient and thus
disposable.[1]

PETA's deliberately cultivated public image does nothing to
quiet such outrage. Their titillating advertisements featuring
curvy Hollywood starlets reinforce the impression that animal
rights is a trendy cause célèbre for shallow show business divas
and beauty pageant contestants. PETA's public representatives
are almost all white—the token of racial diversity is the novelist
Alice Walker, whom many have yet to forgive for her carica-
tured and unsympathetic portrayals of black men in *The Color
Purple*—which deepens the impression that animal rights is a
hobby for upper-middle-class Caucasians with nothing more to
worry about than whether somebody else's dog dies.

Accordingly, many critics accused PETA of trivializing the
history of slavery and Jim Crow. But because PETA thinks the
suffering of animals is profound, the comparison couldn't *triv-
ialize*, at least from their perspective. Indeed, the organization
insists that the angry reaction to its publicity campaigns demonstrates precisely the "speciesism" that the organization is dedicated to resist.

The more apt critique was, somewhat ironically, that of
exploitation. The NAACP's John C. White complained that
"PETA . . . is willing to exploit racism to advance its cause."
Similarly, Scot Esdaile, president of the New Haven NAACP,
remarked, "Once again, black people are being pimped. You
used us." Exploitation is a charge that sticks because so many of
PETA's media efforts have involved thoughtless publicity stunts
rather than thoughtful persuasion. Feminists were dismayed by

PETA's "I'd rather go naked" advertisements and pro-vegan spots that featured nude models wrestling in pureed tofu. In the most literal iteration of the theme, a nude woman poses with her back to the camera, the various parts of her anatomy marked off and labeled as cuts of meat. It's telling that when an almost identical image was posted in a workplace, a female employee considered it a form of sex harassment. Perhaps PETA intended the irony, but because the model—*Baywatch* star Traci Bingham—has made a career striking suggestive poses wearing scanty attire, any potential double entendre was obscure. To feminists, it seemed that PETA would prefer to see women treated as pieces of meat instead of animals.

At best, PETA's Animal Liberation website capitalizes on an antiracist consensus in order to advance an unrelated agenda. At worst—as John C. White's comment suggests—it exploits racism to advance that agenda. Those angered by PETA's comparison of blacks and animals worry that it contains a covert, if unintended, implication: *We've had to give equal rights to the blacks; what the hell, why not chimps and dogs?* Even assuming the purest of intentions, PETA's campaign begins from a dubious presumption: antiracism is so firmly established that it can provide a secure base from which to launch a controversial political agenda. This presumption allows PETA to trade on the capital of racial justice without concern—that battle is over and won; why not build on the victory?

The leaders of civil rights organizations, by contrast, are rarely so sanguine about the security of racial justice. They know that the popular story of inevitable and steady progress toward greater social justice is wishful thinking. The real itinerary is three steps forward and two steps back (or vice versa).

Struggles earlier generations thought won and settled reemerge for their descendants to fight again. The federal civil rights legislation of the 1960s may be safe from repeal, but it is vulnerable to erosion from underenforcement or stingy judicial interpretation. Progressives in the 1970s thought affirmative action was a weak and compromised remedy for generations of exploitation; now they struggle to retain it in the face of a powerful neoconservative backlash. The Voting Rights Act of 1968 faces sustained attack in the courts as reverse discrimination and also faces a political struggle for renewal in 2008. The success and numbers of the black middle class have grown, but so has the isolation and dysfunction of the black underclass. The coattails of racial justice may not be as strong as those seeking to ride them think, and racial minorities who still need the protection of civil rights dare not risk letting its fabric tear from overuse.

RACISM BY ANALOGY

When Oprah tried to explain her experience at Hermès to a national—and predominantly white—audience, she sought solidarity with *everybody who's ever been snubbed because you were not chic enough or the right class or the right color or whatever—I don't know what it was.* Racism, classism, chic-ism—all appear as analogous evils. By her own account, Oprah didn't know what it was, and she implied that it really didn't matter—race, class, fashion sense—what's the difference? If that's right, then why should the law prohibit discrimination on the basis of race but allow fashionable bigots to demean, exclude, and snub on the basis of bad haircuts and frumpy clothing?

The civil rights struggle, like most experiments that work,

spawned imitators. It inspired a host of groups—some sincere and deserving, some cynical and unworthy—to frame their political struggles in similar terms. New identity politics sprouted like dandelions, each the result of a seed spread from older social movements. Feminism borrowed from and influenced the black power and racial justice movements of the 1970s, '80s, and '90s. Italian-Americans, Irish-Americans, Polish-Americans, and others of European descent developed ethnic identity politics—a direct echo of antiracist politics and the black power movement. Gay men and lesbians modeled their struggle for acceptance and dignity on the civil rights movement. Before the ink on the Civil Rights Act of 1964 was dry, conservatives had developed the idea of "reverse racism" to attack any attempt to correct years of deliberate antiblack bias with race-conscious remedial measures.

Some of these struggles are indeed similar to the struggle for racial justice. For instance, modern feminism rightly insists that racial minorities and women often suffer similar forms of employment discrimination and harassment. Advocates of gay rights correctly point out that gay men and lesbians experience housing discrimination and public contempt much like that suffered by racial minorities, and they plausibly—if controversially—argue that the contemporary resistance to same-sex marriage is reminiscent of Jim Crow–era antimiscegenation sentiment. But many of the analogies are strained. Today a host of interest groups, such as the obese, countercultural groups that prefer unconventional grooming, and even dog owners and cigarette smokers have compared their causes to the struggle against racism. In his book *Culture and Equality*, the English philosopher Brian Barry notes that at least one account of the oppressed groups in American society lists:

women, Blacks, Chicanos, Puerto Ricans and other Spanish speaking Americans, American Indians, Jews, lesbians, gay men, Arabs, Asians, old people, working class people, and the physically and mentally disabled.[2]

"This," Barry observes drily, "implies that about 90 percent of Americans are oppressed." Something is amiss when almost everyone in the world's most powerful and prosperous nation claims to be oppressed. The growing number of groups making explicit and implicit analogies to racism also multiplies the potential for disingenuous and questionable claims. These days, everyone can play the race card.

How did we get here? The explosion of racism-by-analogy claims has two causes: one distinctively legal and one cultural and political.

Legal causes

The legal cause is simple: analogy is indispensable to legal argument. The system of legal precedent requires judges to decide if the case at bar is analogous to a previously decided case—and to rule accordingly. It is not surprising that lawyers seeking legal redress on behalf of injured clients have argued that their injuries are analogous to race discrimination. Similarly, activists seeking legislative reform naturally argue that the new civil rights that they wish to advance are similar to established legal protections.

The Civil Rights Act of 1964 prohibits discrimination based on race, color, national origin, religion, and sex. This list reflects the precedent set in constitutional law. The First Amendment protects the free exercise of religion. The equal protection clause of the Fourteenth Amendment, drafted with freed slaves in mind, has been interpreted to prohibit race discrimination, and "national origin" has been widely understood to be almost synonymous with ethnicity and therefore analogous to race.

Sex discrimination—although also addressed in equal protection jurisprudence—made the list through serendipity. An opponent of the legislation—"Judge" Howard W. Smith of Virginia—proposed an amendment to include "sex" in order to make the bill unpalatable to moderates and conservatives. Smith hoped that the amendment would demonstrate the futility and folly of trying to prohibit discrimination based on "natural" differences. Making distinctions based on race, it would suggest, is as natural and inevitable as making distinctions based on sex. A coalition of Southern conservatives who hoped to sink the bill—along with some liberals who hoped to expand it—supported the "sex amendment." We know what happened. The odd coalition of enemies succeeded in amending the bill over the worried objections of the bill's managers in Congress who feared that the opponents were making the better bet. But the liberal upstarts' risky bet paid off, and the act passed, sex and all. Today, the prohibition against sex discrimination has arguably had the most profound effect of any of the prohibited bases of discrimination, countering widespread chauvinism that affects more than half of all Americans and, through the development of sex harassment doctrine, altering the day-to-day norms of civility and decorum in almost every workplace in the nation.

Later civil rights legislation also employed analogies to established social injustices. Both the Age Discrimination in Employment Act (ADEA) and the Americans with Disabilities Act

(ADA) borrowed heavily from the language of Title VII (which deals with discrimination in employment) of the Civil Rights Act, and the debates surrounding them predictably compared discrimination on the basis of age and disability to race discrimination. But the analogies were imperfect. Courts have radically altered the legal rights in practice—expanding some and narrowing others—in order to deal with practical distinctions between the different types of discrimination. For instance, the ADA's requirement that employers offer "reasonable accommodation" to the disabled echoes Title VII's requirement of accommodation for religious practices. In the context of religious discrimination, the courts have limited the requirement to cases where the cost of religious accommodation would be relatively small (*de minimis* in Latin legalese). Disabilities are different: a de minimis limitation in the ADA would exempt employers from most of the types of accommodation disabled people require. The same phrase, "reasonable accommodation," has a different meaning under the ADA: employers are required to balance the costs of accommodation with the benefits to employees. Employers can be required to purchase costly equipment and alter physical facilities—much more than de minimis burdens—in order to comply with the ADA's accommodation mandate.

By using analogies with appropriate attention to their limitations, the courts have balanced expanded civil rights protections with practical constraints and the legitimate interests of businesses. Expanding the definition of accommodation makes sense when the beneficiaries of what amounts to an implicit subsidy are physically disabled persons—blind people who need Seeing Eye dogs or texts in braille, wheelchair-bound paraplegics who require access ramps and accessible restrooms.

But able-bodied people with twenty-twenty vision abuse civil rights analogies, demanding accommodations for the sake of mere comfort and convenience. For instance, pet lovers now insist on bringing their pit bulls, German shepherds, and even barnyard animals such as goats and ducks into restaurants and onto airplanes, claiming that vaguely defined emotional "disabilities" justify exceptions for "emotional support animals." Although the ADA wisely limits mandatory accommodations to animals that are specially trained to assist persons with real disabilities, the Department of Transportation fell for the shaggy dog story and ruled that so-called emotional support animals—trained or not—be given the same access to airplanes and other common carriers as Seeing Eye dogs. Pet owners, emboldened by this success, now demand access to other public places: one able-bodied dog lover incorrectly but confidently insisted, "I can fine people or have them put in jail if they don't let me in a restaurant with my dogs, because they are violating my rights."[3]

Even when owners of "emotional support animals" aren't just putting the lipstick of social justice on the emotional support pig of self-indulgence, their claims belittle and imperil the much more profound needs of people with objectively verifiable needs for support animals. Accommodations for the disabled require other people to make sacrifices. There are good reasons why restaurants and airlines don't allow animals, and each exception imposes a burden on proprietors and other customers. Society can and should make exceptions and bear the accompanying burden for people with real and profound needs, but they must remain *exceptions*. A flood of trivial claims threatens to overwhelm the capacity of businesses and the goodwill of the general public.

Cultural causes

Culturally, racism by analogy is the product of a potent combination of sincere empathy and tactical coalition politics. For instance, it's not an accident that Jews were disproportionately represented among the early white supporters of black civil rights. Antiblack racism looked, sounded, and smelled a lot like anti–Semitism, so Jews were more likely to empathize with black suffering. Today, similar empathies underlie the support of black civil rights leaders for undocumented migrant farmworkers, who work in conditions much like those suffered by black sharecroppers in the era of Jim Crow.

Principled affinities are, of course, sometimes hard to distinguish from expedient logrolling: political allies are obliged to support one another's causes, and it's natural—if not inevitable—that they emphasize similarities to their own concerns. Empathy and coalition building can combine in a peculiar tendency to rope together numerous distinct agendas and insist that they all must stand or fall as a bundle. To some extent, partisan politics is to blame for this kind of thinking. The only reason anyone would link, say, opposition to gay marriage and open borders, as well as support for tax cuts and the war in Iraq is because "conservatives"—more precisely Republicans—have adopted all of these positions. Having adopted them, partisans are likely to develop rhetoric that binds them together: gay marriage, immigration, progressive taxation, and opposition to the war become comparable examples of countercultural licentiousness.

Left-liberal identity politics does something similar, lashing together disparate social injustices with the long and tangled cord of "oppression." Consider this statement by a black feminist group called the Combahee River Collective:

> The most general statement of our politics . . . would be that
> we are actively committed to struggling against racial, sexual,
> heterosexual, and class oppression, and see as our particular
> task the development of integrated analysis and practice based
> upon *the fact that the major systems of oppression are interlocking.*[4]

The interlocking characteristic of the "systems of oppression" is taken as given; it's a "fact" that analysis must be "based on," rather than a hypothesis that analysis might explore and test. It's ruled out in advance that the Combahee River Collectivists might be referring to distinctive social phenomena, each of which would demand attention in its own right and any one of which might persist or collapse, independent of the others. The possibility that racism could persist while homophobia fades into history or that sexism might work independently of class hierarchy isn't worth consideration. This presumption underlies the authors' remarkable assertion that "if black women were free, it would mean that *everyone else would have to be free* since our freedom would necessitate the destruction of *all* the systems of oppression." Such millenarian belief in the relationship of all forms of social hierarchy doesn't *require* one to press unfruitful analogies, but it encourages it. If one takes as given that racism, sexism, homophobia, and class bias are similar enough to be rattled off without distinction in a seriatim list, it's easy to assume that identical civil rights must apply to all of them.

Racism by analogy is both inevitable and problematic. We can't banish analogy, but we must manage and limit it with attention to the significant distinctions among different forms of discrimination. In the abstract, racism, sexism, religious intolerance, bias against the aged, and contempt for the disabled all involve analogous wrongs—bias, intolerance, bigotry—and call for comparable remedies. But in practice each involves different policy choices, different trade-offs, and different legal mandates. Human biology and defensible social norms require distinctions based on sex that we would condemn if they were based on race—sex segregation in sports is okay; race segregation isn't. Accommodation of disabilities often entails expensive mandates; its precursor—accommodation of religion—rarely does. Blithe or tortured analogies obscure these differences and encourage imprecise thinking and ambiguous legal mandates. When it's hard to tell what the law requires, it's easy for people to make good-faith mistakes—to mistakenly violate rights thought narrower than they are and to make accusations based on mistakenly generous views of one's own rights. And it's easy for the unscrupulous and the unsuspecting alike to play the race (or sex, or age, or disability) card.

ANALOGIES AT THE ALTAR

Suite 168 in San Francisco's City Hall is a typical office for a government bureaucracy. There's a long queue of citizens, forms in hand, waiting for one or two public employees. It's a little more pleasant than most government offices, in part because most things in San Francisco are a little more pleasant than similar things elsewhere and in part because the people in line aren't waiting to fix parking tickets, get building permits, or talk their way out of property tax increases. They're waiting to get marriage licenses. Some—dressed in tuxedos and white gowns—are flushed with excitement and dewy-eyed with love's first bloom. They have been or are about to be married in civil ceremonies upstairs in the newly refurbished Beaux Arts rotunda, built with the wealth of the city's first great economic boom—the gold rush of 1849—and restored to its original splendor with the wealth of its last boom, the dot-com rush of 1999. Most of the couples—conspiratorial and anxious—will be married elsewhere by judges, priests, rabbis, ministers, mullahs, Wicca priestesses, or Druidic Pendragons in churches, temples, synagogues, mosques, private homes, public parks, exclusive clubs overlooking the bay, and dive bars with jukeboxes playing Patsy Cline. For them, City Hall is just an item to be struck from a long list of wedding to-dos: the state has little to do with their nuptials, but one does have to make it legal, and that means paperwork and waiting in line.

Two days before Valentine's Day, 2004 , the scene at Suite 168 went from prosaic to operatic. The city and county of San Francisco became the first jurisdiction in the United States to issue marriage licenses to same-sex couples. The change had been in the works for only a few days. The city hurriedly changed marriage license forms to read "first applicant" and "second applicant" instead of "bride" and "groom," but the long-standing wry proviso—"no refunds"—remained. The news spread quickly. Through whispers on the subway and excited exchanges in cafés, grocery stores, bars, and restaurants, it spread through the metropolis of 750,000 like a welcome rumor or a juicy bit of gossip, one person at a time—as well as by way of the press conferences city officials held to announce and take credit for the new policy. Queues that were easily contained within Suite 168 on February 11 grew to cover two floors of City Hall by February 13.

The city took in a record fifty thousand dollars in licensing fees over the next several days. Local merchants scrambled to keep champagne and white rice in stock. Travel agents and hotels offered "marriage specials" as same-sex couples from less-enlightened jurisdictions flew in to tie the knot in the City That Knows How. Television talk-show hostess Rosie O'Donnell flew into town with her longtime partner to finally make it official. And it was official: the city had created a media spectacle.

The atmosphere at City Hall was equal parts raucous party, teary ritual, and righteous protest. The marriages couldn't help but be political statements as well. Only weeks earlier, Republican president George W. Bush, in his State of the Union address, had pledged to support a constitutional amendment banning same-sex marriage. And only a few years earlier, Democratic president Bill Clinton had supported the Defense of Marriage Act, which preemptively barred federal recognition of any same-sex marriage, thereby ensuring that should any state recognize same-sex marriages (none had), the happy couples would not enjoy married status for the purposes of federal law. Religious conservatives had sponsored preemptive defense of marriage legislation in many states, including California, where a successful statewide ballot initiative bluntly insisted, "Only marriage between a man and a woman is valid or recognized in the State of California."

The happy if embattled couples in San Francisco consistently compared their marriages to the victories of the civil rights movement. One couple evoked the struggle of Rosa Parks: "It's a civil rights issue. It's time for us to get off the back of the bus."[5] The comparison came easily. Gay rights organizations had compared gay marriage to interracial marriage for years, citing *Loving v. Virginia*—the 1967 Supreme Court case guaranteeing a right to interracial marriage—for the proposition that social justice and legal principle compelled the recognition of same-sex marriage. San Francisco was the first jurisdiction where the idea resulted in actual marriage licenses: Mayor Gavin Newsom described his decision to license same-sex marriage as "no different from the battles to eradicate laws banning marriage between people of different races."[6]

Loving was one of the last of the landmark civil rights cases of the Warren Court. Experienced civil rights lawyers had avoided challenging miscegenation laws. They insisted that economic and political equality were more pressing needs, and they worried that a case that challenged deep-seated sexual taboos might imperil the movement: *the last thing we need is for people to think this movement is about black men wanting to sleep with white women.* Even in the 1960s, when the Lovings challenged Virginia's anti-miscegenation law, they did so without the help or blessing of the civil rights establishment.

By contrast, in 2005 gay marriage had become *the* defining struggle of the gay rights movement. Support for San Francisco's decision to license same-sex marriage had little to do with marriage; instead, it quickly became a litmus test for homophobia. Almost no one really believed that San Francisco's same-sex marriages would survive legal challenge, but local officials and gay couples still celebrated a civil rights victory. And even people leery or critical of marriage generally felt compelled to support gay marriage as a matter of social justice: *gay couples have the right to spend thousands of dollars on divorce lawyers and alimony just like everyone else!*

Beyond the foam of champagne and the din of well-wishers was a wary and tense conflict, a host of cavils suppressed by a conspiracy of congratulation. This was especially true in the gay, lesbian, bisexual, and transgender "community" itself. In most cities this alliance describes a small group joined by sensibility and common enemies and for that reason makes conceptual and practical sense. But in San Francisco, the spiritual capital of sexual liberation, the "community" had become an urban sprawl: large, diverse, anomic, and often internally conflicted. Despite the outward common front, gay marriage divided the sexuality sprawl like court-ordered busing divided chocolate city from vanilla suburb. The *San Francisco Chronicle* toed the party line and ran upbeat stories about same-sex marriages, stories peppered with worries about their long-term legal viability. But the *Los Angeles Times*, five hundred miles from ground zero, noticed that many same-sex couples were now forced to confront a question that one if not both partners were happy to have avoided: Am I ready to tie the knot? As many straight couples have discovered, a negative answer often ends a relationship that was perfectly happy before the question was posed. Some complained that the marriage "option" suddenly felt compulsory: long-term couples felt an *obligation* to exercise their hard-won civil right to marry.

If for men the dominant issue was commitment, for many women it was feminism. Feminists had spent decades developing a scathing critique of marriage. For feminists, marriage was a trap for women, a toxic cocktail of repressive sexual prescriptions designed to protect male egos against jealousy, and a dependent economic relationship in which male "breadwinners" had the whip hand, underwritten by unrealistic ideals of domesticity and by religious dogma. At best, marriage was glorified prostitution; at worst, slavery by contract. Did all of this change when the spouses were of the same sex? Didn't marriage threaten to import its conventionally regressive norms into same-sex couples? Already, many gay couples had settled into a bland (or volatile) domesticity in which one partner—often younger and less well employed—played the homemaking "wife" and the other the high-earning "breadwinner." But these couples had to acknowledge that their codependence was precarious. The law would not enforce equal division of property or economic support if the couple broke up—that had to be arranged explicitly by contract. Couples entering committed relationships with open hearts were forced to confront the nature of those commitments with open eyes.

Worse yet for these wary onlookers, gay marriage supporters had adopted many of the most moralistic attitudes of mainstream society—anathema to the ethos of sexual liberation that had once been a defining characteristic of gay politics. Gay marriage advocate Jonathan Rauch published several articles defending gay marriage in explicitly conservative terms. He insisted that "marriage is the ultimate commitment for all: the destination to which loving relationships naturally aspire," and he suggested that society should not only allow but "expect" marriage of all romantic couples. For Rauch, a *virtue* of gay marriage was that it would stop the "proliferation of alternatives: civil unions, domestic-partner benefits *and socially approved cohabitation.*"[7] This argument echoed those of other conservative advocates of gay marriage whose positions had split the gay community in the previous decade. Andrew Sullivan, for instance, was famous for condemning the gay "party circuit" and advocating marriage as a "profoundly . . . traditionalizing step"[8] that would bring gays and lesbians into the mainstream. Gabriel Rotello was even more explicit, insisting that same-sex marriage would and should "provide status to those who married and penalize those who did not."[9] This was what many feared: the right to gay marriage would become a duty.

This muted critique of marriage echoed faintly but distinctly outside the gay community. Feminists, veterans of the sexual revolution, and even freethinking moderates quietly hoped that the alternatives to marriage that people like Jonathan Rauch hoped to squelch would not only proliferate among same-sex couples, but would also spread to heterosexual relationships. For every gay conservative who wanted only to emulate mainstream heterosexual domesticity, there were several heterosexual libertines who hoped for universal access to civil unions, domestic partnerships, committed cohabitation, fixed-term renewable marriages (ten years with an option to renew!), communal domestic pacts, polyamorous unions, spouse swapping—anything but the conventional bind of monogamy in the shadow of the law.

And of course there were the conservatives. The muscular extremes were pumped up over gay marriage, which they believed made a mockery of the sacrament and would bring fire, frogs, and locusts swarming across the San Francisco Bay to Mayor Newsom's office at City Hall. But what tipped the scales against gay marriage was the large, soft abdomen of moderate opposition. For this less ardent group, opposition was visceral, not religious or intellectual; it was symbolic, not practical. *Slate*'s legal commentator Dahlia Lithwick suggested that widespread resistance to gay marriage was driven by a reflexive "yuck factor": a lot of people just didn't cotton to the sight of two men swapping tongues in front of a justice of the peace. One parent from the city of Oakley, three hours' drive and half a world away from San Francisco, complained, "I don't want to have to explain this to my kids."[10]

President Bush's definition of marriage as a union of one man and one woman made common sense to such people. And no amount of fancy historical evidence, detailing the numerous ways that "traditional" marriage had diverged from that definition throughout the ages, could put a dent in common sense. Same-sex marriage was a contradiction in terms; it seemed to go against the very nature of the institution. One observer quipped, "God made marriage for Adam and Eve, not Adam and Steve." Many of these opponents of same-sex marriage were not anti-gay. They supported gay rights in employment and housing, and they supported extending many of the legal benefits of marriage to same-sex couples through domestic partnerships. In this, American citizens were way ahead of their elected representatives: Gallup polls taken in 2003 and 2004 found that almost 80 percent of Americans supported equal rights for gay men and lesbians to serve in the military. Almost 90 percent supported gay rights against employment discrimination in the private sector. And as many Americans supported same-sex civil unions as opposed them. But when the question was same-sex marriage, support hovered just above sea level in the low to mid thirties. These numbers sent a clear, if conflicted message: let gay couples do whatever they pleased in private without reprisals. Let them file joint tax returns, share insurance benefits, inherit each other's property. Just don't say it's a marriage.

Of course, that's precisely what gay marriage supporters insisted on shouting from the rooftops of San Francisco. The marriages may have been "merely" symbolic, but symbolism was what gay couples who wanted marriage and their opponents cared most about. The practical minds of the California Supreme Court, however, saw that an issue of far greater importance than gay marriage was implicated in San Francisco's actions. That issue:

the authority of the California Supreme Court. Mayor Newsom argued that the California laws that prohibited same-sex marriage violated the California Constitution, which, according to the mayor, "leaves no room for any form of discrimination."[11] But passing on the constitutionality of legislation is called "judicial review" for a reason: it is the job of judges, not mayors. For the court, Newsom's decision had stakes far beyond gay marriage. If allowed to stand, it would imply that all of the mayors in the state, and perhaps other local officials to boot, would be able to flout any state law that *they* decided was unconstitutional. This threatened chaos. Right-wing local officials could refuse to apply state land-use standards and environmental regulations based on their own interpretations of constitutional property rights; libertarian mayors could ignore state laws prohibiting prostitution, gambling, and narcotics based on untested and untenable theories of constitutionally protected privacy; school boards could alter state-mandated curriculum based on half-baked constitutional theories of religious or expressive liberty. Worst of all, Newsom's theory threatened the authority of the courts; it implied that local officials were entitled to compete with judges, invalidating legislation when the judiciary had declined to do so.

Few were surprised when the California Supreme Court let the gavel drop twenty-nine days after the first license issued to a same-sex couple. The court stopped the nuptials pending review of the legal issues involved. The surprise came later, when the court made it clear that it would not—as the city and gay marriage supporters had hoped—rule on the constitutional question at all. The court insisted that a more immediate question had to be answered first: Did the city have the authority to act in direct contravention of state law absent a judicial invalidation of that law? For the court, that question almost answered itself. Six months after San Francisco issued the nation's first marriage license to a same-sex couple, the court held that the city had exceeded its delegated authority. It unceremoniously invalidated almost four thousand marriage licenses.

Meanwhile, three thousand miles away, in Massachusetts, attorneys had advanced a legal challenge that would ultimately secure the nation's first legally valid same-sex marriages. But as the first vows were taken in Boston, the reception had already started in San Francisco. Everyone in San Francisco knew that gay marriage should have started *there*, not in the puritanical commonwealth that had only just stopped burning witches at the stake, but there, on the nation's leftist coast under the glorious Beaux Arts rotunda of City Hall, officiated by the mayor whom everyone compared to Jack Kennedy. Who could blame San Francisco if the court neglected to RSVP? The city had been left standing at the altar, but at least it had gotten to the church on time.

Was opposition to gay marriage like racism? In some ways it was. The "yuck factor" joins gay marriage opponents and those who outlawed interracial marriage, for whom interracial sex was an abomination, a crime against nature, barely a rung above bestiality. When the Lovings were convicted of miscegenation, the trial court gratuitously opined, "Almighty God created the races, white, black, yellow, malay and red, and he placed them on separate continents . . . The fact that he separated the races shows that he did not intend for the races to mix." Visceral repulsion drove opposition to interracial marriage as it does resistance to gay marriage. And some of the arguments advanced in support of antimiscegenation laws have, sadly, been recycled in support of "defense of marriage" legislation that preemptively forbids gay marriage. For instance, courts that upheld antimiscegenation laws against constitutional challenge argued that the laws were not racially discriminatory. They applied equally to persons of all races: whites were as forbidden to marry outside their race as blacks were to marry outside theirs. Today, opponents of gay marriage make a similar argument. Prohibiting same-sex marriage doesn't discriminate against homosexuals, they say: gay and straight alike are equally free to marry someone of the opposite sex and equally forbidden to marry someone of their own sex. It's also telling that when Massachusetts became the first state in the union to license same-sex marriages, the conservative governor Mitt Romney announced his intention to enforce an old and forgotten law that forbids residents of other states from marrying in the commonwealth if the marriage would not be licensed under the law of their state of residence. This law was originally passed in reaction to—you guessed it—interracial marriage.

But there are important differences. The carnivalesque atmosphere surrounding San Francisco's same-sex marriages couldn't have been less like the attitude surrounding mixed-race marriages in the 1960s. When the Lovings challenged Virginia's antimiscegenation law, they weren't making a symbolic political statement or even hoping to file a joint tax return. They were fighting a one-year jail term, suspended on the condition that they would not return to Virginia together—effective banishment from the state. In many states, interracial couples who could not marry under state law also faced criminal prosecution for cohabitation and fornication. The closest antigay analogy is the criminalization of sodomy, which was held unconstitutional by the Supreme Court in 2003, had been abandoned in all but a handful of states years earlier, and was practically moribund even in the few states where it remained on the books. By 2004 American law had accepted, if not embraced, same-sex intimacy; the struggle was now over the *status* of marriage. By contrast, the resistance to interracial marriage in the 1960s was only part of a larger effort to punish and deter interracial *sex*. The evil that miscegenation laws were designed to prevent was any and all intimate racial mixing; the prime worries were the purity and sexual innocence of white women and the potential emergence of a "mongrel race." Laws against fornication and cohabitation worked hand in glove with antimiscegenation laws, and the threat of lynching supplemented the legal prohibitions.

The stronger analogy between interracial and same-sex marriage doesn't compare racism and homophobia, but rather racial discrimination and sex discrimination. Long before any state had passed legislation prohibiting discrimination on the basis of sexual orientation, some of the earliest gay rights litigators argued that antigay discrimination was really a form of sex discrimination. The argument was simple and formally indisputable: conventional marriage laws discriminate on the basis of *sex* in the same way antimiscegenation laws discriminated on the basis of race. Jim Crow marriage laws prohibited anyone from marrying *outside* their race; today's marriage laws prohibit anyone from marrying *within* their sex. Gay marriage activists lost this fight in part because the prohibition of sex discrimination is not complete— the law allows sex discrimination when it reflects biological differences or deep-seated cultural norms. We have separate bathrooms for ladies and gents, for instance. And their hearts weren't really in it: gay rights activists wanted genuine acceptance on the basis of sexual orientation—not a backhanded and formalistic victory based on sex equality. But the analogy was airtight. By contrast, the analogy between interracial marriage and same-sex marriage springs leaks when the accusation is homophobia rather than sex discrimination. This analogy suggests that just as antimiscegenation laws were motivated by racism, opposition to same-sex marriage is motivated by antigay bias. But the willingness of many opponents of same-sex marriage to support same-sex civil unions and other gay rights suggests that this is only part of the story.

The early same-sex marriage advocates who argued that traditional marriages laws were *sex* discrimination did so for strategic reasons. Antigay discrimination wasn't actionable. But in a deeper sense they were right substantively as well. Many opponents of gay marriage are motivated not by antigay bias, but instead by a commitment to distinctive sex roles. Although resistance to interracial marriage was always motivated by a desire to keep blacks separate from—and socially inferior to—whites, opposition to same-sex marriage sometimes may be motivated by a desire not to distinguish gay from straight, but to distinguish men from women.

Conventional marriage doesn't just exclude gay couples from a special status reserved for straights. It also excludes women from a special status reserved for men—that of husband—and excludes men from a status reserved for women—that of wife. Same-sex marriage would change that. When San Francisco undertook its short-lived experiment with same-sex marriage, it hastily rewrote the form marriage certificates, which had blanks for the names of the "bride" and "groom," to read "first applicant" and "second applicant." This is telling. Many people get married because they want the established sex roles the institution provides: a blushing, beautiful *bride*—white veil and miles of lace—set off against her handsome and chivalrous tuxedoed *groom*. Same-sex marriage seems to undermine those very sex-specific statuses, leaving everyone a sex-neutral "applicant." Sure, we could say same-sex marriages involve two brides or two grooms, but something is lost in the translation: at this point the terms do not describe distinctively gendered *roles* but are merely gendered descriptions of the same role. We could just as well say "male applicant" and "female applicant." This might explain why so many straight people think same-sex marriage will change the nature of marriage for them.

Same-sex marriage poses a threat to conventional sex roles, which almost always make some reference to the social statuses of husband and wife or the closely related biological functions of father and mother. Those roles have already taken quite a beating: sex roles are contested and in flux, battered by feminism's attacks on male privilege and feminine mystique and eroded through sex integration in education, the workplace, and even that last symbolic bastion of male prerogative, the military. Female virtues have been mocked by macho women such as the gun-toting Thelma and Louise, the oversexed Samantha Jones of *Sex and the City*, and the stake and holy water–wielding Buffy the Vampire Slayer. Traditional masculinity has been rejected or lampooned by househusbands, Mr. Moms, and "metrosexual" men.

As men and women alike cast about desperately for appropriate sex role models, the media stocks the pond with caricatures and ideological screeds. Crude male chauvinism takes a ludic form in television programs such as *The Man Show* (where the hosts and audience chug beer at regular intervals and make an ostentatious display of leering at bikini-clad women); and hip-hop offers caricatures of masculinity, equal parts crotch-grabbing bravado and crude misogyny. And while male identity has received more sober treatment in books such as *Iron John*, the need for such sustained exploration is evidence of an identity crisis. Similarly, the Victorian cult of pure womanhood meets the Victoria's Secret lingerie model in women's dating guides, such as *The Rules*, which counsels the single girl to deploy the catty feminine wiles and emotional manipulation learned in junior high school to keep potential suitors on the hook. Modern women's fashion careens between androgynous cargo pants, T-shirts, boyish haircuts, and boxy blazers on the one hand, and drag queen–style stiletto heels, push-up bras, and miniskirts on the other. Even the body itself is the site of crisis as the ideal feminine form no longer develops as nature takes its course, but instead is *built* through cosmetic surgery. And the more high-minded "postfeminist" reactions to gender politics are in large part anxious attempts to redefine and revitalize distinctively feminine roles disparaged by first-wave feminism and eroded by the sexual revolution.

This is a hospitable environment for misguided projects. The desperate effort to retain traditional sex roles (or build them from scratch) is often comical and occasionally pathetic. But it is an understandable, if unrefined, reaction to a real social cataclysm: the erosion of traditional gender hierarchy and with it a comforting, if oppressive, social order. What traditional conservativism lacks in social justice, it makes up for in psychological insight: many people prefer even a hierarchical social order to constant uncertainty and flux. Marriage fills this gender gap: it is one of the few social institutions left that unapologetically divides the sexes into distinctive roles. You may not always know who wears the pants in a marriage, much less who gives and who receives in the matrimonial bed, but at least there is an established model for the relationship. This is why symbolism is as important to the opponents of same-sex marriage as to its advocates. Maybe this desire for stable sex roles is itself a type of prejudice: radical feminists have written volumes arguing as much. But it isn't homophobia.

This is, of course, little comfort to the gay couple who want to be married. They are right to insist that some of the resistance to their union is the result of vicious antigay hatred. And they are right to suspect that the resistance to gay marriage stems, in part, from a widespread refusal to take same-sex commitments and relationships seriously. Many gay men and lesbians have their first and most painful experience with antigay prejudice when they come out to their own families. Some never completely reconcile with parents and siblings who refuse to accept them, their sexuality, or their partners. It may be impossible for some gay marriage proponents to see their opponents except through the lens of such early, devastating encounters. After losing their first family to antigay prejudice, their attempt to build a second family in adulthood faces the same menace in the form of discriminatory marriage laws and so-called defense of marriage legislation.

It should go without saying that the state should not advance antigay prejudice through the force of law. And the state really has no business propping up distinctive sex roles either—that's a job for Wonderbras and Viagra. But if a reactive defense of sex roles, as much as antigay bigotry, underlies much of the opposition to gay marriage, the conventional civil rights analogy may be of limited descriptive and normative value. Tolerance of same-sex relationships and eroticism may not be enough to move people who find same-sex marriage threatening because it might erode *sex* roles. And it's a mistake to equate the nostalgic and probably quixotic defense of embattled gender norms with anti-gay hatred and bigotry.

The good news for gay rights activists is that widespread opposition to same-sex marriage doesn't suggest that civil rights for gay men and lesbians generally are doomed. Opposition to same-sex marriage can be consistent with strong support for gay rights in other contexts. The bad news is that the fight for gay *marriage* may be much more daunting than they had imagined—proponents may need to defeat not only antigay bias, but the desire for stable sex roles too.

Some gay rights activists have begun to ask whether the fight for marriage is worth the resources they've been devoting to it. Maybe it would be better to avoid a war on two fronts and shift focus to civil unions and domestic partnerships—goals that seem attainable in today's political climate. And if marriage remains on top of the gay rights agenda, proponents might be better off trying to engage the large and potentially movable moderate segment of the opposition, rather than indiscriminately attacking them all as bigots.

FAT IS NOT THE NEW BLACK

In the early 2000s, Southwest Airlines was a rare success story in the airline industry. While almost every other major carrier had a regular seat in bankruptcy court, Southwest had turned a healthy profit for over thirty years. Most other major airlines chased the elusive business-class and first-class customer and the last-minute traveler willing to pay full fare. These high fares subsidized low advance economy fares in coach. Southwest made those coach fares profitable, even as they also undercut the competition on price. They did it by cutting costs. For Southwest, profit margins are small, and every nickel counts. Low fares come at the expense of free meals and snacks, assigned seats, movies, fancy frequent-flier programs. While other airlines regularly flew half-empty planes, Southwest flights were usually completely full. They couldn't afford empty seats.

If airline travel was once glamorous and exciting, it is now grubby and harrowing. Even those who couldn't afford the fare remember the halcyon days of the jet set—that Halston-clad airborne aristocracy who passed the time en route to Monaco lounging at the piano bar on the 747's upper deck. The democratization of aviation has turned the lounge in the sky into a bus with wings. Full planes are an unforgiving micro-society of cutthroat competition for space. Those overhead luggage bins are full before half the passengers have passed the gate agent. Seasoned passengers are adept at staking claim to the shared armrest, forcing their neighbors to sit with arms crossed or pressed uncomfortably to their ribs. Then there's the inevitable reclining seat domino effect. When the person in front of you reclines his seat, you *have* to lean back too just in order to preserve a modicum of personal space, and so it goes in a cascade rippling all the way back to the seats next to the overtaxed toilet.

In this Hobbesian war for personal space, the obese passenger is as popular as leprosy. Indeed, several lawsuits have sought damages for physical injury and emotional distress resulting from being crushed between the fuselage and a severely overweight passenger. In 1998 a Continental Airlines passenger whose elbow was "pinned to an armrest by an obese passenger" sued the airline for the cost of tendinitis surgery. In 2002 an Oregon lawyer sued Delta Air Lines when he was seated next to an obese man, claiming that the airline breached an implied contract to provide him with a full seat. In the same year, Virgin Atlantic agreed to pay more than twenty thousand dollars in damages to a woman who suffered blood clots, torn leg muscles, and long-term physical pain after being "squashed" next to an obese woman.[12]

Coincidentally, 2002 was also the year Southwest began regularly enforcing its long-standing "customer of size" policy:

> Customers who are unable to lower the armrests (the definitive boundary between seats) and/or who compromise any portion of adjacent seating should proactively book the number of seats needed during initial reservations. This purchase serves as a notification of an unusual seating need and allows us to process a refund of the additional seating cost after travel (provided the flight doesn't oversell). Most importantly, it ensures that all onboard have access to safe and comfortable seating.[13]

Put simply: overweight people have to buy two tickets to fly Southwest. Other airlines have similar policies, buried deep in company policy manuals; they are almost never enforced. Those airlines typically handle overweight passengers on an ad hoc basis, moving them to a row with an empty seat or, if necessary, upgrading them to business class. But Southwest doesn't have first or business class, and it often doesn't have empty seats. Southwest directed its employees to enforce the policy.

The company traded one type of lawsuit for another. In 2000 Southwest had successfully defended its policy in a California

court. But in 2003, two separate applications of the policy resulted in lawsuits. In May, Trina Blake was pulled aside from a
line of boarding passengers at the Orlando, Florida, airport and
asked if she needed two seats. When she declined the offer, the
employee grabbed a seat-belt extension and followed Ms. Blake
onto the plane, where she was asked to sit down and lower the
armrests while the pilot and two other employees observed. Still
unsatisfied, the supervisor told flight attendants to keep an eye on
Blake and bill her for the second seat if she raised the armrest
during the flight. Ms. Blake sued Southwest for intentional
infliction of emotional distress.[14] A month later, Nadine Thompson, a three-hundred-pound cosmetics executive, boarded a fully
booked Southwest flight in New Hampshire. When an employee noticed that she had the armrest up and was encroaching
on an adjacent seat, they informed her of the company policy.
According to the employee, Thompson became angry and belligerent and refused to consider purchasing the extra seat. Eventually deputy sheriffs were called, and they removed Thompson
from the aircraft as she yelled, "See what they're doing—they're
throwing me off the plane because I'm fat!" Ms. Thompson,
who is also black, sued Southwest for race discrimination,
claiming discriminatory enforcement of the customer-of-size
policy.[15]

Discrimination on the basis of weight is not illegal, save under a handful of state and local laws. The state of Michigan and
the cities of San Francisco, Santa Cruz, and Washington, D.C.,
prohibit it, and some courts have held that the "morbidly obese"
are covered by the Americans with Disabilities Act. But none of
these apply to federally regulated air travel. So the legal theories
underlying the lawsuits are somewhat inventive. Trina Blake sued

for the common law tort of intentional infliction of emotional distress. Basically, she claimed that the airline's employees deliberately harassed her. Nadine Thompson sued for race discrimination; she challenged not the policy itself but its application, claiming that she was singled out because of her race. But when she was asked to leave the plane, Thompson herself thought that her weight was the issue; at the time, she said, "They're kicking me off the plane because I'm fat." Whatever legal posture the claims adopted, the sentiment underlying them is aptly put by Mary Ray Worley of the National Association to Advance Fat Acceptance (NAAFA): "It's discriminatory to make me buy two seats. I believe I am entitled to the space I take up. It's a basic civil rights issue."[16]

Nadine Thompson could accuse Southwest of racism directly; the fat acceptance movement plays the race card by analogy. "Prejudice based on weight is no different from, and no better than, prejudice based on skin color, gender, religion, disability, or sexual orientation," according to the Council on Size and Weight Discrimination.[17] NAAFA's Peggy Howell presses the same point more subtly: "Discrimination against the overweight seems to be one of the last acceptable prejudices."[18] Shelley Bovey—an early leader of the size acceptance movement in the United Kingdom—equated weight and race: "People say losing weight is easy—you just need to stop stuffing your face. But it's almost as difficult as having your skin bleached."[19] And when Bovey was attacked as a traitor by the fat acceptance movement after dieting and losing weight, she evoked racism by analogy again: "Do you have to be black to be against racism?"[20]

When Southwest Airlines addressed the NAAFA annual convention to explain its customer-of-size policy, Mary Ray Worley bristled: "The impression I got was they do not want fat people flying their airline. They don't want our business. They want us to go away." Just like white bigots want blacks to go away? Not really. Unlike Jim Crow laws, Southwest's policy really doesn't discriminate at all. It requires *all* passengers to pay for the seats they occupy. If a passenger carries, say, an antique cello and wishes to have it next to her rather than check it as baggage, she is not entitled to rest part of it in her neighbor's lap. The airline would rightly insist that the cellist pay for an extra seat. Similarly, adults traveling with infants can carry them in their laps, but if they want to strap them into the next seat, they have to buy the little tyke a ticket. This does not constitute discrimination against cellists or parents; it is a simple application of a time-honored principle of capitalist economies: no free rides.

Passengers who need more than one seat but don't buy it deprive the airline of a potential fare. Worse yet, the airline has no way of knowing when that extra seat will be needed. If they must leave an empty seat on every flight, the occasional obese passenger has effectively cost the airline a fare on every flight it operates. If they don't reserve the empty seat, they face either overbooked flights or bad will and lawsuits from passengers put out by an obese person on a full flight. Southwest's policy lets the airline know in advance how many seats are spoken for.

And extra seats aside, heavy passengers are a problem for an airline with slim margins. According to the Centers for Disease Control, Americans gained an average of ten pounds during the 1990s. As a result, airlines spent $275 million to pay for 350 million extra gallons of fuel needed to keep their planes in the sky.[21] Heavier passengers cost more to get off the ground, but (so far) fares are set per person, not per pound. Against the norm of one person, one fare, Southwest's policy looks discriminatory.

But maybe it is an indirect way to make the heaviest passengers pull more of their own weight.

In 2002 Jennifer Portnick applied for a position as a Jazzercise instructor in San Francisco. Her enthusiasm, skill, and physical stamina qualified her for the job. She worked out six times a week and did back-to-back aerobics classes. She had fifteen years of experience doing high-impact aerobics. But there was a problem. The five-foot eight-inch Jennifer Portnick weighed 240 pounds. Jazzercise turned her down, insisting that a "more fit appearance" was a job requirement. Displaying the motivational approach that makes it an industry leader, Jazzercise suggested body-sculpting exercises and changes in diet and opined that if she worked on her figure, Portnick "will be a fabulous instructor someday."

But instead of hitting the Bowflex and counting the carbs, Portnick sued Jazzercise under a San Francisco ordinance that prohibits discrimination on the basis of weight. Portnick's claim made her a minor celebrity in the city and nationwide among activists for the overweight. An aerobics studio might seem an inauspicious target of a weight discrimination claim, but in fact Jazzercise was a perfect target. The company's reasons for rejecting Portnick reflected precisely the type of discrimination that fat acceptance activists had long attacked. Jazzercise conceded that Portnick was a capable instructor, able to lead an aerobics class without tiring or flagging in performance. Her 240 pounds didn't weigh her down, and she was able to move her size-18 frame more adroitly than your typical deskbound endomorph. Jazzercise rejected Portnick not because she couldn't make the right moves, but because she didn't look right for the part. "Jazzercise sells fitness," a company manager opined. "Consequently a Jazzercise applicant must have a higher muscle-to-fat ratio and look leaner than the public. People must believe Jazzercise will help them improve . . . Instructors must set the example and be the role models for Jazzercise enthusiasts."[22]

A weight discrimination case against an exercise studio was perfect for exactly the reason that it sounds ridiculous: everyone thinks aerobics teachers must be thin. Portnick was a heroine to fat activists because she disproved this commonsense stereotype. She was a competent—even excellent—aerobics instructor who was heavy. Fat activists had long advanced the view that weight discrimination was simply a form of irrational and invidious bias, like race discrimination. The Council on Size and Weight Discrimination makes the analogy explicit: "Employers can insist that their public representative be . . . physically capable of doing the job well. But any criterion which excludes an entire group of people—African Americans, people with disabilities, or larger–than–average people—is unacceptable." The idea is to identify some set of objectively job-related criteria—"physical" capabilities—and insist that they are the only legitimate basis for job discrimination. Any other criterion is, like race discrimination, "unacceptable." Portnick was the perfect poster child for the fat acceptance movement because she severed obesity from the physical limitations that accompany it in popular perception. Portnick's complaint seemed to present anti-fat bias in its purest form: a simple aversion to fat people based on nothing other than physical appearance. "I wanted to be judged on my merits, not my measurements," she said.[23]

But Jazzercise insisted that measurements are part of the merits.

The job required more than physical ability. It also required a physical appearance that would inspire the confidence of potential customers.

Is it okay for Jazzercise to discriminate on behalf of its customers? After the passage of the Civil Rights Act, some employers argued that *they* weren't bigots; it was their customers and coworkers who would not accept black employees. Courts recognized that this excuse would make civil rights protections ineffective and duly rejected it. It is now black letter law that "customer preference" is not a valid defense to a claim of discrimination. But there is a difference between Jazzercise's excuse and the customer preference alibi of employers in the Jim Crow South. Some white bigots—who objected to, say, black waiters—thought blacks couldn't do the job, based on a stereotype; others were motivated by a simple aversion to close contact with blacks. Even in the minds of the bigoted customers, though, handing out menus and plates of food had no *intrinsic* relationship to race.

Jazzercise relied on neither type of customer preference. The problem wasn't that customers wouldn't believe that Portnick could effectively teach Jazzercise, nor was it that customers would simply wish to avoid contact with an overweight person. The problem was that customers would not believe that Jazzercise would *help them to lose weight* if the instructor was overweight herself. In this sense, Portnick's physical capability was not only beside the point; it was the problem. Portnick would be living proof that Jazzercise didn't promote weight loss. For many customers, weight loss—not fitness generally but *weight loss* in particular—is the sine qua non of aerobics. Let's face it: many people considering an exercise regime aren't in it for the long-term health benefits; they want to look good in a swimsuit. They don't want to be "physically fit" at their present size; they want to lose weight. In this light, an overweight aerobics instructor is a bit like a substance abuse counselor with delirium tremens.

The real conflict is that Jazzercise sells weight loss and fat activists believe the desire to lose weight is itself just another instance of anti-fat bias. Why lose weight if you can be fit and fat? Because of widespread anti-fat bigotry. To fat activists, Jazzercise was pandering to this invidious social animus. But Jazzercise wasn't just *pandering* to the aversion to obesity; it had made that aversion into a multimillion-dollar business. Fat *acceptance* would directly undermine the market for aerobics classes. The real fight here wasn't over invidious bias on the part of Jazzercise in particular; it was over the role of the fitness industry generally in promoting and exploiting the desire to be thin.

"You can't be too rich or too thin." Is this crude aphorism the moral equivalent of a racist slur? Is the widespread desire to trim down analogous to white supremacy? Despite some intriguing parallels, the analogy between anti-fat sentiment and racism is an uncomfortable stretch. An obvious difference is that weight, unlike race, is generally something people can change. Fat activists beg to differ: Shelley Bovey, for example, insisted that losing weight is "almost as difficult as getting your skin bleached." Some insist that weight is predetermined by genetic predisposition, just as skin color is. Others cite glandular conditions. Genes and glands may account for the extremely obese, but they can't explain most cases. Human genetics change over the course of millennia, whereas the American fat spike happened in less than a single generation. Physicians and biologists do seem to agree that physical metabolism tends to adjust to maintain current weight—eat less and your body will quickly adjust by burning fewer calories. This phenomenon of weight "set points" helps explain why crash dieting doesn't work. But they also concur that sustained changes in diet and exercise can reset those set points, establishing a stable and healthy new weight. For some people, losing weight might be as hard as getting out of their own skin, but for most, it's only moderately challenging, no harder certainly than learning a new language or earning an advanced degree—both of which employers can legally require of employees.

The fat activist might rejoin: Who cares if our weight is within our control? We're fine as we are. Or, as Miriam Berg of the Council on Size and Weight Discrimination puts it, "During the Civil Rights Movement, black children . . . were told 'black is beautiful.' . . . Fat children . . . hear 'maybe we should get you on a diet.' We've got to change that kind of thinking."[24] But the comparison actually demonstrates why race and obesity are not analogous. Race is unlike weight not just because of the ease or difficulty of change, but also because of the *desirability* of change. The reason blacks aren't flocking to Michael Jackson's dermatologist isn't just because getting out of one's own skin would be hard; it's because it would be—as Jackson's case demonstrates—pathetic. The only reason dark skin provokes contempt and social disadvantage is irrational prejudice, so there's no good reason for anyone to change it. But unlike dark skin and curly hair, obesity is a condition that we have good reasons to worry about. We can agree with the Council on Size and Weight Discrimination's mission statement that "happy and attractive people come in all shapes and sizes," but it does not follow that obesity should be a matter of indifference. Leaving aside aesthetic considerations, obesity causes illness and exacerbates disease. Although there are exceptions, overweight people are generally less able to perform many physical tasks than thinner people. And, as any coach-class airline passenger knows, extremely obese people present practical challenges in cramped spaces.

The Southwest Airlines policy was designed to protect its profit margins and its passengers. It's not just irrational prejudice that makes passengers cringe when a fat person sits next to them; it's often cramped muscles and pinched nerves. Similarly, Jazzercise wasn't just pandering to bigotry by insisting that its instructors be thin; it was cultivating a social preference that was indispensable to its business. Asking Jazzercise to hire fat instructors is not like asking a lunch counter to hire blacks; it's more like asking a cosmetics company to hire models with severe acne.

Fat activists are curiously silent about the supersized food business, well fed by government subsidies that artificially increase the supply of everything from artery-clogging animal fat to high-fructose corn syrup. According to nutritionist Marion Nestle, Big Food now produces 3,800 calories for every person in the United States. A healthy and physically active adult needs only about 2,500 calories a day—a typical sedentary adult needs fewer, as, obviously, do children. Some of those extra calories go into trash bins, but many of them go straight onto plates and then to expanding waistlines. As the burger kingpins devise new and devious means to turn us into junk-food junkies (Nestle reports that Big Food spends $36 billion a year on marketing), the fashion, entertainment, and dieting industries work just as hard to convince us that only the rail-thin and super-fit are worthy of success, esteem, and affection.

There is an injustice here. But a legal entitlement to "as much space as I take up" will only exacerbate it. The fat acceptance movement is right to point out that contempt for the overweight is is both cruel and counterproductive. But it asks society to accept a wishful fantasy when it insists that obesity is unrelated to physical health and physical capabilities. And it demands not equal treatment, but rather a covert subsidy when it insists that employers, insurers, and common carriers ignore the objective costs associated with obesity. The hollow notion of "acceptance" cannot justify this subsidy, which rich and poor obese people alike would enjoy at the expense of everyone else, rich and poor. Worst of all, by ignoring hard facts about obesity, the fat acceptance movement obscures the role that irresponsible government policy and socially indifferent industries play in encouraging the lifestyle that leads to this unfortunate and often avoidable condition.

KEEPING DOWN APPEARANCES

In the winter of 1992 the city of Santa Cruz, California, was in the midst of a social transition typical of cities on the Left Coast. The coastal commune was home to an assortment of post-1967 idealists: beach bums, skate punks, ex-hippies, burnouts, dropouts, New Age spiritualists, and evangelical Holy Rollers. These free spirits and nonconformists had, in time-honored American tradition, rejected the lifestyle and norms of Middle America and kept moving west until they ran out of land. As the veterans of the Summer of Love aged and mellowed, like the fine wines that took the place of more potent narcotics, the alternative lifestyle was carried on by a new generation. Instead of long hair, they had purple and pink buzz cuts; instead of beads and sandals, they had pierced noses and Doc Martens combat boots. But the spirit was the same: individual expression as an imperative, antistyle as the highest form of fashion, personal grooming as protest, and hashed-out haberdashery as a social statement that read, as best as the squares and the straights could make out, "Up yours."

Of course Santa Cruz, like any other town, also had its conventional bourgeoisie. And the alternative lifestyle had proved very profitable for some members of the counterculture: hippie communes had morphed into multi-acre private estates; beach huts had been transformed into profitable cafés, surfboard shops, real estate brokerages. The city's laid-back vibe attracted over-caffeinated venture capitalists and insomniac software engineers from beyond the Santa Cruz Mountains in Silicon Valley. Like a shot of espresso after a bong hit, this was an unnerving mix. Self-employed millionaires waited in line with growing annoyance at the organic-coffee shops as unemployed burnouts leisurely pondered the relative merits of chai tea and chamomile; BMWs roared over the dotted yellow line on Highway 1 to pass diesel engine VW buses. Like Berkeley to the north, where the craftsman cottages that once housed day-trippers and Deadheads now sold for upward of a cool million, and like Santa Monica to the south, where camping and clambakes on the beach had given way to ocean-side condos for Hollywood executives and crab salad at The Ivy, the times they were a-changin' in Santa Cruz.

The "ugly law" was a manifesto for countercultural Santa Cruz. It was going to outlaw discrimination on the basis of *per-*

sonal appearance. The idea came from a group called the Body Image Task Force, which started off going after discrimination on the basis of height and weight. But now they wanted to do more than that. They also wanted to attack the "simple bigotry" that led employers to discriminate in favor of pretty faces and conventional grooming.

The ugly law was what you got when the counterculture took control of the state. After decades of complaining about bourgeois morality, it turned out that the members of the counterculture were just as moralistic as any graying burgher with a mortgage. Santa Cruz was the site of a collision of the New Age and the evangelical, and its counterculture reflected these influences, combining New Ageism's focus on self-actualization with an evangelist's zeal and sense of moral fervor. The combination wasn't as incongruous as it may seem. New Left New Ageism and right-wing Christian fundamentalism have a lot in common: charismatic leaders, insular communes, the priority of the supernatural over the material and of faith over reason, and *especially* the centrality of righteousness. This isn't mere coincidence. As Tom Wolfe noticed, it was the hippies who revitalized evangelical Christianity in the 1970s. A lot of people saw God after dropping acid, and for some, the experience stuck. And ironically, New Age spiritual cults—ESP practitioners, UFO believers, and the self-actualization movements of the Me Decade—all owed a debt to Christianity, itself considered a cult until Constantine got religion.

A common goal of many of the movements of the New Left—New Age spirituality, hippie Christian evangelism, and, more recently, left-wing multiculturalism, with its emphasis on cultural authenticity—was, as Wolfe puts it, to "strip away all of the shams and excess baggage of society . . . in order to find the

Real Me . . . a spark of the light of God. In most mortals that spark is asleep . . . all but smothered by the facades and general falseness of society . . ."[25] In each instance, the conventions and norms identified with "society"—the scientific method, the theory of evolution, the separation of church and state, Western medicine, Western culture—were dismissed as sham and subterfuge, impediments to the discovery and flourishing of the Real Me. And if "society" didn't like the looks of the Real Me—green hair, pierced nostrils, gangbanger tattoos, do-rags, black nail polish on my upturned middle finger—well, that was society's hang-up.

A former psychiatric aide named Cooper Hazen earned the dubious honor of unofficial poster boy for Santa Cruz's proposed ugly law. He had kept his job despite purple hair, five earrings, and a nose ring, but his pierced tongue had the stud that broke the camel's back. The Associated Press reported Hazen's account of his termination: "Thith ith wha gah me thierd."[26] Another supporter—a woman with a partially shaved head and a black diagonal line drawn across her face—said that she was tired of being portrayed as an extremist and went on to wax belligerent and sociological: "I wish I had blue hair tonight. There's such a national fear of people having blue hair."[27] A man with a Fidel Castro beard, long hair tied in a ponytail, and a button reading PROUDLY SERVING MY CORPORATE MASTERS supported the ordinance because it "gets everyone down to an equal level."[28]

This type of equality recalled Senator Roman Hruska's notorious defense of the failed Supreme Court nominee Harold Carswell: "Even if he is mediocre," argued Hruska, "there are a lot of mediocre judges and people and lawyers. They are entitled to a little representation, aren't they?" Opponents of the ugly law thought society should reward those willing to make an effort in their personal grooming. "If someone looks and acts as if they don't care what others think, they risk being rejected," one local business owner insisted.[29] The free market, they thought, encourages people to improve, to pull themselves *up* to compete with the best. The ordinance would destroy these incentives and pull everyone *down* to an "equal level" with the worst.

Casting call" read the full-page ad announcing job openings at the Clift Hotel in San Francisco. The recently renovated Clift was opening at the peak of the city's high-tech economic boom. It was the latest ultrahip hotel in a chain that included trendy properties in New York, London, Miami, and Los Angeles. Opening night was studded with minor stars, the crowd buzzing in anticipation of the arrival of the English actress Elizabeth Hurley, San Francisco's celebrity mayor Willie Brown, and the hotelier and celebrity in his own right Ian Schrager. The interior was designed by the enfant terrible of contemporary design, Philippe Starck. Lights were dim. Walls were covered with plasma screens showing avant-garde video art. The bar served twenty different types of martinis—they had lavender martinis, lychee martinis, green tea martinis, chocolate ambrosia espresso upside-down martinis. If you asked for gin, vermouth, and an olive, they had bouncers ready to show you the sidewalk on Geary Street.

A job interview was good enough for other hotels, but staffing up the Clift entailed a casting call. Anyone who was to don the hotel's designer uniforms had to do more than a job;

they had to play a role. The hotel lobby wasn't a place to park your luggage and wait for a bellhop; it was a stage. The corridors were Seventh Avenue catwalks, and it was always Fashion Week. Hospitality industry skills were all well and good, but first and foremost, staff at the Clift had to look the part. A female employee was invariably tall and lithe, with high cheekbones; she wore full makeup, a French manicure, and a pout. Men were clean-shaven, muscular, and lantern-jawed or clean-shaven, lanky, and vaguely androgynous. The archetypes were the young Brad Pitt and the young David Bowie. The person behind the bar wasn't a bartender (as a sip of the cocktails proved), but he had probably played one on TV.

Before its renovation, the Clift Hotel had an extraordinarily skilled and professional—but not especially good-looking— staff. Afterward, it had an extraordinarily good-looking, but not especially skilled or professional, staff. The trade-off was obvious: one could find either looks or skills easily enough, but it was hard to find both inhabiting the same body. The Clift's new management went for looks, and it transformed a struggling grande dame of faded elegance into one of the hottest dates in the city.

Other successful hotels may not vet for supermodel bone structure, but they do impose detailed grooming codes to insure that employees conform to a refined corporate image. At the Ritz-Carlton hotel, for instance,

> employees find that if they want to keep their jobs, they have to check their personal style at the door of their workplace. Everything about their appearance . . . is . . . preordained by a . . . corporate personnel or human resources

department . . . guidelines require that hair be a "natural color," . . . other forbidden looks: beards and goatees, "mutton chop" sideburns, dreadlocks, big hair (buns, twists or bangs higher than 3 inches from the top of the head), earrings larger than . . . a quarter, more than two rings on each hand, skirt lengths higher than 2 inches above the top of the knee and long fingernails.[30]

"Appearance discrimination" isn't always a simple preference for the conventionally beautiful. Sometimes it may be more a matter of having the right look for the job. The Clift wanted chic and stylish employees, not steamy sexpots. The right look was a Seventh Avenue fashion house, not the Playboy Mansion. The Ritz-Carlton prohibited shorts skirts, big hair, long nails, and jewelry not because they are unattractive but, one might say, because they are too attractive—overly sexy and therefore inappropriate for a business-oriented hotel. Beauty is not only in the eye of the beholder, it's also in the light of context.

Former Harvard librarian Desiree Goodwin learned this the hard way. In her lawsuit against Harvard, Goodwin claimed that she was the victim of both race and sex discrimination. But the accusation that made headlines was her claim that she was unfairly "seen merely as a pretty girl who wore sexy outfits, low cut blouses, and tight pants."[31] Goodwin claimed that she was denied promotion because she was too pretty. Predictably, this provoked groans and the rolling of eyes. It is hard to believe that discrimination against good-looking people is a pressing social problem that demands judicial attention. The claim also, predictably, invited critical evaluations of Goodwin's looks: color photos of her, caught on good days and bad, inevitably accompanied the stories and fueled speculation and critique. Jokes involving sexy librarians flooded the Internet. Conservative bloggers and Harvard loyalists unanimously declared that Goodwin's looks belied her claim.

In fact, Goodwin was an attractive young woman with soft features, full lips, and clear olive skin. It isn't hard to imagine her, dressed in even mildly provocative clothing, creating a stir among randy undergraduates and oversexed professors. We can imagine senior staff, resentful and repressed, punishing the innocent and lovely Goodwin, whose only offense was that she reminded them daily of their own inadequacies and frustrations. Alternatively, we can imagine a sensitive administration's concern that Goodwin's youthful charms and insouciant attire would distract patrons and staff alike from the serious business of scholarly research. Or perhaps people influenced by the stereotype that looks and brains are mutually exclusive simply couldn't take her seriously.

Unfortunately for Goodwin, discrimination on the basis of good looks is not actionable in Massachusetts (and Harvard won in court on the claims of race and sex discrimination), but the law of the commonwealth aside, if Goodwin *was* a victim of appearance discrimination, should she have a legal case? If Goodwin's clothing and demeanor were the problem, it would seem fair to expect her to conform to the norms of her workplace. But this might be harder to do than it sounds. Unlike the Ritz-Carlton, which offers employees a detailed dress code, elite universities give no guidance in matters of appearance. One is expected to know what not to wear. Maybe rigid grooming codes aren't so bad—at least they offer all employees a clear and attainable goal. In their absence, inappropriate attire and grooming are usually taken as symptoms of deeper faults: a crude sensibility, poor taste, bad upbringing. Success in the establishment often owes as much to style as to substance. And it's the rare Gatsby-like figure who can learn this style in adulthood; typically, one is to the manner born.

It's possible that Goodwin faced not race or sex discrimination, as she alleged in court, and not exactly looksism, as she asserted in the press, but a form of class bias. Discrimination on the basis of elusive traits such as demeanor and poise may well work to disadvantage entire socioeconomic groups. But it is hard to imagine how the law could define or identify, much less prevent, such discrimination. Discrimination on the basis of appearance *sounds* more objective—more like discrimination on the basis of race.

Of Santa Cruz's ugly law, one pundit asked rhetorically, "Is a law banning discrimination for reasons of personal appearance really necessary? Has there been a rash of unfair, unjustified terminations by employers based on looks? Are landlords throwing people out of their homes because they are ugly?"[32] Actually, the answer to some of these rhetorical questions is yes. Studies have shown that attractive job applicants were offered higher salaries than non-attractive applicants were offered for the same jobs.[33] Professional personnel officers evaluating résumés with photos attached preferred attractive to unattractive applicants with similar objective qualifications.[34] Looks matter not only in the image-obsessed entertainment and fashion industries but also in skilled professions where one might expect the importance of expertise and training to overwhelm the effects of physical attractiveness. One study found a prettiness premium in the salaries of elite law school graduates: attractive lawyers earned significantly more than average-looking or "homely" lawyers with the same qualifications and educational pedigree.[35] "Appearance discrimination" wasn't just a crackpot idea of ideological extremists and grungy burnouts. The clean-scrubbed, mainstream careerists of the *Harvard Law Review* even weighed in on the question: a note by a member of the *Review* proposed in 1987 that federal law should prohibit appearance discrimination.[36]

"It gets everyone down to an equal level" wasn't an inspiring slogan. But the law's sponsor, Councilman Neal Coonerty, had a better one: "People should be judged on the basis of real criteria, their ability to perform the job or pay the rent, and that should be the sole criteria," he insisted. "What this ordinance is really saying is, hire the best qualified person."[37] So the ugly law would not put the talented on the same level with the inept or equalize the rewards given to the industrious with those of the shiftless. It would not get everyone down to an equal level. Instead, it would ensure that people were sorted according to their objective qualifications rather than their superficial appearance.

But employers like the Ritz-Carlton and the Clift would insist that appearance *is* a job qualification. The Clift's gorgeous new staff and designer uniforms were as important to its image as its remodeled guest rooms and designer lobby. The Ritz-Carlton's customers expect elegance and refinement, not the working-class flash of big hair and press-on nails or the trendy bohemianism of goatees and muttonchop sideburns.

Can physical appearance be a job qualification? Or is it—like race—a personal characteristic that employers and customers should ignore? It helps in answering these questions to notice that grooming is unlike race, in that it is within individual control. So "discrimination" on the basis of grooming is really just a rule about employee behavior. And control over behavior is of course exactly what employees must relinquish to their employers in return for wages. A requirement that employees conform to a dress code is no different from any other job requirement.

There are exceptions. A dress code could be an underhanded way to deter members of minority groups from taking a job. An employer is within its rights to insist on certain hairstyles and grooming, but if an employer banned, say, all-braided hairstyles for the *purpose* of pushing black women out of its workforce, it would be liable for race discrimination "by proxy." The law also requires employers to accommodate religious observance when the burden of doing so is small. An employer might have to make exceptions to a grooming code for religiously required headscarves, turbans, and yarmulkes. And some dress codes might be sexually demeaning: for example, courts have found that a requirement that women wear uniforms while men are allowed to wear business suits and a requirement that women wear sexually provocative attire in a professional setting were unlawful sex discrimination. But for the most part, employers are free to establish workplace dress codes. Even the Santa Cruz "ugly law" was amended to allow dress codes before it was enacted.

But what about physical features that—like race—can't easily be changed? Is it like racism for employers to vet potential employees for supermodel good looks? The ancients thought that good looks reflected less visible virtues such as kindness and integrity, and physical beauty was itself considered a form of virtue. Aristotle reportedly said that personal beauty was a better introduction than any letter. In the Middle Ages, it was widely believed that truthfulness could be determined from a person's facial features. The premise of Oscar Wilde's famous novel *The Picture of Dorian Gray* is that cruelty and vice make themselves known in visible form as blemishes, wrinkles, and scars. For the aesthetes of the nineteenth century, the taste for corporeal beauty was one of the many compulsions—like the closely related tastes for intoxicating drink and for sex—that defy rational justfication but nevertheless demand respect because they define our humanity. They are what make us more than brains on stilts, machines without the ghost. The famous aesthete Wilde—characteristically droll but not facetious—wrote, "It is only shallow people who do not judge by appearances. The true mystery of the world is the visible, not the invisible."

Thankfully, few people today endorse the belief that physical appearance corresponds to inward virtue. But most people value good looks in and of themselves. All other things being equal, most people prefer beauty. And many people choose to endure other faults for the sake of appearances: drivers stand on the shoulders of highways next to roadsters that are no less stylish with hoods raised, belching steam; homeowners squirm on couches and chairs that resemble modern sculpture and are as comfortable to sit on; women teeter about in sexy shoes that will help podiatrists finance lavish retirements; lovers endure the company of vain and selfish partners who inspire the lust and envy of passersby. It's fair enough to think these people silly and impractical, but should we outlaw their preferences? If a proprietor can fill a restaurant, bar, or hotel with paying customers who prefer attractive staff even to competent service (if you think this isn't possible, you've obviously never been to Manhattan, Los Angeles, or Miami), should the law condemn him?

If the complaint is that good looks are the gift of fortuity rather than the fruit of labor, it should worry us that those who issue the righteous call to prohibit discrimination on the basis of looks are happy to leave other unearned advantages to lie where they fall. Lawyers and academics are quick to condemn the "superficial" preference for beauty—a quality we as a group have in relatively short supply—but I have yet to hear a pointy-headed intellectual suggest that it is unjust to reward inherited intelligence. We all work with what we have: should those blessed with high IQs be free to capitalize on their native intelligence while those blessed with high cheekbones be denied their natural advantages?

CULTURAL DISCRIMINATION: A RACE CARD WITH NO LIMIT

"Our Hair is Nappy because the Universe is in coils, just like our hair, which makes for a connection of 'Positive Energy' that we receive and give back to the Universe, our Life Force" reads the first sentence of a website dedicated to black women's hair. This is a lot to attribute to so many dead strands of protein, vestiges of the fur that warmed our bodies in an earlier stage of evolution. But such sentiments are an understandable counterreaction to decades of frankly racist denigration of the characteristics of black hair. Conventional slang dubbed straight or wavy hair "good hair," with the unavoidable implication that coarse or "nappy" hair is bad. For many blacks—especially women, whose gender leaves them more vulnerable to extant social norms of beauty—the morning grooming ritual is also a painful struggle with racial contempt. Anyone who hasn't taken a preemptive strike and shaved it all off has to give some thought to her hair. Most women fret about it, noting their good hair days with satisfaction and lamenting the inevitable occasions when too much humidity, wind, sun, or smog, or a thousand other unavoidable conditions, make for a bad hair day. But for many black women it is all of this plus the stubborn fact that their hair refuses to conform to social expectations. Naturally long and flowing hair is rare among all but the most fortunate women of European and Asian decent. Among black women it is almost unheard of. Yet that is what society— not to mention the boys of all races—seems to like. What's a girl to do?

For many, capitalism and technology provide an answer. Modern cosmetology offers a gauntlet of innovative treatments marketed to fix "bad" hair, but which may be better suited to extracting confessions of heresy in the course of a religious inquisition: lye- or acid-based chemical straighteners, hot combs, irons, curlers and presses, high-tech Japanese perma-straightening techniques, and sixteen-hour processes in which individual strands of luxurious hair, purchased and imported at great cost from raven-haired maidens of the Far East, are woven by hand to augment the customer's own inadequate supply.

Renewing our faith in the human spirit, many black women rebelled against this thumbscrews-and-rack approach to hair care. But as the history of oppression and injustice demonstrates on too many occasions, the reaction can be almost as vicious as the original offense. The tyranny of "good hair" has given way to the despotism of "authenticity." Black women who want to straighten their hair are derided as self-hating sellouts. God help the daring black woman who dyes it blond or experiments with colored contact lenses. Scholarly treatises and online screeds singing the praises of naturally black hair rarely resist a dig at the benighted bimbos who still condition theirs. The possibility that hair is simply personal style, unburdened by political significance, is as popular as dandruff in a beauty parlor.

In the late 1970s Renee Rogers made a federal case of her hairstyle, arguing (unsuccessfully) in the Southern District of New York that the all-braided hairstyle forbidden by her employer's grooming code was "the cultural and historical essence of Black American women."[38] In 1987 the Hyatt Hotel in Washington, D.C., was picketed and threatened with boycotts when its grooming code was applied to prohibit all-braided or "cornrow" hairstyles. The nation's law reviews published several articles condemning such grooming codes as race discrimination. Antiracists in the legal community were almost unanimous in this view, although the precise legal theory according to which a universally applied grooming code became racial discrimination was obscure. For some, the grooming codes gave rise to an inescapable inference of discriminatory intent: the employers imposed the grooming codes in order to injure or repel black women. For others, intent was irrelevant. Banning braids was racism per se because the hairstyle, it was argued, was a racial characteristic, like dark skin or a broad nose. For still others, the grooming codes had a discriminatory effect. Because black women disproportionately favored the cornrow hairstyle, banning it would affect a disproportionate number of black women.

Each of these legal theories had its weaknesses. The industries in question—airlines and hotels—had strict grooming codes that applied to all of their employees and proscribed a wide variety of hairstyles and grooming options. They were equal opportunity sticklers when it came to grooming. In the 1970s airlines were heavily regulated. Fares and schedules were largely dictated from Washington, D.C., so the airlines tried to distinguish themselves on the details of service and corporate image. The flight attendant of the seventies was a nurse in the sky, a surrogate wife for lonely business passengers, a fantasy sexpot ("coffee, tea, or me"), and a fashion model. In the late 1960s Delta Air Lines required flight attendants to be "between 20 and 26 years of age, between 5'2" and 5'8" . . . not over 135 lbs., never married and in radiant good health."[39] Airlines invested in designer uniforms to evoke the glamour of the jet set. The now defunct Braniff Airways hired Emilio Pucci—Italian fashionista to "it" girls and international bright young things—to make its uniforms, teasing potential customers in its 1966 advertisement: "Does your wife know you're flying with us?" Southwest Airlines branded itself the "love airline" and put its stewardesses in hot pants and go-go boots. Some of the more stringent and blatantly sexist requirements were later rejected by courts in litigation and by labor unions in collective bargaining, but many survived.

The court that heard and rejected Renee Rogers's discrimination lawsuit noted that American Airlines had given her the option of keeping her braids and wearing a hairpiece while at work. This, the court implied, suggested that the airline was not using its grooming code to force black women from its workforce. Critics condemned the hairpiece option as racist and demeaning (one article critical of the *Rogers* decision was even titled "A Hair Piece"). But the hairpiece was the standard option that airlines—famous for detailed-bordering-on-obsessive regulation of hairstyles—offered to women of all races who didn't want to permanently change their civilian coifs. The 1972 book *Flying High: What It's Like to Be an Airline Stewardess* advises potential stewardesses:

> Don't let your hopes soar about keeping your waist length hair. Count on its being cut to perhaps an inch or two below your collar, and then later, if you are lucky enough to conceal longer hair in a chignon or knot, you can be happy. Many training schools offer hairpieces at a discount price, and the instructors will show you how to manage them.[40]

But the critics insisted that forbidding the cornrow hairstyle was race discrimination because, as Rogers had put it, cornrows were the "cultural and historical essence of black women." The more ambitious version of this claim hypothesized that the prohibition against race discrimination extended to more than the phenotypical attributes of race. It also prohibited discrimination based on the "cultural attributes" of race. Discrimination against "black culture," according to this theory, was as objectionable— and as illegal—as discrimination against black skin.

Renee Rogers and her cornrows were just the beginning. A flood of legal scholarship proposed to forbid "cultural discrimination." Scores of law review articles insisted that the Civil Rights Act, properly interpreted, *already* prohibited it. Articles championed the race discrimination claim of a Mexican-American radio announcer who demanded to speak Spanish on the air even though his audience did not include a significant number of Spanish speakers. Others condemned an employer who required bilingual employees to speak English while on the production line after black and Asian coworkers complained that these employees had harassed them using Spanish as a means of exclusion and secrecy. Still others insisted that a church-based club for at-risk girls was guilty of race discrimination when it applied a long-standing policy that required employees to be good "role models" and fired a black guidance counselor who had become pregnant out of wedlock. The claim was that out-of-wedlock pregnancy was a black cultural practice.

Legal multiculturalism had its roots in black nationalism, with all its stylistic excess and quixotic ambition. But there was a more moderate impulse behind legal multiculturalism: the desire to make civil rights more responsive to the concerns of nonblack minority groups. Multiculturalist legal scholars complained that civil rights were stuck in the past, based on a "black/white racial paradigm" that "excluded" and "marginalized" other racial groups and ignored their distinctive concerns. Multicultural rights, because they redefined invidious discrimination as bias against culture rather than color, would offer relief to fair-skinned Latinos reviled for their accents and mixed-race Native Americans who wanted to maintain (or rediscover) traditional practices. Civil rights remodeled for the twenty-first century would have to redefine race itself as a collection of practices, political commitments, attitudes, and affects—as culture. The alternative, the multiculturalists insisted, was to leave Latinos—now the largest racial minority group in the United States—Native Americans, and Asians out of the civil rights revolution.

Sometimes bigots use such cultural differences as a proxy or a cloak for invidious prejudices: for example, a racist might disingenuously claim not to understand a potential employee with a Spanish accent or might refuse to hire people with limited English mastery as a way of screening Latinos out of the workforce. Obviously such alibis must be condemned as forcefully as the prejudice that motivates them.

But multiculturalists went further than this. They came close to insisting that any injury suffered by a racial group was *by definition* a racial injustice: many Asians face discrimination because of language; Asians are a racial group; therefore language discrimination is a form of race discrimination. This proves too much. The valid attempt to ensure that civil rights, developed with blacks in mind, also addressed analogous concerns of other racial groups was too easily used to preempt discussion of more complicated, nonracial conflicts.

The multiculturalists suggested that we should condemn discrimination on the basis of "ethnicity" as harshly as discrimination on the basis of race. In one sense this seems a mild extension of existing prohibitions against discrimination on the basis of race and national origin. But "ethnicity" is ambiguous. If such a prohibition is limited to ethnic *status*—prohibiting employers from refusing to hire "Mexicans" or "Chinese" or "Asians"—then it is superfluous. Existing laws against race and national origin discrimination already prohibit this. On the other hand, if the prohibition is to extend, as some argued it should, to "ethnic *traits*," then it raises practical and conceptual questions. Practically speaking, some "ethnic traits"—such as language skills and accents—may affect an employee's ability to do a job. Language barriers can be proxies for invidious prejudice, but they also pose practical difficulties and can create innocent misunderstandings. The employer who insists on mastery of English, or worries about a heavy accent when filling a position that requires intensive communication with an English-speaking public, should not be condemned as a bigot.

And many ethnic traits—unlike race—are readily malleable. People can assimilate to a workplace culture if they try. Should they try? Assimilation is a dirty word to multiculturalists, and for some good reasons. Immigrants have historically faced a stark choice: assimilate or face rampant and severe discrimination. Many of those who could assimilate, and "pass" as Anglo-Saxon stock, did. Over time, as ethnic prejudices waned, many Americans who had abandoned the distinctive culture of their European ancestors watched their children reclaim it when white ethnic pride emerged in the 1970s (a direct, if not intentional, echo of black-is-beautiful racial pride).

Multiculturalists have interpreted this history of discrimination and the pragmatic reaction of immigrants to it as evidence of a societal "demand for assimilation." But bigots of past generations did not demand or even want recent immigrants to assimilate. They wanted them to stay confined to ethnic ghettos and menial jobs. Assimilation was one of the many sacrifices that some immigrants made in order to improve their lot in life—and for many, hardly the biggest. For others, assimilation was not a decision at all, but a slow and almost imperceptible social process of adaptation.

When cultural difference is just a trigger for racial prejudice, it's obvious that no one should discriminate because of it. But it's inconsistent to insist that culture is too insignificant ever to matter to a business, but is so important to employees that we need to make a federal case of it. Sometimes cultural differences are trivial and sometimes they are profound—for both employers and employees, for both landlords and tenants, and for both recent immigrants and third-generation natives. Most professions and workplaces have fairly distinctive norms of behavior, standards of grooming, dominant and expected modes of inter-action—what we could call a professional "culture." There's nothing in the civil rights tradition that would suggest that such norms are unacceptable, much less invidious. "Culture" de-scribes almost everything that sets human beings apart from one another. Saying that we can't discriminate on the basis of culture comes very close to saying that we must limit our evaluations to the objectively quantifiable. This goes far beyond prohibiting bigotry. It threatens to impose a bloodless technocratic value system from the bench.

A lot of the things that the legal multiculturalists insisted were racial or cultural "traits" looked to everyone else an awful lot like freely chosen behavior. Renee Rogers's claim, stripped of the toupee of "black culture," was that she had a right to defy an evenhanded workplace dress code. Would employees resist "Eurocentric" company uniforms next? It was one thing to attack an English-only rule when applied to someone whose only language was Spanish, but the cultural rights agenda wanted to attack the rule even when the employees were flu-ent in English and therefore could easily comply. The injury these plaintiffs suffered wasn't discrimination or exclusion—it was that they found the rules annoying or inconvenient. But if work were never a bother, they wouldn't have to pay you for it.

The notion that civil rights law should forbid employers from discriminating on the basis of *behavior* underlies a flood of new claims of racism by analogy. If, as the legal multiculturalists claim, racism is a failure to tolerate nonmainstream norms and practices, then the loser of almost any social or political conflict can claim to be the victim of racism-like bias. An aerobics studio requires its instructors to stay slim? Such a preference for aesthetic uniformity and conventional beauty is as hurtful to people who tend toward the heavy side as a WHITES ONLY sign is to racial minorities. The boss has a rule against your Mohawk coif or fluorescent pink hair? He'd never get away with a "similar" rule against black people. The city bans smoking in bars and restaurants, consigning smokers to chilly outdoor patios and huddling on the sidewalk? It's a new Jim Crow. The public park restricts off-leash dogs to a few fenced-in areas, which quickly become trampled and strewn with feces because of the presence of unsupervised dogs? It's segregation. It's a concentration camp! (Think I'm exaggerating? Each of these analogies has been publicly advanced by some interest group or interested person.)

From the far side of the multicultural looking glass, these arguments didn't seem far-fetched. In fact, they seemed to be logical applications of civil rights principles. And that's exactly what should worry us. Just about the worst thing that could happen to the cause of racial justice would be for the multiculturalists to convince a significant number of people that civil rights legislation required their agenda. The proponents of multicultural rights are inspired by a worldview and commitments that few Americans of any race share. Even as the nation has become increasingly skeptical of social justice claims, multiculturalists blithely advance a radical agenda that would force employers and businesses to effectively subsidize ethnic and racial nationalism—a worldview most Americans find abhorrent.

This is a grave tactical mistake. The multiculturalists assume that if they can tie their agenda to civil rights, the nation will have to accept it. In fact, with the two bound together, the nation would have a choice—accept both civil rights and its multicultural sidecar or send them both to the wrecking yard. The laws that prohibit discrimination in employment, housing, and public accommodations are not mandated by a Supreme Being or even a Supreme Court: they are acts of Congress—legislation of the popular branch of government. As such, should they become unpopular, they can be amended, watered down, or even repealed. If the Hobson's choice were put to *me*, I'd swallow ethnic nationalism in order to protect the civil rights guarantees we still profoundly need. I have no confidence that a majority of Americans would make the same call.

WHY EMPLOYERS SHOULDN'T HAVE TO HIRE THE "BEST PERSON"

All of the groups pressing racism-by-analogy claims concede that employers and businesses are entitled to discriminate—to make and act on distinctions between individuals. They wish only to take *certain* distinctions out of play. Renee Rogers didn't insist that American Airlines eliminate its dress code. She only wanted an exception for her cornrows. Jennifer Portnick was the perfect poster child for the fat acceptance movement precisely because she could do everything a typical aerobics teacher could do—except look thin while doing it. Neal Coonerty— the sponsor of Santa Cruz's ugly law—insisted that the law would actually help businesses discriminate appropriately by eliminating distractions from "real criteria, the ability to perform the job or pay the rent."

Implicit in the uncontroversial but vague admonishment to focus only on "real criteria" is a more specific and more controversial idea: that there's a morally relevant difference between some congenital virtues, like intelligence or natural talent—which deserve reward—and other native advantages, like good looks or height, which do not. A federal court put it this way:

> In our society we too often form opinions of people on the basis of skin color, religion, national origin, style of dress, hair length, and other superficial features. That tendency to stereotype people is at the root of some of the social ills that afflict the country, and in adopting the Civil Rights Act of 1964, Congress intended to attack these stereotyped characterizations so that people would be judged by their *intrinsic worth*.[41]

According to this idea, racism and looksism are morally equivalent evils: both fail to limit judgment to intrinsic worth. When San Francisco considered an appearance discrimination law, supporters argued that employer dress codes "smack of the kind of mentality that kept blacks and other minorities out of the public eye for years until civil rights protections were passed."[42] After all, racism rewards the superficial advantage of fair skin and sharp features; how is this morally different from looksism, which rewards the superficial advantage of conventional attractiveness? Outlawing looksism is logically compelled by the moral commitment to reward intrinsic worth underlying the Civil Rights Act.

The idea of intrinsic worth is seductive. We'd all like to think that deep within we have the spark of virtue, genius, or charm that makes us worthy of the respect of our peers, the love of those we desire, the grace of God. And we'd like to think that society distributes its largesse based on those virtues—that it rewards individuals based on who they really are deep down inside. The cult of the Real Me is a religion of meritocracy.

But the Civil Rights Act reflects a more limited and earthly aspiration. It was not meant to mandate judgment based on intrinsic worth; it was meant to forbid judgments based on a handful of specific and enumerated bases. Congress was no doubt well aware that unfairness, subjectivity, and idiosyncrasy of every imaginable kind were rampant in the market economy, but it chose to outlaw only a few specific types of unfairness. The Civil Rights Act of 1964 prohibits discrimination on the basis of race, color, sex, national origin, and religion. Why this list?

All of these items describe groups that, in American society, were the targets of explicit, vicious, and pervasive bigotry. Individual members of these groups were victims of discrete cases of unfair treatment, but worse yet, entire social groups were turned into permanent outcasts. If I'm denied a job because I'm too short or because I remind the boss of a hated ex-husband, that's unfair. But it is unlikely that the next employer will share this idiosyncratic bias. And it's even less likely that I'll return home from my unsuccessful interview and find that my sister has been turned down by a different employer for the same bad reason. By contrast, when a black job seeker in the 1960s was denied a job because of his race, it was almost certain that he would face numerous rejections for precisely the same reason. And so would his wife, his siblings, his parents, and most of the people in the segregated neighborhood where he lived. Racism, xenophobia, and religious bias keep entire families and interdependent communities down. Practices that create a permanent underclass are unjust in a different and more profound way than isolated arbitrariness. And they are not only unjust; they are dangerous. Religious wars in Europe and race riots in the United States (perpetrated by both white racism and minority discontent) prove that widespread social bigotry is a threat to social peace and order. So egalitarian liberals and social conservatives alike could support antidiscrimination legislation. Social justice and social order required it.

By contrast, discrimination based on weight, looks, or "culture" may be pervasive, but it is rarely as explicit or as severe as racism. "Fat" and "ugly" people—with the exception of those few who have joined fat acceptance political movements—don't think of themselves as a discrete social group, and no one else thinks of them that way either. There are no segregated ghettos populated by the ugly. The world has never seen a "weight riot," nor has any society suffered social unrest caused by animus toward people with beady eyes or bad acne. Fat and unattractive people are spread pretty evenly across families and social classes, so the ill effects of bias against them are often ameliorated by other social advantages. And good looks are hardly a requirement for success in politics or business, as a glance at either house of Congress or a stroll down Wall Street will confirm. Weightism and looksism aren't problems of social order or of *social* injustice.

And there's a practical distinction that justifies the list Congress wrote into the Civil Rights Act: racism, sexism, and xenophobia are irrational in the sense that they can't be justified on the basis of facts and logic. They are also, in part for that reason, potentially tractable. Civil rights legislation disrupted what had become a self-reinforcing system that propped up bad ideas and counterproductive customs. Segregation ensured that whites would never have sustained contact with blacks, and as a result, whites had nothing with which to evaluate racist propaganda and inherited prejudices. Integration's explicit purpose was to end this reign of ignorance that nurtured mutual suspicion and mistrust between the races. Customary discrimination denied minorities the chance to test their abilities and industriousness in many fields of labor; antidiscrimination laws gave minorities a chance to prove their merit. The belief underlying civil rights legislation was that stereotypes and prejudice would wither in the light of lived experience. There is evidence to support this optimism. Political scientists Paul Sniderman and Thomas Piazza have shown that although racial prejudice remains a significant problem, such attitudes are pliable: people can be talked out of their original prejudices, and racial attitudes are influenced by elite opinion and issue framing.[43]

By contrast, many of the claims of racism by analogy lack these important characteristics. Obesity is objectively relevant to many jobs and enterprises. Unlike racism or sexism, the distaste for obesity based on its objective costs is unlikely to be dislodged. Grooming, because it is a matter of individual choice, is often a good indicator of other virtues such as industriousness, detail orientation, and sociability; for this reason, discrimination based on it will be hard to change. Although some aspects of what we consider physically attractive are culturally determined, others are probably hardwired into our consciousness through eons of evolution: facial symmetry suggests good health and the absence of disease, for example. And while many of the specific standards of beauty may change, the preference for beauty in some form seems to be a constant. Legally induced changes in standards of beauty might not improve social justice: they might just give different people the short end of the ugly stick. Any awkward teenager or homely wallflower will confirm that the taste for physical beauty is unfair. But legal intervention is unlikely to eliminate it.

There are risks to trying, as the memorable defense of Santa Cruz's ugly law—it "gets everybody *down* to an equal level"—reveals. Santa Cruz's ugly law foreshadows the dystopia of Kurt Vonnegut's short story "Harrison Bergeron":

> Everybody was finally equal. They weren't only equal before God and the law. They were equal in every which way. Nobody was smarter than anybody else. Nobody was better looking than anyone else. All this equality was due to the 211th, 212th, and 213th Amendments to the Constitution, and to the unceasing vigilance of agents of the United States Handicapper General . . . [There were laws] to keep [smart] people . . . from taking unfair advantage of their brains . . . Ballerinas . . . were burdened with sashweights and bags of birdshot, and their faces were masked, so that no one, seeing a free and graceful gesture or a pretty face, would feel like something the cat drug in.[44]

Weightism and looksism depart from the ideal that people should be judged according to intrinsic merit rather than accidents of birth or superficial traits. But that doesn't distinguish the problems of overweight or "ugly" people from the disadvantages suffered by people who, through no fault of their own, are burdened with inbred obnoxiousness, inherited physical weakness, or lower-than-average native intelligence. These maladies too will affect an individual's success and esteem in society. They too are inherited rather than earned. But a legal order that forbade us to consider all unearned virtues—that really got "everyone down to an equal level"—would be the dystopia of the Handicapper General.

Almost every religion is based on the idea that all human beings have a core "self"—the Real Me, the immortal soul—that exists apart from the crude stuff of flesh and bone, and that it is on this and this alone they deserved to be—and ultimately will be—judged. Philosophers have debated whether it is better to be loved for one's traits—beauty, intelligence, kindness, skill—or despite them. If one is loved for these traits, some worry, isn't it really the *traits* that are loved rather than the person herself? But for anyone other than a professional philosopher or a theologian, what could it mean to love someone *despite* his traits? What else is there? We judge people on their attributes, deserved or not. Indeed, if we suspend the seductive but questionable notion of the Real Me, we might say that people are nothing more than the sum of their attributes. As Kingsley Amis's "Lucky" Jim Dixon understood when considering the relative virtues of two eligible female acquaintances, virtues caused by luck are virtues just the same:

> Christine's more normal, i.e., less unworkable, character no
> doubt resulted, in part at any rate, from having been lucky
> with her face and figure. But that was simply that. To write
> things down as luck wasn't the same as writing them off as
> non-existent or in some way beneath consideration. Christine

was still nicer and prettier than Margaret, and all of the deductions that could be drawn from the fact should be drawn.[45]

Some might think it wise or even morally required that we ignore physical attractiveness in friends or even lovers ("beauty is only skin-deep"), but it would be the rare lover or friend who would also ignore personality. Similarly, some argue that employers should ignore looks, weight, and height because they are not "job related," but so far no one has demanded that employers ignore inherited personality traits—say, hire the congenitally surly as readily as the naturally charming and ingratiating. Yet these are also arguably not "job related"—a surly waiter can still take your order and bring the food to the table before it cools; indeed, a few big-city restaurants are known for their grouchy servers. The trouble with the notion of "intrinsic merit" is that, as with the Deity, although most people are believers, there's no agreement on the specifics.

SOCIAL INSECURITY: CLAIMING "BIAS" TO GET AN EDGE IN A CUTTHROAT ECONOMY

Sixty–two-year-old Walter Biggins had worked for the Hazen Paper Company for almost ten years when he got his pink slip. "Almost" is the operative term: had he worked for precisely ten years—just a few weeks more than he did—he would have been entitled to pension benefits on his retirement. Biggins thought this timing was suspicious. He believed that he was not fired for cause as his employer claimed, but because his pension was about to vest. The Hazen Paper Company confirmed this suspicion when it offered to retain Biggins as a "consultant"—a position that would not include pension benefits.

Biggins sued for age discrimination. A jury agreed that he had been fired in order to cheat him of his pension, and the First Circuit Court of Appeals opined that his employer indeed discriminated against Biggins on the basis of his age : "If it were not for [his] age, sixty-two, his pension rights would not have been within a hairbreadth of vesting. [Biggins] was fifty-two years old when he was hired; his pension rights vested in ten years."

The United States Supreme Court overturned the judgment for Biggins. Justice Sandra Day O'Connor explained the Court's decision with a primer on the meaning of discrimination:

> It is the very essence of age discrimination for an older employee to be fired because the employer believes that productivity declines with old age . . . on the basis of inaccurate and stigmatizing stereotypes . . . [But] when the employer's decision is wholly motivated by factors other than age, the problem . . . disappears. This is true even if the motivating factor is correlated with age, as pension status typically is. Pension plans typically . . . become nonforfeitable or "vested" once the employee completes a certain number of years of service with the employer. On average, an older employee has had more years in the work force than a younger employee . . . Yet an employee's age is analytically distinct from his years of service . . . Because age and years of service are analytically distinct, an employer can take account of one while ignoring the other . . . it is incorrect to say that a decision based on years of service is necessarily "age-based" . . . The decision would not be the result of an inaccurate and denigrating gen-

eralization about age, but would rather represent an accurate judgment about the employee—that he indeed is "close to vesting."[46]

Civil rights lawyers groaned and rolled their eyes in unison after reading this. The main obstacle older employees faced was the perception—often accurate—that they could be replaced by less expensive younger workers. The stereotype that older workers were *less productive* than younger workers wasn't the problem. The problem was that older workers, because of lock-step salary structures and pensions that vested only after long terms of service, often were *more expensive.*

So what's wrong with firing a worker who costs more than he's worth? In many industries it is widely understood that a substantial amount of compensation is deferred in order to provide incentives for loyalty: new employees accept less than they merit initially in exchange for the promise of retirement benefits and escalating compensation even after their productivity has peaked. This gives employees an incentive to stick with their current jobs, but it also gives employers an incentive to fire older workers because their current level of productivity can't justify their higher salaries and the expected cost of retirement benefits. Viewed in isolation, the termination is a rational business decision: to cut an employee whose expected cost to the firm is greater than her productivity. But viewed in context, it is a breach of an implicit promise, a cruel bait and switch.

Still, "cruel" is not the same as "discriminatory." Justice O'Connor pointed out that, in theory, a worker too young to enjoy the protection of the Age Discrimination in Employment Act (the law applies only to workers of at least the age of forty) could find himself in Biggins's position—about to enjoy a vested pension—and might be fired for precisely the reason Biggins was. Biggins was playing the age card.

Firing someone because their pension will cost the firm more than their continued efforts are worth isn't intentional age discrimination. But it is illegal anyway: the Court did not overturn Hazen Paper Company's liability under the Employee Retirement Income Security Act, which regulates employee pensions. Biggins's age discrimination lawsuit demonstrates how thin the line between invidious discrimination and plain old unfairness can be. Because it is so thin, employees who suffer at the hands of greedy, mean-spirited, or vengeful bosses might be tempted to fight back by claiming discrimination.

The casting couch (it's not just for Hollywood anymore)

California's prison guards enjoy the support of one of the most powerful public unions in the state. Tough-guy prosecutors, the war on drugs, and "three strikes and you're out" criminal penalties have put more and more of the Golden State's citizens behind bars for longer periods of time. More than 160,000 people enjoyed the hospitality of California's correctional facilities in 2004. More prisoners means more prisons, which means more guards, which means more clout for the California Correctional Peace Officers Association.

"The union runs the prison system," lamented Thelton Henderson, the federal judge who presided over lawsuits involving the notorious "super-maximum-security" Pelican Bay State Prison.[47] Inmates at Pelican Bay have accused prison officials of violent abuse, intimidation, and a code of silence that impedes investigations against sadistic guards. Inmates claim that prison guards deliberately incited gang violence within the prison, used rival gangs to subdue each other and settle scores for guards, and regularly wagered on the outcome of the jail yard fights they were supposed to prevent. The United Nations called conditions at Pelican Bay "inhuman."

Compared with Pelican Bay, the Central California Women's Facility is a Holiday Inn. If you were a female employee working under Deputy Warden Lewis Kuykendall in the 1990s, the right comparison might have been a roadside motel with hourly rates. When Edna Miller started working there in 1994, she heard the rumors: Kuykendall was sleeping with an associate warden, Debbie Patrick, *and* with his secretary, Kathy Bibb.[48] Later another female employee, Cagie Brown, told Miller that she was sleeping with Kuykendall too. Kuykendall had discovered a job perk the union didn't publicize.

A year later, Kuykendall's extraordinary on-the-job performance resulted in a promotion to warden at the Valley State Prison for Women. Edna Miller was transferred to Valley State and served on a committee that evaluated candidates for promotion and transfer to Valley State. One of the candidates applying for transfer to the prison run by Kuykendall was Kathy Bibb. According to Miller, when the committee rejected Bibb, Kuykendall intervened to make sure that his girlfriend was able to relocate within groping distance. "Make it happen," he demanded. Soon enough Debbie Patrick was also transferred to Valley State Prison for Women, where she also worked under Kuykendall.

Kuykendall's third paramour, Cagie Brown, also found her way to Valley State, where she quickly took full advantage of her special relationship with the warden. When Edna Miller and Brown were in competition for a promotion, Miller was the obvious favorite. She had a higher rank, better education, and more experience as a prison official. Other officers who were consulted about the promotion recommended Miller. But Brown had an ace up her skirt: she told Miller that Kuykendall would have to give her, Brown, the promotion because she knew "every scar on his body" and would "take him down" if she was denied. Brown got her promotion. And a little over a year later Brown became associate warden—and Edna Miller's direct supervisor.

Morale among the prison guards—at least those who weren't sleeping with Kuykendall—was low. An internal affairs investigation reported that other employees asked, "What do I have to do, fuck my way to the top?" Cagie Brown seemed to think the answer was yes. Rumor among prison employees had it that she even hedged her bets and began an affair with the new chief deputy warden, Vicky Yamamoto.[49] Meanwhile, Yamamoto—perhaps emulating Kuykendall's management style—repeatedly asked Edna Miller to dinner. When Miller refused, Yamamoto retaliated. She undermined Miller's authority in front of subordinates and kept Miller from seeing the warden on prison business. When Miller complained to an internal affairs investigator, Yamamoto enlisted Brown in a campaign of bullying and harassment. When Miller complained to Kuykendall, he did nothing. After Miller complained again, this time to an intensifying internal affairs investigation, Brown found Miller and lambasted her for hours, eventually following her home. At one point Kuykendall ruefully admitted that because of his sexual relationship with Brown, he could do nothing to stop the harassment: "I should have chosen *you*," Kuykendall confided to an appalled Miller. Miller quit in August 1998 and filed a sex discrimination lawsuit against the Department of Corrections, alleging unlawful sex harassment.

There was plenty of harassment and there was plenty of sex, but was there sex harassment? The trial court thought not and summarily found for the department. The court of appeals affirmed: granting favors to a sexual favorite was not, according to these courts, sex harassment under California law. Sex harassment is a form of sex discrimination; the theory underlying the law is that sexual advances or sexual taunting can be a particularly effective method of driving women from the workforce. And even if the intent is not to repel, a boss who demands sexual favors from women discriminates on the basis of sex: men advance on the strength of their performance in the boardroom while women must also perform in the bedroom.

Sex harassment law prohibits two types of behavior. One is harassment so severe as to create a hostile environment. For instance, one successful plaintiff in federal court, Teresa Harris, was the target of an ongoing campaign of taunting and humiliation directly related to her sex. The company president belittled her, saying, "You're a woman, what do you know? We need a man as the rental manager" (Harris's position), and he referred to her as a "dumb-ass woman." He suggested openly, in front of coworkers, that they "go to the Holiday Inn to negotiate [her] raise." He asked Harris and other female employees to get objects from his front pants pocket.[50] He created a hostile work environment for women. The second type of sex harassment has been informally dubbed quid pro quo harassment. Here someone in a supervisory capacity makes sex a condition of some workplace privilege or career advancement: "Sleep with me and I'll help you get that promotion" or "Sleep with me if you want to keep your job."

So wasn't Kuykendall a textbook sex harasser? Actually no. None of the women who Kuykendall slept with or made advances toward complained about it. They were willing partners who, it seems, even competed with one another for his affections. The law doesn't forbid sexual relations between coworkers—even when one supervises the other. It forbids only unwelcome sexual advances that create a hostile environment or overtures that come with job-related threats or promises attached. Had Kathy Bibb, Debbie Patrick, or Cagie Brown objected to Kuykendall's overtures, *they* might have had a case for quid pro quo sex harassment. But they didn't object. These women weren't victims—they were opportunists.

Edna Miller *was* a victim. She was denied a promotion she merited, and she was harassed as an indirect result of Kuykendall's numerous affairs. Isn't that enough? The California Court of Appeals thought not. It reasoned that Miller was in the same position as any employee Kuykendall *wasn't* sleeping with— male or female. Miller wasn't a victim of *sex* discrimination— she was a victim of favoritism that hurt men and women alike and of an equal opportunity campaign of harassment, directed at *anyone* who offended Kuykendall's girlfriends: "Plaintiffs have demonstrated unfair conduct [but] . . . plaintiffs were not themselves subjected to sexual advances, and were not treated any differently than male employees."

Federal courts that have addressed the question have come to a similar conclusion: an employer who favors a lover over other employees does not unlawfully discriminate on the basis of sex. For instance, when a hospital administrator promoted his girl-friend over several male employees, the Second Circuit Court of Appeals found no sex discrimination: "[The male employees] were not prejudiced because of their status as males, rather they were discriminated against because [the administrator] preferred his paramour . . . the same predicament as that faced by any woman applicant for the promotion: No one but [the girl-friend] could be considered for the appointment."[51]

This may seem like legalistic hairsplitting, but it makes sense. Suppose Kuykendall had finagled jobs for his relatives or old college buddies and preferred them for promotion? And sup-pose these nonsexual favorites undertook a similar campaign of harassment against anyone who complained of their illegitimate favored status. Edna Miller would have suffered an identical injury—the loss of a promotion she merited and harassment by her unworthy superiors. But in these circumstances a claim of sex harassment would be a nonstarter. Miller's case is analogous: the sexual nature of the relationship between Kuykendall and his favorites doesn't transform the injury suffered by *Miller* into sex discrimination.

Still, some federal courts have held that sexual favoritism can create a sexually discriminatory hostile environment for other employees if it is severe and widespread enough to send the message that management views women as "sexual playthings." And the federal Equal Employment Opportunity Commission guidelines suggest that widespread sexual favoritism can be an "implicit" quid pro quo by implying that the only way for women to advance is to—as some of Miller's colleagues put it—fuck their way to the top.

Relying on these authorities, the California Supreme Court reversed the state court of appeals and held that Miller did have a valid case of sex discrimination under California law. It's tempting to applaud this decision because the outcome—redress for Edna Miller—is so obviously just. Edna Miller was the victim of unfair treatment. But not of sex discrimination. The authorities the California Supreme Court relied on don't quite fit the facts of Miller's case. Kuykendall's dangerous liaisons didn't really send the discriminatory message that Kuykendall thought of all women as sexual playthings. It sent the message that those women who were in fact his sexual playthings would receive favored treatment, and everyone else—male and female—had better keep on their good side. Kuykendall discriminated on the basis of sex, but only in the sense that he chose only women as his lovers. He treated everyone else equally badly. There was no indication that the women who *weren't* sleeping with Kuykendall were any worse off than the men who weren't sleeping with him. It would make sense to claim that Kuykendall's behavior created a hostile environment *for women* if the only way women could advance was through sex while men could advance by merit. But in Kuykendall's prison both men and women were equally able (or unable) to advance by merit, while some women were also able to sleep their way to the top. One could argue, perversely, that it was *men*—precluded *by their sex* from "fucking their way to top"—who were the real victims of sex discrimination: women had two routes to advancement; men were limited to only one.

Treating simple favoritism as sex discrimination helped Edna Miller get her well-deserved recompense, but it doesn't address the larger problem she faced—a problem that can have nothing to do with sex or sexism. Many employers and managers can and do pick favorites for reasons that have nothing to do with the job. Union and civil service rules typically prevent such abuses by requiring merit promotions, but nonunion employees enjoy no such protections. And in this case the union may have been part of the problem: the inordinate power of the California Correctional Peace Officers Association made it easy for abuses of power by its members to go unchecked. "The union runs the prison system," according to federal judge Thelton Henderson. That's not discrimination, but it is a big problem for inmates at Pelican Bay and for employees like Edna Miller at Valley State Prison for Women.

Racial minorities and women need civil rights guarantees because they can't always rely on the free market to treat them fairly or on unions to protect them against discrimination by management. In fact, some of the early employment discrimination lawsuits were brought against unions, which often reserved the best job opportunities for whites or excluded racial minorities altogether. The law—as unreliable and cumbersome as it is and always has been—is often their only ally against pervasive and systematic bigotry perpetrated by management and organized labor alike. Historically, most other Americans have relied on powerful and responsive unions, the goodwill and loyalty of management, and—best of all—a strong labor market for job security. Only members of the most reviled and marginalized groups in society needed to go to court to keep their jobs.

Today, good jobs for people without advanced degrees are few, competition is fierce, layoffs are commonplace, and unions are weak. While people who lost their jobs in the 1950s and '60s could usually find comparable jobs, today they have to settle for less—often much less. People who have good jobs are desperate to keep them.

And the good jobs in the new economy aren't like the old ones. For instance, manufacturing jobs required hard skills that could be measured and quantified. How well can you use the forklift? How quickly can you assemble the engine? Most of the good jobs in the new economy (and most of the bad ones, for that matter) are in the service sector and require what management science calls "soft skills": charm, attitude, charisma, team spirit. When the job requirement is as subjective as a "good attitude," it's easy for management to claim that you don't measure up. You can't offer your stellar test scores or top performance record to refute the boss's claim that you lack "interpersonal virtues." And those soft skills can look an awful lot like simple prejudices: Are you insufficiently "charismatic" for that upper-management job or are you too macho? Or too old? Or too fat? Or too short? When that dreaded pink slip arrives, a discrimination lawsuit—once a second-best remedy for society's downtrodden and outcast—looks pretty good. When arbitrary layoffs are the norm, anyone can feel like a victim.

THE RACE CARD AS WILD CARD

The success of federal civil rights legislation makes it tempting to apply the model to a growing list of injustices. But the civil rights model doesn't fit all sizes. The core civil rights victories of the 1960s removed irrational barriers to free trade that remained due to ignorance and inertia: by allowing businesses to find broader labor and consumer markets, civil rights legislation can actually benefit the businesses it regulates. By contrast, later iterations of civil rights began to impose real costs; for instance, providing access for the disabled requires expensive physical alterations of facilities. We ask businesses, and by extension their customers, to bear the costs because the disabled are uniquely entitled to our sympathy and uniquely in need of accommodations. While earlier civil rights policies undermined only irrational bigotry, these policies involved difficult trade-offs. Civil rights protection for some meant inefficiency, added expense, surveillance, and curtailed freedom for others.

Most of the racism-by-analogy claims seek such costly accommodations. Cultural rights would overturn reasonable attempts to maintain uniform standards of grooming and would punish policies promoting a common workplace ethos. Laws against weight discrimination would make innocent bystanders (or sitters) endure physical discomfort and could undermine the few industries that encourage a healthy and active lifestyle. Laws against appearance discrimination would thwart the satisfaction of subjective but defensible aesthetic tastes. This doesn't necessarily mean that we should reject the claims, but it does require a cool-headed cost-benefit analysis that the heated rhetoric of bias does not facilitate.

Because many of these second-generation civil rights would impose real costs on businesses, resistance to them is understandably greater. Costs can't just be "tolerated"; they must be either absorbed by equity holders or passed along to customers: in most cases, a bit of both. There are only so many expensive regulations we can expect investors and consumers to bear. We should choose them carefully. And even when the racism-by-analogy argument calls only for "sensitivity," there are practical limits of human attention and sympathy. The good-natured humanitarian who listens attentively to the first claim of social injustice will become an impatient curmudgeon after multiple similar admonishments. Busy corporate executives, business managers paid according to productivity, and professionals who bill by the hour will sit through only so many sensitivity training sessions. If goodwill is exhausted and popular opinion sours, the coercive force of law will be of little effect. And a business community united in frustration at a bloated civil rights regime could become a powerful political force for reform or even repeal. Will such frustrated critics distinguish the stronger claims from the weaker when the proponents did not? The growing number of social groups making claims to civil rights protection threatens the political and practical viability of civil rights for those who need them most.

The law can identify a small set of social prejudices—race, sex, religion, national origin, age, and disability—that are so unjustified and so socially destructive that we're confident that the benefits of prohibiting them outweigh the costs. The list may not be complete: I think we should add sexual orientation, for instance. But there are limits. For the most part, we have to leave it to institutions and businesses to decide how to hire employees and price services, confident that successful enterprises are usually better able to make this call than legislatures or judges. It's a mistake to transform civil rights prohibiting truly invidious discrimination into an omnibus requirement that we reward "intrinsic merit"—an idea that is compelling to precisely the extent that it remains pliable and ambiguous. Short of creating the Office of the Handicapper General, the law can't stop people from discriminating on the basis of all morally irrelevant characteristics. The fantastic aspiration to somehow make society perfectly "fair" through force of law reflects a dangerous combination of gauzy idealism, narcissistic entitlement, and reckless hubris. And it lets almost everyone play the race card.

■ THREE
CALLING A SPADE A SPADE: DEFINING DISCRIMINATION

In 1962 the city of Jackson, Mississippi, operated five public swimming pools, four exclusively for the use of whites and one reserved for blacks. Black Jacksonians sued the city and won a judgment that this violated their rights under the equal protection clause of the Fourteenth Amendment to the United States Constitution. The city council, faced with liability if it continued to segregate the pools, voted to close them all. Black residents sued the city again, claiming that the decision to close the pools was obviously motivated by "ideological opposition to racial integration." If this wasn't obvious enough on its face, the mayor of Jackson removed any ambiguity and announced as much: "We are not going to have any intermingling," he insisted in defense of the decision.

An easy case. But not in the way you might think. The Supreme Court held in *Palmer v. Thompson* that the city's decision to close the pools did *not* violate the civil rights of black residents. Writing for the Court, Justice Hugo Black insisted that the city's discriminatory motivations were irrelevant: "No case in this Court has held that a legislative act may violate equal protection solely because of the motivations of the men who voted for it." Justice Black cautioned of the "hazards of declaring a law unconstitutional because of the motivations of its sponsors . . . It is extremely difficult for a court to ascertain the motivation or collection of motivations, that lie behind a legislative enactment . . . Furthermore, there is an element of futility in a judicial attempt to invalidate a law because of the bad motives of its supporters . . . *rather than because of its facial content or effect* . . . it would presumably be valid as soon as the . . . relevant governing body repassed it for different reasons."

Justice Black wasn't simply saying that the plaintiffs hadn't proved discriminatory intent, or that the city had good, nonracist reasons for closing the pools. He was saying that it *didn't matter why* the city closed the pools; all that mattered was that they closed them to everybody, regardless of race. For Justice Black, closing the pools altogether wasn't race discrimination. Blacks and whites alike would have to swelter in the Mississippi sun or find a private pool in which to cool off. To be discriminatory, the law would have to treat blacks and whites differently—to exclude blacks from public facilities or segregate them based on race as the city had done in the past. In such cases there is no need to ponder motivations—such laws are *facially* discriminatory. But for Black and a majority of the Supreme Court it was not discrimination to treat all races equally badly, even if the reason was that the government would rather deprive whites of the pools than see them shared with blacks.

THREE CONCEPTS OF DISCRIMINATION

Most people think unlawful discrimination is a decision *motivated* by animus or bias. So far our examples have involved such claims. But state of mind is not the sine qua non of wrongful discrimination. A decision can be motivated by bias but not be discriminatory. And invidious discrimination need not involve bias or animus.

As Justice Black's opinion in *Palmer* suggests, the most obvious type of discrimination is *facial* discrimination: a policy that explicity assigns preferences or shabby treatment on the basis of race. Today, facial discrimination is rare. Because the law flatly forbids it with very few exceptions and because it is conspicuous when it happens, few people pass facially discriminatory laws or adopt facially discriminatory policies. But there are some cases where most people would agree that facial discrimination is justified. For instance, suppose a police department begins a manhunt for a fugitive Dr. Richard Kimble and directs officers to stop and question "middle-aged *white* males between five feet nine and six feet tall." It has adopted a facially discriminatory policy: stop white males, but not males of other races. Or consider a more controversial case: suppose a university seeks to increase racial diversity and prefers black, Native American, and Latino applicants to otherwise equally competitive white and Asian applicants. That's a facially discriminatory policy, yet many of the most outspoken critics of race discrimination support it.

Not only isn't all facial discrimination objectionable; not all objectionable discrimination is discriminatory on its face. Justice Black's opinion in *Palmer v. Thompson*[1] has been widely criticized, and rightly so. It can't be sufficient for the law to prohibit facial discrimination. Suppose a restaurant posted a sign that read BLACKS BELONG IN AFRICA, BUT AS LONG AS YOU'RE HERE, SIT DOWN AND EAT over its door. And it politely served every black person who was willing to walk past the sign. Under Justice Black's rationale, the restaurant isn't discriminating: whites and blacks alike have to walk past the offensive sign. Black customers may argue that the sign was posted because of ideological opposition to racial integration, but according to Justice Black's logic in *Palmer,* that doesn't matter.

There are two reasons that, sometimes, we might want to prohibit facially equal treatment: the underlying discriminatory intent and the likely discriminatory effects. Let's consider discriminatory intent. Although we can't prohibit racist attitudes, we can and should prohibit racists from deliberately making life hard for racial minorities. The dissent in *Palmer* made just this argument against Jackson's decision to close the public swimming pools. Justice Byron White complained that "shutting down the pools was nothing more or less than a most effective expression of official policy that Negroes and whites must not be permitted to mingle together." That expression, White opined, violated the equal protection clause of the Fourteenth Amendment.

Why should we care about motivations? An obvious reason is that we think motivations are pretty good predictors of tangible consequences: discriminatory intent yields *discriminatory effects.*

For instance, one might object to Jackson's decision to close the pools because it will *affect* blacks more severely than whites. At first blush this seems wrong: both groups will suffer precisely the same deprivation—no public pools. Let's try a little harder: it might be that blacks are on average less likely to have access to alternative swimming pools—less likely to belong to private clubs or have access to private homes with pools. Losing access to the public pools will be worse for blacks as a group than for whites as a group. But this goes too far. If we were to take this argument to its logical conclusion, most decisions to discontinue public amenities—whether due to budget constraints, rising costs, or changing tastes—would be actionable as discrimination because on average blacks have less disposable income than whites and hence less access to private alternatives.

A stronger argument might insist that the decision weighs more heavily on blacks because of the underlying social meaning: closing the pools in order to avoid desegregation suggests that racial mixing in the swimming pools is so odious that whites should forgo the amenity altogether rather than accept it on an integrated basis. This is a plausible interpretation of the city's actions given the social context: public swimming pools promote just the sort of quasi-intimate proximity that provoked Jim Crow's most compulsive aversions.

The social meaning of Jackson's decision to close the pools might affect blacks in two ways. One, it might do so indirectly, as a form of antiblack propaganda. It might convince whites, who would otherwise be open to egalitarian contact with blacks, that blacks do not merit equal treatment. Two, it might affect blacks directly—blacks will be forced to endure the stigmatizing message that their presence will make the public pools unfit for others to use.

This brings us almost full circle, back to intent. The decision has a discriminatory effect because of its social meaning. That social meaning is a statement that blacks are inferior and their presence will ruin the public pools. But that statement doesn't injure Jackson's black population directly because *they* might be convinced that it's true; it injures them directly because they will, correctly, believe *that other people believe it.* The direct injury is not that of propaganda, it is that of an insult. And an insult is insulting because it reflects the speaker's attitudes—her intent.

We have three *distinct but related* theories of discrimination: formal discrimination, discriminatory intent, and discriminatory effects. Part of the reason we object to facial discrimination and intentional discrimination is because of their effects, but one of the reasons an action may have a discriminatory effect is because of what it suggests about the actors' intentions. Despite this interdependence, they are distinct theories: actions that are objectionable under one theory can be okay under the others. When we need to decide whether a conflict involves racism or whether someone is just playing the race card, we face a conceptual question as much as a factual one.

DISCRIMINATORY INTENT

When Stephin Merritt's band The Magnetic Fields released the album *69 Love Songs,* he was compared to some of the most renowned lyricists in the American musical canon. *Rolling Stone* magazine said he was "the Cole Porter of his generation." He was asked to play at Lincoln Center as part of its American Songbook series. Merritt had become a member of popular music's avant-garde. But music critics found Merritt's personality somewhat less charming than his lyrics. Like many talented people, Merritt is prickly and opinionated. When asked about another member of pop music's aristocracy—the Icelandic musician Björk—in an interview for the online journal *Salon,* Merritt was contemptuous. Whereas many critics praised Björk's unstructured phrasing as a cutting-edge innovation, Merritt called it "rambling." "Formlessness," he sneered, "is not the way to go."[2] He went on to compare Björk, unfavorably, to the 1970s pop group Fleetwood Mac, who he insisted pioneered many of Björk's extolled techniques decades earlier.

Merritt was no more enamored of hip-hop's gritty and authentic urban beat than of Björk's quirky and ethereal Icelandic melodies. In the same *Salon* interview Merritt said, "I liked the first two years of rap, and after that, it kind of got boring . . . I thought, 'Why aren't they singing yet?' If they can't sing, what's the point? . . . Who wants to hear pop without melody?" About a hit single by a critically praised rap duo Merritt said, "I probably tapped my foot along the first hundred times I heard the goddammed thing . . . [but] I'm desperately sick of hearing it." When the interviewer, desperate to find something Merritt liked, played what he considered a particularly accomplished rap song, Merritt stopped the song and complained, "It's shocking that we're not allowed to play coon songs anymore, but people, both white and black, behave in more vicious caricatures of African-Americans than they had in the nineteenth century. It's grotesque . . . That accent, that vocal presentation . . . would probably have been considered too tasteless for the Christy Minstrels."

Merritt was far from the first person to notice that rap music often conducts a dangerous trade in racial stereotypes. No less an eminent racial authority than Stanley Crouch lambasted "the gangster-rap wing of hip-hop for reiterating a kind of min-strelsy in which black youth was defined as truly 'authentic' in the most illiterate, vulgar, anarchic and ignorant manifesta-tions . . . such material [is] popular among whites because such 'authentic' Negroes, however hip-hopped up, [are] aggressively reinstituting the folklore of white supremacy."

One might think Merritt's sensitivity to racial stereotypes would be prima facie evidence of his goodwill, but some critics perceived racial bias lurking beneath his disdain for rap music. This perception was reinforced when, several years hence, Mer-ritt confessed his affection for the song "Zip-A-Dee-Doo-Dah" from Disney's animated musical *Song of the South*—a film that many consider to be a de facto apology for Jim Crow (he went on to describe the film itself as "unwatchable").

Merritt went from critic's darling to suspected racist on the strength of these disconnected statements. The debate spread through the blogosphere. Some cited as further evidence for the prosecution Merritt's published list of the best albums of the twentieth century, which, with a total of one hundred albums—one for each year—included "only" eleven works by black artists. *The New Yorker*'s music critic Sasha Frere-Jones pointed to a *New York* magazine interview in which Merritt dis-missed the work of rap duo OutKast as "innocuous party music for suburban teenagers"; sniped that Beyoncé Knowles "is not famous for her songs; she's famous for that outfit"; opined that Britney Spears "would be absolutely meaningless if we didn't see pictures of her"; and, continuing the theme, quipped that Justin Timberlake "gives good photo shoot."

For those readers unfamiliar with the transitory luminaries of early-twenty-first-century pop music, OutKast and Beyoncé are black; Spears and Timberlake are white. How is this evidence of *racial* bias? Frere-Jones scrutinized the dregs of the Darjeeling for obscure signs and portents: "Two women, three people of color and one white artist openly in love with black American music [Timberlake had recently released an album obviously inspired by white-glove-era Michael Jackson, complete with pictures of Timberlake wearing a white glove.] That's who he's biased against. You could say there's no pattern here."[3] But Frere-Jones worked up a sweat to suggest otherwise: Britney Spears is white, but she's a woman (women and blacks provoke the same bias?). Justin Timberlake is a white man, but he's "openly in love with black American music."

With two more degrees of separation you could make Dick Cheney into an honorary black person. Merritt may or may not be a bigot, but the evidence cited by his critics suggests the latter. Instead, he would seem to be an opinionated romantic with a cogent if somewhat unoriginal critique of the entertainment industry. He dislikes marketing. He insists on the primacy of substance over style, authenticity over polish. And one of the many marketing techniques Merritt dislikes is the racial segmentation of popular music. In another interview (which, to his credit, Frere-Jones cites in his anti-Merritt blog) Merritt made this old-fashioned plea for a melting pot: "What I'd like to see in the year 2000 is the abandonment of music being categorized by the race of the artist, or the perceived race of the audience. It's disgusting, and I would like to be amazed that it's still happening . . . [Eliminating] racism and sexism would be major improvements, and it would make an enormous difference in the music industry. It would be really nifty if black people were allowed to make records that didn't have to constantly refer to very recent traditions of black radio." Far from being a racist, Merritt seems to be sensitive to racial issues and willing to discuss them.

This is refreshing given that most white commentators steer clear of racial politics for fear of . . . being called racist. Merritt has a controversial view but one shared by many people deeply committed to racial justice: he is critical of racially targeted niche marketing and the stereotypes it too often encourages.

One observer of the Merritt controversy complained, "The . . . attack against Merritt is founded on the dangerous and stupid notion that one's taste in music can be interrogated for signs of racist intent the way a university admissions policy can: If the number of black artists in your iPod falls too far below 12.5 percent of the total, then you are violating someone's civil rights."[4] (As it happens, and as we'll see in a few pages, the law at least does not evaluate university admissions according to such a standard—far from it.)

Even if your iPod puts you in the clear, you'd better not relax; similar litmus tests can be applied to other aesthetic preferences. When the film *Brokeback Mountain*—a story involving a romantic relationship between two men—lost for Best Picture at the Oscars, some said it was evidence of rampant antigay prejudice. The author of the short story on which the film was based penned a lengthy screed for *The Guardian* newspaper, which began by describing the antigay protests outside the award ceremony, went on to lambaste the members of the Academy as narrow-minded octogenarians cloistered "in deluxe rest homes, out of touch . . . with the yeasty ferment that is America," and disparaged the winning film as a "safe pick . . . for the heffalumps." More pointedly, the *Los Angeles Times* film critic Kenneth Turan wrote, "In the privacy of the voting booth . . . people are free to act out the unspoken fears and unconscious prejudices that they would never breathe to another soul, or, likely, acknowledge to themselves. And at least this year, that acting out doomed *Brokeback Mountain.*"[5] And in the *LA Weekly,* columnist Nikki Finke fumed, "Hollywood's homophobia could be on par with Pat Robertson's."[6]

There's an irony in this line of reasoning. *Crash*, the film that won Best Picture and was as a result the object of contempt for many *Brokeback Mountain* supporters, was no feel-good romantic comedy or crowd-pleasing swashbuckler; it was a film about *racism.* And by all creditable accounts it was a very good film. In the wake of the accusations, some spoke out to defend the winner. The *Chicago Sun-Times* critic Roger Ebert insisted, "I chose *Crash* as the best film . . . because it was a better film." If a vote against *Brokeback Mountain* is evidence of antigay bias, wouldn't a vote against *Crash*—to say nothing of the vitriol directed at it by some *Brokeback Mountain* supporters—suggest racism? What's an unbiased, open-minded critic to do?

The Subconscious on Trial

Almost anyone could be tarred as some kind of a bigot on the basis of her subjective aesthetic preferences. We should all strive for and expect equal treatment when it comes to jobs, housing, and access to public places, but are we really obliged to vet our record collections and Netflix rental queues for hidden bias? What led otherwise fair-minded and thoughtful professionals to leap to uncharitable conclusions based on such scanty and ambiguous evidence?

There's a larger idea that underlies these accusations: the idea that racial injustice and a growing list of analogous injustices are, first and foremost, problems of bad intentions—diseases of the mind, of the heart, perhaps of the soul. Such accusations are often controversial and contested because this state of mind is usually inscrutable. Only the accused party can know for certain whether he was motivated by bigotry, and he, for obvious reasons, can't be trusted to give an honest answer.

If the scales of justice pivot on a distinct but inscrutable state of mind—call it bias, prejudice, bigotry—we *have to* make much ado about little or nothing. If the pivotal issue is bias, but bias is hard to prove and easy to conceal, then we must look for the faintest of patterns, sniff out the weakest of scents, call on obscure and capricious oracles, devise ever more ingenious if indirect tests. Casual statements, unguarded turns of phrase, and everyday behavior without obvious social significance must be scrutinized for obscure signs of bias.

Sasha Frere-Jones asked, in his criticism of Stephin Merritt, "Is it possible to look at your own preferences and find something your consciousness was not letting you in on?" Harvard psychologists Mahzarin Banaji and Anthony Greenwald think so. They've developed a test designed to tease the unconscious out of its shadowy lair. The test requires the subject to match words and images by pressing keys on a computer keyboard. The images are of human faces—some black and some white. The words have either positive or negative meanings or connotations: "good," "love," "peace," "success," "beautiful" versus "evil," "hate," "failure," "ugly." The subject is instructed to press the *e* key when either white faces or "good" words appear, press the *i* key when either black faces or "bad" words appear. Later the test switches the pairing: the subject is to press *e* when either black faces or "good" words appear and *i* when white faces or "bad" words appear. The test asks the subject to complete the exercise as quickly as possible. The computer times each response and records the number of "mistakes." If you find it easier to associate good terms with white faces and bad terms with black faces—meaning you make the associations more quickly and with fewer mistakes— then you probably harbor what Banaji and Greenwald call an implicit bias in favor of whites and against blacks. (You can take this test online at *implicit.harvard.edu.implicit.* Pack for the guilt trip: 88 percent of white subjects tested positive for antiblack bias, as did half of *black* subjects. Most people also test positive for antigay, anti-elderly, and anti-Muslim bias.) The website for the Implicit Association Test (IAT) includes this quotation from Fyodor Dostoyevsky: "Every man has reminiscences which he would not tell to everyone but only his friends. He has other matters in his mind which he would not reveal even to his friends, but only to himself, and that in secret. But there are other things which a man is afraid to tell even to himself, and every decent man has a number of such things stored away in his mind."

All of the ambiguous racial incidents I've explored so far in this book might have been caused by unconscious bias. Why not use the IAT as a racism polygraph? When politicians, employers, shop clerks, cabdrivers, bouncers, and restaurant hostesses deny that they are racists in the face of credible accusations, let them take the test and prove it. If we could have stopped Clarence Thomas's confirmation hearings and given the Judiciary Committee the IAT, perhaps we'd have had a better idea whether their inquisitiveness about Anita Hill's sexual allegations was a racially motivated "high-tech lynching." When Hermès defended its Parisian employee, what if Oprah had asked her to take the IAT right there on national television? The New York Taxi and Limousine Commission could equip officers with laptops loaded with the IAT to administer to taxi drivers suspected of refusing service on the basis of race. Some commentators have proposed using the IAT to screen biased jurors from serving in trials with minority defendants and to remove biased cops from police forces.

The authors of the IAT have rebuffed such proposals: indeed, Banaji and Greenwald have vowed to testify in court *against* the use of their test to "prove" discriminatory intent. They insist that the value of the IAT lies in raising public awareness of the prevalence of bias in society and of the possibility of a beast within: an IAT booster called it "unconsciousness raising."

Why *not* use the IAT to unmask hidden bias in active conflicts? Banaji points out that the test can't prove *discrimination* in a specific case—only implicit bias, which can be counteracted through conscious effort. If bias can be asymptomatic—people who "test" positive for bias might not act on it—and if almost everyone is at least a little bit biased, then what does the IAT's conception of bias really tell us?

In the film *The Incredibles* the school-age superhero, Dash, is admonished not to show off his talents for fear of making his classmates feel inferior. "*Everyone's* special, Dash," his mother chides. Dash answers with the sharp insight of youth: "Which is another way of saying that nobody is." Racism is similar. If almost everyone is racist, then, in a sense, nobody is. If "racism" comes to describe an almost universally held, unintentional associative bias that may have no tangible effect, it loses its appropriate connotation of moral censure. As IAT skeptic Philip Tetlock of the University of California at Berkeley insists, "We've come a long way from Selma, Alabama, if we have to calibrate prejudice in milliseconds."

The mere presence of "bias" deep in the recesses of the unconscious mind should be distressing. But frankly, it should not be surprising. The modern commitment to racial equality is only a generation old. Plenty of people have attitudes formed during an era of explicit and state-sanctioned racism, and they've passed those attitudes on to their children. In the recent past, mass media perpetuated racial stereotypes on a daily basis: spend a few hours with a crime drama from the 1970s or 1980s and prepare to confront some nasty racial images. In many respects, things are better today. But while mainstream media, in the face of sustained and deserved criticism, has moved away from the crude racial stereotyping of past decades, many blacks have filled the void, perpetuating such stereotypes with impunity under the sham of inner-city ghetto "authenticity." These efforts have had their pernicious effect on individual psychology. As the IAT suggests, many people reflexively make negative associations with blacks and other minorities. The IAT tells us that we have a ways to go to eliminate racial bias *as a society*. But it doesn't tell us much about individual culpability.

It's also worth noting that the IAT presents race in an extremely stylized way. The test flashes images of faces deliberately cropped so as to exclude hairlines, chins, and cheekbones. The rules instruct the subject to look at the faces for only an instant before pressing the appropriate key. It's rare that we encounter actual people in such circumstances: divorced from social context; bereft of the telling nuances of grooming, attire, and demeanor that guide us in social encounters. The closest real life comes to the conditions of the IAT is when a taxicab driver assesses a potential fare at forty miles an hour, and even then the driver can glean additional information from surroundings, attire, and posture. Of course, the test's authors would insist that this is the point: the faces are cropped so as to isolate race as the sole variable. It's the point, but it's also the problem. Real people aren't walking avatars of their racial identity. Real people have a lot of other relevant characteristics as well, so associative bias may often be outweighed by other individual characteristics.

And on a personal level, there's something invasive and uncharitable about the IAT, which evaluates us based on our most primal and unguarded impulses rather than on those improved and refined by conscious effort. The truest self is not necessarily the unguarded self. Just as an author deserves to be judged on his carefully edited final manuscript and not on a surreptitiously obtained first draft, so too perhaps critics should wait for the finished product—outward behavior—rather than seek access to the unedited, unconscious mind. As Banaji and Greenwald are careful to point out, people can overcome implicit biases through deliberate effort. Maybe one can live a virtuous life by remaining on guard against invidious biases and checking their effects. In and of itself, implicit bias doesn't demand condemnation, much less legal intervention.

Before it was passed into law, opponents of the Civil Rights Act criticized it as "thought control." They claimed the act would punish employers for their attitudes. The skeptical reactions of people like Professor Tetlock and, more tellingly, Professors Banaji's and Greenwald's own reluctance to apply the unconscious bias idea to specific conflicts with real stakes reflect a similar concern. Mandatory testing for implicit bias sounds like a job for the thought police. American law has tried and for the most part succeeded in making a rigorous distinction between the universe of tangible actions and the inner sanctum of thought. People should be held responsible for their behavior, but, as Dostoyevsky's quotation suggests, few of us would like to publicize all of our *conscious* thoughts, much less try to defend or explain unconscious biases we didn't even know we had. A defendant in a criminal trial cannot be compelled to testify, in large part because there's something dehumanizing about using a person's own memories as a weapon against him. Isn't it worse to turn someone's own unconscious mind against him?

Ridding society of unconscious bias is a job for poets, pundits, writers, and artists—not lawyers and judges. As Professors Banaji and Greenwald acknowledge, attitudes don't respond to legislative edict, they change the same way they are formed: through evocative narratives, images, and experiences. Positive experiences with racial minorities can counter the effect of previously internalized negative stereotypes. Professor Banaji noticed that the results of the IAT improved when subjects were exposed to positive images of blacks before the test: the Reverend Martin Luther King, Jr.'s, "I Have a Dream" speech, Tiger Woods winning the U.S. Open, or Michael Jordan sinking a basket from mid-court. And whites with at least one close black friend were less likely to exhibit implicit bias than those with racially homogeneous social circles. Public policy can help to reduce bias by promoting social integration and sponsoring racially sensitive education and artistic expression. (Let's have a public service ad campaign: "Just say no to bigotry!") But the best the law can realistically *require* of individuals is that they keep whatever biases they have in check.

The theory of unconscious bias reinforces the reassuring belief that disputes about racism are fundamentally disputes about facts—we could achieve uncontroversial solutions if we just had more information—rather than intrinsically controversial ideological disputes about the requirements of social justice and the limits of social engineering. The lawyers who want to use the

IAT as evidence seem to think the case is closed if unconscious bias is established as a matter of fact. But most racial controversies aren't just factual, they're ideological. As Professor Tetlock suggests, the theory of unconscious bias begs rather than answers the question "Where are we going to set our threshold of proof for saying that something represents prejudice?"

The law has struggled with just this question for more than a century. The Thirteenth, Fourteenth, and Fifteenth amendments to the Constitution were each attempts to address the evils of slavery and speed the assimilation of black former slaves into full citizenship in the republic. Most germane to our concerns, the equal protection guarantee of the Fourteenth Amendment was the legal basis of successful challenges to many racially discriminatory laws and practices. But it famously did not prohibit Jim Crow laws that required racial segregation in public places, conveyances, and schools, which were upheld under the unfortunate doctrine "separate but equal." In the mid-twentieth century, as Fourteenth Amendment jurisprudence began to evolve away from the moral knuckle dragging of "separate but equal" and toward the ethically upright posture of the civil rights revolution, constitutional law established the framework for the legal prohibition of racial discrimination.

The courts and Congress have expanded and reinforced this edifice in the forty-plus years of litigation since the Civil Rights Act of 1964. Some of the earliest cases under Title VII of the Civil Rights Act, which prohibits discrimination in employment, involved blatant instances of bias. But employers and their agents quickly realized that it was a bad idea to announce their biases. Rather than insisting on direct proof of often obscure (and deliberately obscured) discriminatory motivations, the law turned to a technique that Sherlock Holmes would have approved of: deductive reasoning based on circumstantial evidence. When an employer makes a contested decision in circumstances that suggest bias, we ask her to justify it. If the employer offers a plausible justification for the decision, the disgruntled employee can try to prove that the employer is lying and that the real explanation involves illegal bias, or he can try to establish that the employer's justification is only part of the story and that illegal bias was involved as well. The Supreme Court developed this evidentiary framework for intentional discrimination in 1973 in *McDonnell Douglas v. Green*.

Percy Green had worked for McDonnell Douglas in Saint Louis, Missouri, for almost ten years when he was laid off in 1964. Green, a committed civil rights activist, believed that the layoff was racially motivated. He organized a protest against his former employer (the Civil Rights Act wasn't effective until July 2, 1965, so he couldn't sue for race discrimination yet). Green and members of a civil rights group called the Congress for Racial Equality staged a "stall-in," where "five teams, each consisting of four cars would 'tie-up' five main access roads into McDonnell at the . . . morning rush hour. The drivers of the cars [would] stop their cars, turn off the engines, pull the emergency brake, raise all windows, lock the doors, and remain in their cars until the police arrived . . . [Green's] car was towed away by the police, and he was arrested for obstructing traffic . . . [he] pleaded guilty to the charge . . . and was fined."

Less than a year later, McDonnell Douglas advertised openings for new employees in Green's trade. When Green applied to get his old job back, McDonnell Douglas balked: Green was a troublemaker who illegally tied up traffic at the Saint Louis factory. Why would they invite this snake back into the nest? Green believed that McDonnell Douglas's refusal to rehire him confirmed the racial bias he suspected had motivated the layoff a year earlier. He believed that the company had used the excuse of workforce reduction in order to get rid of black employees who would stand up for their rights; now, less than a year later, they were replacing Green and his cohort with more docile, probably white, employees. For Green, the layoffs and the rehiring were all part of one drawn-out discriminatory decision. But this time Green didn't need to stage another protest. He sued McDonnell Douglas for race discrimination under Title VII of the Civil Rights Act of 1964.

The federal courts hearing the case had to sort through a welter of evidence. Green was qualified for the position McDonnell Douglas was hiring to fill. He was also a black civil rights activist. Since Green's qualifications couldn't be the reason the company didn't want him, maybe his race and racial politics were. But McDonnell Douglas had suffered Green's "stall-in" less than a year ago. Wasn't this a nonracial reason for refusing to rehire him? Or was it just an alibi, put forward to hide the defendant's true, racially discriminatory motivations?

Green's case was appealed all the way to the Supreme Court, which set out a procedure for thinking through the problem of discriminatory intent—a *method*, much like the method the estimable Mr. Holmes endeavored to teach Dr. Watson. The Court instructed that one must address the evidence in stages. In the first stage, one considers the evidence that might suggest, on first impression, that the challenged decision was discriminatory. In Green's case, this evidence was as follows:

1. Green is black—a member of a minority group that is often the target of racial prejudice.
2. Green applied for and was qualified for the job—so we can eliminate the most common reason an employer would reject a job applicant: that the applicant isn't qualified.
3. The employer rejected Green. This is the action Green challenged as racially discriminatory.
4. The position remained open and the employer continued to seek applications—so we can eliminate the possibility that the employer rejected Green because its needs changed.

These four elements comprise the plaintiff's prima facie case. *Prima facie* is Latin for "first face": the "first face" of the evidence appears to support the plaintiff's complaint that the challenged action was discriminatory. The elements will differ according to the specific accusation: for instance, if the claim involved firing rather than hiring, element 3 would substitute "fired" for "rejected" and we'd strike element 2. But the function of the prima facie case would remain the same: to establish that racial discrimination is likely by showing that the plaintiff is a plausible target of the type of discrimination he or she has alleged and by eliminating the most common nondiscriminatory reasons that might explain the challenged action.

The prima facie case establishes what lawyers call a "rebuttable presumption" in favor of the plaintiff. At this point the defendant must offer some innocent explanation for its actions in order to avoid liability. This effectively *requires* the defendant to put forward some explanation—and thereby open its motivations to further scrutiny. At this point—in the third and final stage—the plaintiff may try to prove that the defendant's alibi is a "pretext" and that the real reason for the challenged action was racial prejudice.

Practically speaking, the stages of evidence establish the legal definition of discriminatory intent. Discriminatory intent is very hard to prove. The IAT notwithstanding, we really have no way of reading people's motivations unless they announce them: we know only what a person does, not why he does it. If the law required direct proof of discriminatory intent, few plaintiffs could ever prevail. The *McDonnell Douglas* methodology helps juries and judges decide when it is reasonable to *infer* discriminatory intent from what we do know. In that sense, the *McDonnell Douglas* structure is not simply a way of evaluating evidence; it is also a way of defining discrimination. *McDonnell Douglas* means that a suspicious employment decision (one that satisfies the prima facie case) that a defendant cannot or refuses to justify *is* discriminatory as a matter of law.

But suppose a defendant lies in order to hide embarrassing but nondiscriminatory motivations? In that case the *McDonnell Douglas* presumption would be inappropriate. In 1993 the Court heard such a case: *St. Mary's Honor Center v. Hicks.* Melvin Hicks was fired from his job as a shift commander at St. Mary's Honor Center—a halfway house for parolees in Missouri— after what looked like a long vendetta against him resulted in a demotion and culminated in a heated exchange with his immediate supervisor. Hicks sued St. Mary's for racial discrimination. St. Mary's responded that Hicks had been demoted because he didn't effectively discipline the employees under his direct supervision and that he had been fired because he threatened his immediate supervisor. The district court didn't buy this excuse: Hicks was the only supervisor disciplined for rule violations by subordinates, even though such violations were common. And the supervisor Hicks had supposedly threatened had picked a fight with Hicks in order to provoke him. St. Mary's had not offered a convincing explanation for demoting or firing Hicks. But the district court didn't think Hicks had proved that he had been fired because of his race: "Although [Hicks] has proven the existence of a crusade to terminate him, he has not proven that the crusade was racially rather than personally motivated." The Eighth Circuit Court of Appeals reversed. Applying the *McDonnell Douglas* method, it reasoned that "because all of defendants' proffered reasons were discredited, defendants were in a position of having offered . . . no rebuttal to an established inference that they had discriminated against plaintiff on the basis of his race."

Five justices of the Supreme Court reversed the court of appeals, vindicating the decision of the district court. Writing for the Court, Justice Antonin Scalia pointed out that the typical Title VII defendant was not an individual who could testify to his own state of mind, but rather a company or organization made up of many individuals. Such a corporate defendant has to rely on the testimony of the managers and supervisors responsible for the challenged action as to their motivations: here St. Mary's had to rely on the word of Hicks's supervisor, who testified that Hicks was fired for cause. The district court didn't believe him, but did it follow, as the court of appeals believed, that St. Mary's discriminated on the basis of race? Scalia thought not. A supervisor might lie in order to hide embarrassing or unethical—but not race-related—motivations, but a grudge that is personal rather than racially motivated does not violate Title VII. If the supervisor is guilty of perjury, the state can prosecute him for *that* offense, but the court should not impose liability for discriminatory conduct that has not been proved. And the defendant should not be held liable for discrimination because it, perhaps unknowingly, suborned its employee's deception.

This threatened to undo the twenty-year-old *McDonnell Douglas* deductive method of proof. The genius of *McDonnell Douglas* was that it narrowed down a potentially limitless inquiry into potential motivations, first by eliminating the most common innocent reasons for the challenged action through the prima facie case and finally by narrowing the field to two possibilities—either the defendant's proffered explanation was true or it was a "pretext" for discrimination. But if the defendant's explanation didn't exhaust the universe of possible innocent explanations, the plaintiff could never prove discrimination by such a process of elimination. What good is the *McDonnell Douglas* requirement that the defendant explain its actions, Justice David Souter asked in dissent, if the defendant isn't bound by its explanation? Souter complained that Scalia's reasoning allowed the trial judge or jury to "roam the record, searching for some nondiscriminatory explanation that the defendant has not raised and that the plaintiff has had no fair opportunity to disprove." It threatened to "saddle the victims of discrimination with the burden of . . . eliminating the entire universe of possible nondiscriminatory reasons for a personnel decision."

The somewhat testy disagreement between Scalia and Souter had predictable ideological stakes. Justice Scalia was the mastermind of the Court's right wing and widely esteemed as a powerful and principled thinker. He was also a verbal pugilist, known for his sharp wit and his openly contemptuous treatment of lawyers and colleagues with whom he disagreed. Justice Souter, a moderate *political* conservative appointed by the first President Bush, was also a staunch *judicial* conservative who placed a high value on continuity and respect for past precedent—whether politically liberal or politically conservative. Souter the *judicial* conservative quickly angered *political* conservatives by defending liberal precedent on questions such as abortion and affirmative action.

Conservatives saw civil rights law as a threat to employer prerogatives, and they believed the threat had to be contained. For conservatives, one of the great—if rapidly waning—strengths of the American economy was the traditional laissez-faire regime of employment at will. In the nineteenth century—a golden age before the corruptions of the New Deal and the Warren Court—employment law was based on a formal symmetry between employer and employee. Just as an employee could quit a job without explaining his reasons, so too could an employer discipline or fire an employee for a good reason, a bad reason, or no reason at all. Most employers did not act capriciously: a wise employer valued good employees as much as the employees valued their jobs. But employers, like employees, often had reasons for their personnel decisions that they would be hard-pressed to articulate to laypersons unfamiliar with their particular businesses. Nineteenth-century judges understood that judicial oversight of the employment relationship would interfere with the freedom of employers and employees to strike the bargains they chose and would replace the time-tested expertise of the business owner with the dilettantism of the judge. After all, nothing prevented both parties from negotiating to include job-security provisions in the employment contract. The intermeddling of courts would make both employers and employees worse off: by rewriting voluntary contracts to include job security, the courts would encourage employers to try to make up for the loss by slashing wages, altering other job conditions for the worse, or replacing human labor with machine automation.

Conservatives complained that this noble rule had been rendered almost impotent—like Gulliver by the Lilliputians—by a host of petty limitations. Union demands for job security forced many employers to prove that any firing was for "cause" or to pay exorbitant damages for wrongful termination. Now it was safer just to carry the lazy and incompetent (which was, they said, what the unions wanted all along). Civil service rules effectively made public employees wards of the state for life. Academic tenure maintained a reserve army of socialist theorists whose main occupation was to bite the hand that was obliged to keep feeding them. And if that wasn't bad enough, antidiscrimination law in the hands of the liberals would err so heavily on the side of plaintiffs that no sane employer would dare ever fire a member of one of the growing number of "protected groups." A modest legal prohibition covering a few severe and blatant prejudices now threatened to unfurl and cover more questionably disadvantaged groups and more ambiguous situations. Garden-variety personality conflicts were repackaged by lawyers as ever more rare and exotic types of invidious discrimination.

Scalia's opinion in *Hicks* reflected these characteristic conservative concerns. It was predictable that some supervisors would not confess to a host of nondiscriminatory but ignoble motives and instead would offer unconvincing excuses. And even if they did confess, many juries, outraged at such "unfair"—but not discriminatory—treatment, would find the defendants liable anyway. Title VII didn't cover personality conflicts or personal grudges—only discrimination. But in these circumstances Title VII would guarantee life tenure for anyone who could make out a prima facie case under *McDonnell Douglas.*

Souter's dissent in *Hicks* reflected his respect for precedent and a lawyer's sense of the practical limitations of fact-finding. Discriminatory intent is extremely hard to prove. Occasionally an employer slipped up and announced his prejudice in mixed company or memorialized it in a memo, but this was rare. When it did happen, it made the newspapers. The *McDonnell Douglas* method offered a sensible, fair, and predictable way to uncover discriminatory intent that employers had every incentive to hide. The employer had a chance to explain suspicious behavior and an obligation to present accurate testimony at trial. If it failed to do either, it was reasonable to assume the worst. For Souter, Scalia's opinion in *Hicks* undermined this orderly procedure and replaced it with a free-for-all.

Both Scalia and Souter were as concerned with institutional priorities as with individual attitudes. For Scalia, a large organization could not be treated as an individual with a single state of mind: a fabricated alibi did not imply guilt, because an individual supervisor might dissemble to hide his own non–race-related sins rather than racial transgressions attributable to the entire company. A rule that automatically made the employer liable when a jury or judge didn't buy its explanation might capture more discrimination, but it would do so only by turning Title VII into a guarantee of life tenure for members of protected groups. This was too high a price to pay: better to let some discriminators get away with it.

For Souter, an employer was responsible for its employee's testimony. The employer was in the best position to unearth the truth and had an obligation to do so. If the employer "acted for a reason it is too embarrassed to reveal *or for a reason it fails to discover,* the plaintiff is entitled to judgment." For both justices, the definition of discrimination was as much a matter of incentives as a question of fact. Scalia worried that a more plaintiff-friendly rule would push employers to a tenure system for racial minorities and women, while Souter worried that a more defendant-friendly rule would eliminate the incentives for employers to investigate and reveal the reasons for questionable personnel decisions.

Hicks wasn't the first case to undermine *McDonnell Douglas*. In 1989 the Court confronted another scenario that threatened to undo the neat *McDonnell Douglas* method of deduction under which we infer discriminatory intent from the absence of plausible, nondiscriminatory motivations: it encountered a defendant that was motivated by legitimate reasons *and* prejudice. Ann Hopkins was an associate of the Price Waterhouse accounting firm when she came up for partnership. She had recently landed a $25 million contract with the State Department and had glowing references from the partners in her office and from clients who described her as "an outstanding professional" with a "deft touch," "strong character, independence and integrity"; as "extremely competent, intelligent"; and as "very productive, energetic, and creative." Despite these credentials, Hopkins was not made partner: she was "held" for reconsideration the following year.

It turned out that Hopkins wasn't the dream team player the positive evaluations made her out to be. Many complained that she was not simply assertive and energetic, but also abrasive, aggressive, and rude. Some staff claimed that she was abusive to subordinates. One partner insisted that she was "universally disliked" by staff, and even some of her supporters agreed that she was "unduly harsh, difficult to work with, and impatient." Price Waterhouse claimed that these faults doomed her partnership bid.

Hopkins argued that the real reason she was passed over was her sex. She cited a number of comments that made note of her sex and slipped into sex stereotypes. One partner said she was too "macho." Another advised her to go to "charm school." The partner who explained the company's decision to delay her promotion offered the kind of advice a beauty pageant hopeful might expect: he told Hopkins to "walk more femininely, talk more femininely, wear make-up, have her hair styled, and wear jewelry."

The *Price Waterhouse* case revealed all the shortcomings of the *McDonnell Douglas* method. *McDonnell Douglas* assumed that the defendant had one and only one reason for the challenged decision—it was either motivated by discriminatory intent *or* it was motivated by a legitimate consideration. The case envisioned a single decision maker whose state of mind could be attributed to the defendant. But *Price Waterhouse* involved a large organization that made personnel decisions collectively. Partnership review at Price Waterhouse didn't involve a simple decision by a personnel officer or supervisor; it was a multistage moon launch of a process in which every partner in the firm nationwide was invited to comment on the candidate. The file was reviewed by two separate committees and finally submitted to the entire partnership for a vote. Hopkins was "held" by the second committee, which based its decision on the comments of 32 partners who commented on her candidacy—13 supported her, 8 opposed her, 8 hadn't formed an opinion, and 3 recommended that she be "held." Both supporters and detractors made sex-specific comments, such as that Hopkins should be more "ladylike," and supporters and detractors also made sex-neutral criticisms such as that Hopkins was abrasive and difficult to work with. It was impossible to identify a single decision maker with a discrete state of mind, much less to use a deductive process to isolate the one and only motivation underlying the decision. In Chapter One we encountered the problem of racism without racists. *Price Waterhouse* raised the possibility of the inverse problem: sexists (or sex-specific attitudes) without sexism (a sex discriminatory outcome).

The *McDonnell Douglas* method was useless here. Hopkins could easily establish a prima facie case. Price Waterhouse could just as easily offer a believable innocent explanation for its decision—Hopkins was passed over for lack of interpersonal virtues. But this settled nothing: Hopkins insisted that her interpersonal shortcomings alone did not explain the decision; sexism also played a role. According to Hopkins, the best one could say for Price Waterhouse was that it was motivated by legitimate reasons *and* sexism: it should still be held responsible for the sexism. Price Waterhouse countered that even if some partners had sexist attitudes, their sexism wasn't responsible for the decision not to make Hopkins a partner; it was her own bad personality. She was trying to make Price Waterhouse liable not for sex *discrimination*, but for sexism. But the law didn't prohibit sexism: in fact, the First Amendment *protected* ideas—even sexist ideas—and their expression *from* governmental regulation. Hopkins's theory of the case would turn Title VII into a muzzle or, worse yet, a penalty for "bad thoughts." The Supreme Court seemed to face a Hobson's choice: it could find for Hopkins and turn Title VII into thought control, or it could find for Price Waterhouse and effectively inoculate any discriminating employer that also had a legitimate reason for its decision.

The controversy fractured the Court. Although six justices

agreed that Price Waterhouse was liable for sex discrimination, a majority of the justices could not agree as to *why*. The four most liberal justices—William J. Brennan, Thurgood Marshall, Harry Blackmun, and John Paul Stevens—delivered one opinion; Justices Byron White and Sandra Day O'Connor concurred in the judgment, but each delivered separate opinions advancing different legal theories to explain that judgment. Justices Anthony Kennedy, Antonin Scalia, and William Rehnquist filed a frustrated and angry dissent.

All nine justices agreed that Hopkins had to show that she was passed over for partnership because of her sex. But the Court fractured over what "because of" meant. The dissenting justices insisted that "because of" meant that the prohibited motive was the "but for" cause of the challenged decision: Hopkins needed to prove that, *but for* sexism, she would have been promoted to partner. As it was, Hopkins had shown only that sexism was "in the air." Some partners had expressed sexist views that might or might not have affected her candidacy. This wasn't actionable.

In a plurality opinion, Justice Brennan rejected such a requirement of "but for" causation. Brennan offered a physical analogy to explain why he did:

> Suppose two physical forces act upon and move an object, and suppose that either force acting alone would have moved the object. As the dissent would have it, neither physical force was a "cause" of the motion unless we can show that but for one or both of them, the object would not have moved . . . Events that are causally overdetermined . . . may not have any "cause" at all. This cannot be so.

He concluded that if sexism was a factor in the decision, it was reasonable to say that sexism "caused" it. For Brennan, a decision is "because of" sex and therefore violates the law if the plaintiff can show that the decision was "tainted by awareness of sex . . . in any way," even if legitimate reasons were at work as well. He concluded that if sex was a factor in the decision, the defendant was liable for sex discrimination unless it could prove that it would have made the same decision even if sexism hadn't been in play.

While Justice O'Connor agreed that Price Waterhouse discriminated against Hopkins because of her sex, she disagreed sharply with Brennan's reasoning. She, like the dissent, insisted that the plaintiff had to prove that sex was the "but for" cause of the decision. O'Connor insisted that sexist "stray remarks," "statements by non decisionmakers," and even "statements by decisionmakers that were unrelated to the decisional process" were not enough to prove sex discrimination. This was merely sexism in the air.

But O'Connor believed that Hopkins had established that the sexism at Price Waterhouse had come to earth and affected her candidacy for partnership:

> It is as if Ann Hopkins were sitting in the hall outside the room where partnership decisions were being made. As the partners filed in to consider her candidacy, she heard several of them make sexist remarks in discussing her suitability for partnership. As the decisionmakers exited the room, she was told by one of those privy to the decisionmaking process that her gender was a major reason for the rejection of her partnership bid.

If Justice Brennan's opinion in *Price Waterhouse* read like an undergraduate "Intro to Philosophy" lecture, with its digression into the metaphysics of physical causation (if two trees fall simultaneously in the forest, which one causes the noise?), Justice O'Connor's concurrence was a made-for-TV movie, with its maudlin image of a beleaguered Hopkins skulking outside the boardroom as the partners made sexist jokes. These flourishes added drama, but they also, unfortunately, added confusion. Despite Brennan's extended disquisition on the subject, causation had almost nothing to do with the *Price Waterhouse* controversy. The real controversy involved the extent of the employer's duty to purify the workplace of prejudice. Justice Brennan and the liberals would presume discriminatory intent anytime bias had plausibly played a role in the challenged decision "in any way." The effect of such a rule is to require employers to police the comments of their employees and punish or actively repudiate sexist comments. (Brennan emphasized that Price Waterhouse "in no way disclaimed reliance on" the comments that reflected sex stereotypes.)

Justice O'Connor, by contrast, thought this went too far, turning Title VII into "thought control." She would presume discriminatory intent only if sex stereotypes infected "the decision-making process"—which for O'Connor was a discrete entity, separate from the workaday life of the firm, as suggested by her metaphor of a physically distinct corporate boardroom outside of which Hopkins waited. O'Connor's rule would effectively require employers to keep sexism out of this metaphorical room. But despite O'Connor's demand for "but for" causation, this too has nothing to do with whether sex caused the specific decision. Instead, it—like Brennan's opinion—

defines the extent of an employer's *ongoing* duty to safeguard against discrimination.

The difference between the two opinions is simply that O'Connor narrows the scope of that duty. For O'Connor, only comments made in connection with some discrete "decision-making process" count as proof of discriminatory intent. But many employees are the victims of bias, not in formal decision-making processes, but long before a formal review or promotion occurs. They suffer because of supervisors who give them "grunt work" instead of challenging assignments that offer the chance to impress and advance. They suffer subtle race- and sex-motivated slights and insinuations—what O'Connor dismisses as "stray comments"—that will harm their reputations. This type of discrimination, much more than overt bigotry in a formal process, is a pervasive impediment to true equality of opportunity for women and racial minorities.

O'Connor downplays these types of bias, not because they can't cause injuries, but because employers can't eliminate them without intrusive policing of their employee's speech and perhaps even their thoughts. O'Connor's fear that civil rights law could become a form of state-imposed thought control is perfectly valid. But it has nothing to do with distinguishing those cases where sex bias "caused" a decision from those where it did not. Instead, O' Connor effectively defines discrimination pragmatically, in order to strike a balance between equal opportunity and freedom of expression.

While Brennan's approach would try to reach every case where illicit motivations may have played a role in a decision, O'Connor's pragmatic approach to antidiscrimination simply lets some discrimination go unaddressed because the costs of remedying it are too high. Viewed this way, O'Connor's approach may seem unsatisfying and even callous, a beady-eyed expediency inappropriate to matters of civil rights. But perhaps the same pragmatism that informed her concurrence in *Price Waterhouse* also motivated her majority opinion upholding affirmative action in *Grutter v. Bollinger*. In a sense, the two positions are practical complements: given that the law cannot identify and prevent or punish every instance of invidious discrimination, affirmative action looks less like favoritism and more like a sensible response to the discrimination that escapes the law's reach.

So far we've encountered three quite different definitions of intentional discrimination. The first defines intentional discrimination as a mental state. The Implicit Association Test is inspired by a commonsense idea of bias as a discrete state of mind. It tries to establish the existence of this state of mind by testing an individual's reflexive associations with race or sex. It seems to follow that someone who exhibits bias on the IAT will be influenced by bias in her daily life—she'll discriminate. But evocative as it is, the IAT cannot prove that an individual has discriminated or will discriminate in the future, as its authors readily admit. The relationship between a subjective state of mind and the phenomenon of discrimination isn't straightforward.

The second definition finds intentional discrimination in the absence of good cause. The *McDonnell Douglas* method is almost indifferent to state of mind: it infers discriminatory conduct from surrounding facts. Justice Scalia's opinion in *Hicks* was less an attempt to isolate a mental state than an effort to defend the employer prerogatives against a requirement that all terminations be made only for cause. And Justice Souter, dissenting in *Hicks,* wanted to defend the orderly procedural regime of *McDonnell Douglas against* open-ended speculation as to state of mind.

The third definition finds discrimination in the failure to take adequate precautions against animus and stereotypes. Both Justice Brennan's and Justice O'Connor's opinions in *Price Waterhouse* sought to balance the expressive liberties and managerial prerogatives of employers against the antisexist and antiracist interests of employees. They did so not by isolating the influence of a prohibited state of mind on the challenged decision, but by defining the extent of management's duty to banish, mute, or counteract bigotry.

To say that the IAT and the incongruous opinions in *McDonnell Douglas, Hicks,* and *Price Waterhouse* all concern one question— "discrimination"—is scarcely more accurate than to say that every published opinion of the Supreme Court is concerned with the single question of "justice." Claims of intentional discrimination do not turn on a simple factual question of whether a prohibited state of mind caused a decision. They turn on more nuanced policy questions that require courts to balance the liberties of employers against the rights of employees; the interests of society in vibrant free markets against the interests of society in social justice; the value of expressive and associative liberty against the value of equal opportunity and race and sex integration. Whether a conflict involves a case of discrimination or a case of playing the race card can be a matter of opinion and perspective.

DISCRIMINATORY EFFECT OR "DISPARATE IMPACT"

The very first opinion in which the Supreme Court applied Title VII—*Griggs v. Duke Power Company*—had nothing to do with either facial or intentional discrimination. Willie Griggs was a black employee of the Duke Power Company. He challenged a policy that required a high school education and passing scores on two standardized tests in order to transfer to certain jobs. The Duke Power Company applied this policy to all of the employees in its North Carolina plant without regard to race.

But Duke Power had openly discriminated on the basis of race right up until the effective date of the Civil Rights Act. It had a formal policy that restricted blacks to "labor"—the least remunerative job category. When the Civil Rights Act became effective, the company stopped openly discriminating and started requiring the standardized tests and a high school education for assignment to any position other than "labor." Whites scored far better than blacks on the standardized tests. One contemporaneous study conducted by the Equal Employment Opportunity Commission found that 58 percent of whites, as compared with only 6 percent of blacks, passed a battery of standardized tests that included the two used by Duke Power. Why did blacks do so poorly on the tests? Chief Justice Warren E. Burger believed that the difference in performance was "directly traceable to race . . . Negroes . . . have long received inferior education in segregated schools."

Willie Griggs drew attention to the following stark facts: on the very day it was legally required to drop a long-standing policy of racial segregation, Duke Power implemented a test that required skills that the law had long denied blacks the chance to develop; as a result, the company excluded roughly twelve times as many black as white applicants from its better jobs. Did this show that Duke Power discriminated on the basis of race? The district court thought not: it found that there was no proof that a racial purpose motivated Duke Power's decision to use the tests. The court of appeals agreed and held that, lacking discriminatory purpose, there was no violation of Title VII.

The Supreme Court reversed this holding and insisted that an employer could violate Title VII without discriminatory intent. Writing for a unanimous Court, Chief Justice Burger insisted that the "absence of discriminatory intent does not redeem employment procedures . . . that act as 'built-in headwinds' for minority groups and are unrelated to job capability." The first case in which the Supreme Court of the United States found an employer liable for discrimination did not involve bigotry or discriminatory intent.[7]

Justice Burger identified two elements of unlawful discriminatory effect. The first: The challenged policy must "act as built-in headwinds for minority groups"—in other words it must screen out a disproportionate number of minorities—and it must be "unrelated to job capability." The second element is actually a defense. Once the plaintiff shows that the policy he challenged had a numerically discriminatory effect, the defendant must prove that that it is "job related" in order to avoid liability. Because many unobjectionable policies can have a numerically discriminatory effect, this second element is critical.

What counts as "job related"? The *Griggs* Court insisted that the criteria must measure "the person for the job and not the person in the abstract." It explained that Duke Power's criteria were not job related because "employees who have not finished high school or taken the tests have continued to perform satisfactorily . . . History is filled with examples of men and women who rendered highly effective performance without the conventional badges of accomplishment in terms of certificates, diplomas or degrees." This suggests that a tight fit between job and criteria is required: any criteria that would screen out qualified employees is not "job related."

The ideal job criteria would always measure the employee for the job. The ideal job interview would involve an on-the-job assessment, an audition. Of course, even auditions can't measure how well the applicant will perform every real-life task. Some people might perform well for a short period of time but lack stamina, or they might happen to be unrepresentatively good (or bad) at the task assigned during the audition. A better way of measuring the employee would be to have her do the job for a whole day, or even a week. We often evaluate law professors this way. When considering hiring an established professor from another school, the conventional process involves a "visiting offer"—the candidate actually moves house and works for a month, semester, or even year at the school, and the faculty interacts with her, observers her teaching, and enjoys (hopefully) her collegiality. We actually watch the candidate do the job.

This method has its drawbacks. It's extremely expensive. The law school has to pay to bring the professor out, help her find housing, set her up with an office, and pay her salary for the period of the visit. Such an interview can cost well over $100,000. And that doesn't count the cost to the candidate, who must uproot, leaving home, friends, favorite restaurants, trusted therapists or bartenders, and in some cases even families. We do this because the stakes are very high. Hiring an established professor usually means an offer with tenure, and accepting the offer means relinquishing tenure at the old school. A mistake could be very costly for employer and employee.

Now consider a typical job where no one expects either employee loyalty or job security. No one—employer or applicant—

would want to invest a lot in the selection process. Here an employer might want to measure the person "in the abstract"— using a standardized test score or paper credentials—because doing so is cheaper than measuring the person for the job. Few tests are a perfect match for a given job. The typical written test can do no more than evaluate abstract qualities, such as "analytic skills" or "critical thinking," that will be applied in concrete situations on the job. It's easy to attack such tests as insufficiently job related. The EEOC has developed detailed guidelines for determining whether a given test is sufficiently "job related" to survive a disparate impact challenge, but these "validation" methods are often complex and expensive—an industry of validation consultants emerged in the wake of *Griggs*. Many tests that provide useful information do not meet the EEOC validation guidelines. And because the whole point of standardized testing is to acquire information quickly and inexpensively, the need for costly validation is often enough to defeat the purpose of using even those tests that might meet the guidelines.

Thirty-five years after *Griggs*, the theory of discriminatory effect or "disparate impact" established by the case remains the most controversial doctrine in contemporary civil rights. It is still not perfectly clear how—or whether—the disparate impact theory relates to intentional discrimination. Immediately after *Griggs* many legal scholars thought that the disparate impact theory was developed because intentional discrimination is often difficult to prove. The underlying legal violation according to these scholars was still intentional discrimination. Disparate impact was just a way of establishing intentional discrimination by inference: if a policy effectively screened women or minorities from the workforce and wasn't job related, it was reasonable to assume that it was motivated by discriminatory intent. *Griggs* seemed to bear this out. The suspicious timing of Duke Power's new test requirements suggested bad motives. But the *Griggs* Court expressly denied that the ruling rested on a suspicion of intentional discrimination.

Later cases confirmed that no hint of intentional discrimination was required. A 1982 Supreme Court case, *Connecticut v. Teal*, involved a challenge to a two-step promotion process used by the state. A candidate had to pass a standardized test in order to be considered for promotion; those who passed the test were then evaluated according to recommendations from their supervisors, their work records, and seniority. Fifty-four percent of black candidates passed the standardized test as compared with 80 percent of white candidates. Four black employees who failed the test sued the state for race discrimination, insisting that the state was obliged to demonstrate that the test was job related or abandon it.

Connecticut pointed out that the plaintiffs' claim focused only on the first step of a two-step process. The second step—which actually determined who was promoted—included an affirmative action policy that favored blacks. As a result, almost 23 percent of black candidates were actually promoted as compared with 13.5 percent of white candidates. The process as a whole didn't discriminate against blacks. Not only was it implausible that Connecticut was *trying* to screen blacks out of upper management; it did not in fact do so. A greater proportion of black than of white candidates received promotions. At the bottom line, Connecticut argued, there was no discriminatory effect.

But the Supreme Court held that Connecticut could be liable for the discriminatory effect of the standardized test alone. Justice Brennan argued that looking only at the "bottom line" would allow an employer to discriminate against some employees—those blacks who flunked the standardized test—as long as it treated *other* members of the same group favorably—those blacks who passed the test and benefited from the affirmative action policy. This violated the *individual* rights of the employees who were discriminated against by means of the test. A hypothetical may help clarify Brennan's point: suppose an employer discriminated *against* blacks with darker skin, but in *favor* of blacks with lighter skin, so the bottom line was a racially integrated workforce. The bottom line should not preclude the darker-skinned blacks' claim of race discrimination. Brennan insisted that Title VII guarantees each *individual* equal employment opportunities. "Congress," he opined, "never intended to give an employer license to discriminate against some employees on the basis of race or sex merely because he favorably treats other members of the employee's group." The plaintiffs who flunked the test and were hence ineligible for promotion were entitled to challenge the part of the promotion process that disproportionately excluded blacks, even if the promotion process as a whole did not disadvantage blacks.

Brennan's opinion in *Teal* provoked a blistering dissent: Justice Lewis F. Powell, joined by Justices O'Connor and Rehnquist, insisted that it made no sense to say—as Brennan had—that Connecticut's standardized test discriminated against the *individual* blacks who failed; the only reason we call a facially neutral test "discriminatory" at all is because of its effect on a *group*. Powell argued that the Court should look at the employer's "total selection process"—which in the case at bar did not have a disparate impact on blacks. To return to our hypothetical, discrimination against darker-skinned blacks is *facial* race discrimination; an evenhanded use of a standardized test isn't. The disparate impact claim, by its very nature, required proof of a policy's disproportionate effect on a *group*—not an individual. For Powell, proof that the selection process as a whole did not disproportionately affect the group was exculpatory: "Having undertaken to prove a violation of his rights by reference to group figures [the plaintiff] cannot deny [the defendant] the opportunity to rebut his evidence by introducing figures of the same kind." Powell described *Teal* as "a long and unhappy step in the direction of confusion."

Teal took a straightforward and intuitive conception of discrimination and warped it into something abstract and arcane. Before *Teal*, we could think of discriminatory effects theory in one of two ways. One, it was a way of attacking concealed intentional discrimination: the facts of *Griggs* suggested discriminatory intent. Two, it promoted integration by requiring employers to avoid policies that unnecessarily segregate the workplace. The law would require employers to spend a little more time and money on closely job-related criteria whenever more loosely job-related criteria had discriminatory effects. *Teal* throws both of these intuitively plausible rationales into doubt. An employer—like the state of Connecticut—that offsets the exclusionary effects of a standardized test with an affirmative action policy is almost certainly not motivated by animus or prejudice. And if the end result or "bottom line" of the selection process is a workforce that has as many (or more) blacks as it would have if candidates were randomly selected, no integrationist goal is served by forcing the employer to abandon it.

Worse yet from the perspective of employers, *Teal* insists on micromanaging personnel decisions. After *Teal*, it is not enough that employers avoid intentional discrimination and incidental segregation—now the federal courts and administrative agencies will tell employers exactly *how* they must avoid them. The employer who wants to use a standardized test as a quick and easy screening device and prefers to correct for any resulting racial impact in another way is forbidden from doing so.

There are good reasons to dislike standardized tests. Much of the problem isn't the content of the tests themselves but rather the claims made on their behalf. The testing industry—like any other merchant in a competitive market—has every incentive to exaggerate. Their names announce that standardized tests measure "aptitude," "achievement," or even "intelligence." In fact they can only rank performance in a highly contrived and controlled competition. And as tests proliferate and their influence grows, so does the flesh-and-blood resistance, which understandably takes the form of a ritual slaying: *These tests—bloodless and obscure—aren't infallible after all. They can't take the measure of a man—in fact, they can't even measure the qualifications for the job!*

But if the real problem is standardized testing generally, let's attack it directly. Standardized tests are overused, and our confidence in them is often misplaced. But they are indispensable to modern society, which needs cheap, reliable, and consistent—if imperfect—methods of evaluation. We use standardized testing because we must. But the common belief that the tests measure merit and dispense just deserts should yield to a recognition that they are a yardstick of expedience and dole out rough justice.

How does this square with the idea that the tests must be "job related"? *Objectively* speaking, any policy that is worth more than it costs to implement is job related. We can expect the non-bigoted employer to drop requirements that truly aren't job related without the threat of legal liability because screening for truly irrelevant traits will actually make the workforce worse: if a law school screened its professors for height or looks (God forbid!) it would eliminate some very good short and homely professors and as a result wind up with a less competent faculty. If we can eliminate the possibility that a test is being used as cloak for intentional discrimination—as we can when the employer offsets any exclusionary effect in later stages of the selection process—we should defer to the typically superior judgment of the employer as to the objective requirements of the job. The notion that courts, rather than the people who created the job, should decide what is and is not "job related" is a supersizing of the ambition underlying civil rights. This idea has led directly to the explosion of racism-by-analogy discrimination claims I discussed in Chapter Two. After all, if the courts know better than the employer whether or not a standardized test is "job related," why can't they also decide whether grooming, physical appearance, and obesity are sufficiently job related for an employer to consider them?

But the legal doctrine of "job relatedness" isn't entirely superfluous or wrongheaded. It's just misnamed. Legally, "job relatedness" isn't an objective question—it's a policy question. The real meaning of "job related" involves a trade-off between the benefits of the challenged policy and the benefits of integration. Although we can expect most non-bigoted employers to drop truly arbitrary criteria out of self-interest, we can't expect them to drop useful criteria, even when they have profound exclusionary effects, because we can't assume that employers will value integration. If we as a society value it (I hope we do), we have to make sure that businesses consider it when devising their personnel policies. Accordingly, "job related" means *sufficiently job related that its value to the business outweighs its cost to society in terms of segregation or exclusion.* Despite the detailed statistical methods developed by the EEOC to validate standardized tests, this can't be more than a rough and subjective guess, because the trade-off involves incommensurable values. There is no way to objectively compare the benefits of cheaper or more effective employee screening with race and sex integration.

I would propose a blunt and unsentimental justification for discriminatory effects analysis. It's a trade-off: race and sex integration are important enough to justify extra employee screening costs. By contrast, the current muddled definition of discriminatory effects—expressed in Justice Brennan's opinion in *Teal*—denies that there are trade-offs to be made. It assumes that the challenged policies are worthless unless they are "job related" according to the current legal standard. But the legal standard for job relatedness is too stringent for this to be true. There are many tests that offer valuable general information but would not qualify under the law as job related. It is unlikely that the average person who flunks a general aptitude test is as good at most jobs as the average person who passes it. But this is what the *Teal* theory requires us to believe.

It's easy to shoot a messenger as obnoxious as a standardized test. And everyone of goodwill wants to believe that there are no objectively relevant differences in job qualifications between the races or sexes. It's natural and even commendable to insist that tests that suggest otherwise must be biased: they're measuring "culturally specific" traits rather than job-related skills; they're discriminatory. This blind faith flows from a generous egalitarianism, but it also betrays a willful ignorance of the harsh effects of social prejudice. Generations of explicit discrimination and pervasive social bias have taken their toll: the groups that suffer these evils are *worse off*—not only in terms of wealth and status but also in terms of education and skills—than those that do not. Righting this social injustice will require more than simply overcoming irrational biases and correcting misjudgments. The discriminatory effects theory is on its firmest footing when it acknowledges this. In *Griggs*, for instance, the Court recognized that discrimination and bias had kept blacks from acquiring the credentials and skills that whites enjoyed, and it insisted that businesses make small concessions in terms of screening costs to ensure that they did not perpetuate this historical social injustice. So conservatives are right to insist that the doctrine of discriminatory effect does not, strictly speaking, simply prohibit discrimination. It also requires scrupulously evenhanded employers to change practices that happen to disadvantage minorities as a group, even at some cost.

But the conservatives are wrong to insist that this is necessarily a bad thing. Civil rights law does this in other contexts too. Title VII requires businesses to accommodate religious practices even when their resistance to doing so is not biased. For instance, businesses must rearrange schedules to allow the faithful to observe holy days when doing so would not be overly costly. More dramatically, the Americans with Disabilities Act can require businesses to remodel facilities and provide costly special equipment in order to help disabled employees do their jobs.

Civil rights advocates often say that these provisions simply protect employees from discrimination on the basis of religion or disability: making a Seventh Day Adventist work on Saturday is the same as firing him because of his faith; refusing to provide work-related texts in braille for a blind employee is the same as firing her because she can't see. If the religious employee does good work Sunday through Friday, he deserves the job; if the blind employee does a good work once she has the braille translations, she deserves the job. It's easy to understand why someone would feel this way. But it's only half true. From the perspective of the employee, it's true that the accommodations shouldn't matter. She's producing just as much as anyone else; she's just as good. But from the perspective of the employer, the accommodations do matter. For the employer, the value of an employee is not measured in terms of productivity alone—it's measured in terms of productivity *minus costs*. Every employee is expensive to employ: employees require workspaces, uniforms, offices, equipment, and of course wages. To be valuable to the employer, an employee must produce more than he costs. And if two employees are equally productive, but one is less expensive, the cheaper employee is more valuable. It's not discriminatory to prefer the cheaper yet equally productive employee—it's good business.

If employers obeyed only the profit motive, they'd hire very few people with disabilities. In many cases, even very competent disabled people who required accommodations could not compete with people of modest competence who did not. The cost of the accommodations would overwhelm the benefit of their extra competence. The law requires employers to bear *and ignore* the cost of modest accommodations. This requirement does more than eliminate irrational discrimination against the disabled. It actively promotes the integration of disabled people into the workplace. Similarly, although less dramatically, the discriminatory effects theory promotes race and sex integration by requiring employers to use more refined and often more expensive selection criteria that measure the person for the job if measuring the person in the abstract would screen out disproportionate numbers of minorities or women.

Conservatives often complain that such policies are social engineering. Government has no business promoting integration, they say—once civil rights law eliminates irrational bias, its job is done. This reaction is wrong for two reasons. One, there's nothing wrong with so-called social engineering. In a sense, all law is social engineering. We want to engineer a society where people honor their bargains, so we enforce contracts in court. We want to engineer a society where people are careful not to injure others, so we make people pay for recklessly caused accidents. We want to engineer a society where fathers support their children, so we garnish the wages of "deadbeat dads" and use the proceeds to feed and clothe their offspring. No one calls these policies social engineering, because the goals are uncontroversial. People start grousing about "social engineering" only when they have doubts about the goals. But we shouldn't have doubts about integration as a goal—it's the only way we'll achieve meaningful racial equality and lasting racial harmony. I'll have more to say about this in Chapter Four. For now, it's worth noting that we'd almost certainly have more integrated workplaces if not for our long, sad history of explicit racial bias.

This brings me to the second reason critics are wrong to complain that the mild pro-integration policy of employment discrimination law is social engineering. The critics insist that once the law eliminates irrational bias, all is fair: we should let the chips lie where they fall. But civil rights law does not eliminate irrational bias. As we've seen, the law strikes a balance between equal opportunity for women and minorities and other competing goals, such as employer prerogatives and freedom of expression. The law deliberately errs on the side of the defendant: the employee has to *prove* discriminatory intent. Sometimes she won't be able to do so even when it actually occurred. The law doesn't try to *eliminate* bias, because to do so would be too costly in terms of wrongfully imposed liability, invasive investigations, restrictions on employer flexibility, and freedom of expression. But we need to do something to counteract the bias we can't eliminate directly. The discriminatory effect theory does this in two ways: it requires employers to revise job criteria that *might* be motivated by bias—even when the employee can't prove it—and it promotes workplace integration to make up for the cases where undetected bias keeps workplaces segregated.

The theory of discriminatory effect is a distinct theory of discrimination that has almost nothing to do with state of mind. Disparate impact theory forbids businesses from *inadvertently* perpetuating racial disadvantage. Conservatives universally hate the idea of discriminatory effect for just this reason: they insist that it is inconsistent with the text of the Civil Rights Act and that it defies common sense to say that someone can "discriminate" unintentionally. They complain that it's affirmative action traveling under an alias.

But even if the disparate impact theory was a questionable interpretation of the law when the Supreme Court first adopted it, in 1971, Congress has since explicitly endorsed it in the Civil Rights Act of 1991, which actually *strengthens* the disparate impact prohibition. And the basic idea of "unintentional discrimination" isn't hard to understand. Someone could unintentionally discriminate in one of two ways. A policy might piggyback on disadvantages that came about during the period of explicit discrimination. *Griggs* was such a case: blacks did less well on the standardized tests because they were forced into inferior schools by Jim Crow laws. Using the standardized tests as a barrier to better jobs effectively perpetuated the disadvantages of Jim Crow, whether Duke Power intended to do so or not. A plausible interpretation of the facts in *Griggs* is that Duke Power imposed the standardized test requirement not in order to keep its workforce segregated, but in order to discover whether blacks from inferior high schools had the skills necessary to do the more demanding jobs. Before the Civil Rights Act, the managers of Duke Power considered a high school education sufficient because they believed it consistently met a certain standard. They didn't need to consider the quality of the segregated all-black schools, because they never accepted applicants who had attended those schools. Once they could no longer discriminate, they had to ask whether a high school education from a black school with inferior resources meant the same thing as a high school education from a white school. Worried that it didn't, they imposed the standardized tests. It is important to emphasize that this worry need not have been inspired by a racist stereotype that blacks are inherently inferior (although it certainly may have been). It could as easily have been inspired by a realistic assessment of the quality of underfunded and demoralized black schools. The worry needn't have been that blacks with the same credentials still weren't as good as whites. The worry could have been that blacks couldn't have the same credentials—a high school education at a white school was better than a high school education at a black school.

There's a cruel irony here. For decades, the Jim Crow South had segregated the public schools by force of law under the doctrine "separate but equal." But when white businesses had to evaluate the black graduates of these supposedly equal schools, they tacitly acknowledged what civil rights activists had argued all along: the separate schools were not equal at all. The doctrine of discriminatory effects prohibited employers from callously perpetuating the disadvantages of Jim Crow. They didn't have to hire less competent blacks, but they couldn't use broad and unspecific criteria that blacks were less likely to have: the law required them to prove that such criteria matched the job. This was an added burden for employers who preferred imperfect information on the cheap to specific and detailed information at a dear price. But it was the only way to make good the promise of equal opportunity. A trade-off to be sure, but an easy one to defend.

There's a second way nondiscriminatory policies might further disadvantage historically disadvantaged groups. Generations of deliberate discrimination have shaped the practices and habits of evaluation. Segregated institutions developed practices and policies without nonwhites and women in mind. Sometimes, keeping those practices and policies in place will unfairly disadvantage these previously excluded groups, even if that's not what anyone intends. It's easy to see this if we use sex as an example. Suppose a males-only health club decides to admit women for the first time. Because it was males-only when its facilities were built, it has only one restroom, with eight urinals and one standard toilet. It's not enough for the club to stop intentionally discriminating. It won't be a hospitable environment for women unless the club also remodels to add a women's room with more stalls. If it doesn't, women won't want to join, and the club will remain segregated.

Here's an example that involves race. Everyone has encountered those infrared sensor mechanisms that turn the faucet on and off in public restrooms. In theory, you simply hold your hand in front of the faucet and it turns on and stays on as long as your hand is still there. In practice, sometimes it turns on, and sometimes it doesn't; sometimes it stays on, and sometimes it shuts off before you can lather up—another mod con that's actually less convenient than the old-fashioned mechanism it replaced. Now, I'll bet some of my readers are wondering what I'm griping about: those faucet sensors work perfectly. I'll bet those readers have relatively pale skin. Am I about to suggest a racist conspiracy? Did the faucet manufacturer deliberately program the faucets to ignore black people? Of course not. But the principle on which they operate is that the faucet will be triggered when your hand reflects light back to a sensor. Lighter objects reflect light, while darker objects absorb it. So lighter-skinned people will trigger the mechanism more easily and more consistently than people with dark skin.

It's not hard to imagine how we wound up with these irritating faucets. Some bright young inventor proposed "touchless" faucets. Seemed like a good idea. They were developed and tested, and they worked brilliantly. It just never occurred to anyone that they'd be a problem for blacks. And even if it did, that would have seemed a minor glitch in an otherwise flawless improvement. If we lived in a society where 85 percent of the population had skin as dark as mine, this first generation of touchless faucets would not have made it out of the development stage. If the team that developed the faucets included blacks, they probably would have noticed the problem right away. But the faucets worked well for 85 percent of the population, and no one thought much about the unfortunate darker 15 percent.

Shouldn't Congress pass a law to ban those racist bathroom faucets? Well, no. Apparently, new technology has solved the invisible man problem, so it's only a matter of time before all of the offending faucets are replaced with color-blind models. And balky faucets are a minor inconvenience in the broader scheme of things. (Those ineffectual hot air hand dryers obviously deserve the higher legislative priority.) But sometimes it's reasonable to call this kind of inadvertently caused disadvantage "discrimination." When the difference isn't an annoying extra few minutes in the loo, but instead access to gainful employment, legal intervention is appropriate.

To make good the promise of equality, sometimes we will need to reconsider practices and policies developed in segregated contexts. Deciding whether a neutral policy adopted for respectable reasons is effectively discriminatory is not a simple question of facts. It's a complicated question of trade-offs and predictions; it requires us to weigh the costs of changing or abandoning policies that make beady-eyed economic sense against the harm such policies do to the causes of social justice and of integration—without a perfect measure of either. Unless we're willing to abandon any hope of achieving racial justice, we can't do without some idea of discriminatory effects. But because such claims involve contested factual questions, close judgment calls, and ethical nuances, they will always be controversial. They'll be a source of legitimate and sincere disagreement. And they'll provide some with excuses to play the race card.

FACIAL DISCRIMINATION: RACIAL PROFILING AND AFFIRMATIVE ACTION

Several times a year something like this happens. A stranger paces up and down the hallway of the faculty wing at Stanford Law School, where I work, alternating anxious glances at her watch and at the names posted over office doors. "Do you know where I can find, umm . . . oh, I can't remember his name . . . He's a professor here . . . he's tall, short, cropped hair . . . I think he was wearing a tweed jacket . . ." So far this describes 70 percent of the male faculty at the law school, and several of the female, whom I've eliminated only because of the gendered pronoun. "Well, what does he teach?" I ask. "I think he teaches copyright—or is international law? Could be land use." I try another tack: "Younger or older?" I query. "Well. I think he's a little older than you." I start naming names. "He's a nice-looking man . . . uuuuhh . . . he's black . . ." I groan, audibly unless I catch myself. There are forty-five professors at the law school. Four are black, including me. Had my politically correct interlocutor mentioned this salient fact at the outset, we'd have narrowed the field to three right away.

Why do people do this? Perhaps some people have taken the legal ideal of "color blindness" too literally. Others may feel that race—or at least non-Caucasian race—is some type of handicap or deformity that it would be impolite to mention, like a lisp or a cleft palate. Still others may simply be uncomfortable with a racial etiquette that's constantly in flux. I'm too young to have been called a colored person or a Negro, but I do remember when the right term was "black." But some people complained that we *aren't* actually—we're various shades of brown, ocher, tan, olive—and anyway shouldn't we really be talking about culture and not color? So it became "Afro-American." But then some folks started to grouse that they didn't want to be named after a haircut (the etymology has to be the reverse, but never mind), and it became African-American. But that's a little vague, isn't it? I mean, Africa is an awfully big place, and there are a lot of immigrants actually from Africa, so it's confusing too—can Kwame Anthony Appiah, the philosopher raised in Ghana, and I, born in New York, both be African-American? So we switched to "people of color," which has the added appeal of including Latinos and Asians so it's one big rainbow coalition (never mind precision). At this point one might be forgiven for transposing the terms and saying "colored people"— but you won't be, so don't do it.

If we can't even agree on terminology, but lots of people are quick to take offense when anyone gets it "wrong," is it better just to avoid the topic altogether? In their zeal to avoid giving offense, too many people also manage to overlook the obvious. For better and, by and large, for worse, we've divided society into groups based on common physical characteristics and common ancestry—races. These groups matter less often than many people think, but they do matter sometimes. As long as we have to put up with the numerous downsides of race, we might as well enjoy its scanty benefits, one of which is that race is a widely understood shorthand for physical description.

But suppose, rather than a lost visitor to the law school, I was confronted by an armed police officer. And rather than an embarrassed exchange in which race figures by its conspicuous absence, I was subjected to a time-consuming, humiliating, and invasive interrogation and search that was provoked by my race.

The Usual Suspects

Oneonta is a small town in upstate New York. Its website describes it as "a friendly community . . . proud of its diversity . . . a . . . community . . . where everyone knows everyone else." In

1992 "everyone" in Oneonta was about 10,000 people, and another 7,500 students attended the neighboring State University of New York. "Diversity" meant fewer than 300 black people. On September 4, a seventy-seven-year-old Oneonta resident was the victim of a burglary and attempted rape. She told the police that the assailant was a young black man and that he had cut his hand during the assault. Because it was dark when the attack occurred, she could not offer the police a more detailed description. The police deployed a canine unit, which tracked the assailant's scent to the university. Then the trail went cold. With no leads, the police obtained a list of all of the black male students enrolled in the university and tried to question them *all* and examine their hands for cuts. That effort yielded no suspects, so the police conducted a sweep of the town. They stopped and questioned two hundred nonwhites on the streets of Oneonta.[8]

The police tried to round up and question every single black man in Oneonta! Yet a federal court held that the Oneonta police had not discriminated. "[The police department's] policy was race neutral on its face," the court explained. "Their policy was to investigate crimes by interviewing the victim, getting a description of the assailant, and seeking out persons who matched that description." But this dodges the issue: witnesses are typically *asked* to identify suspects according to sex, height, weight, age, *and race.* And even if police didn't deliberately elicit a racial description, they deliberately used it.

Rounding up all black men and only black men for a questioning is race discrimination in its purest form. But it makes sense to use race in this way for the same reason it would make sense for anxious white folks to go ahead and tell me they're looking for a black person rather than waste my time with a less useful, race-neutral description. Race is a good way to identify people. It's convenient shorthand for a host of conspicuous physical characteristics that would be cumbersome to list. And in many settings race is very effective in winnowing a group down. There are only four black professors at Stanford Law School; there were fewer than eighty black students on the Oneonta campus and fewer than three hundred black residents in the entire city.

My colleague at Stanford, Professor Richard Banks, poses this question: If it's okay to use race when searching for a specific criminal, isn't it also okay to use it when searching for members of a *group* of criminals?[9] Suppose a criminal gang is on a looting spree. Police know that the gang is racially exclusive: all of its members are Asian males. Given the *Oneonta* decision, can police target Asian men when searching for the fruits of the crime? Legally, the answer is yes—this is similar to a search for a specific suspect in a specific crime. Now, suppose the gang isn't racially exclusive, but predominantly Asian with a few white and Latino members. Race is still a pretty good way of narrowing down potential suspects. *Most* of the suspects are Asian, so again, targeting Asians for questioning in this case is not very different from doing so when one specific suspect is Asian.

If police can use race to round up suspects based on the membership of a local gang, can they use race to round up suspects based on the demographics of a local, statewide, or nationwide criminal population? Suppose police have reliable data that a disproportionate number of drug couriers in their jurisdiction are black. Does that information justify stopping black people based on their race and searching them or their cars for drugs? What if race is only one element of a statistical composite of a typical drug courier. Is it okay for police to use a composite—they'd probably call it a "profile"—to conduct roadside stops and searches for contraband?

Racial profiling has gotten a deserved bad rap in the press and among politicians. More than twenty states have prohibited it, as have most federal agencies (with exceptions for national security investigations). Conservative and liberal politicians alike have publicly denounced the practice, and few police departments will publicly admit that they use it. At worst, "racial profiling" is just a euphemism for a crude racial stereotype—black people are natural-born criminals—that has contributed to a history of antagonism between law enforcement and black communities. That's why civil rights activists call with one voice for its repudiation. For example, the ACLU's Racial Justice Project condemns racial profiling in unequivocal terms, calling it an "outrageous form of racial discrimination" and demanding its eradication.

Racial profiling inevitably ensnares the innocent along with the guilty. For instance, in May 1992, Robert Wilkins, a Harvard Law School graduate returning from a relative's funeral, was stopped and forced to stand in a torrential rain as Maryland State Police searched his car. He sued the Maryland State Police and settled out of court for ninety-six thousand dollars and an agreement that police keep records of the race of individuals whom they stop.[10] In August 1998 U.S. Army Master Sergeant Rossano Gerald, a decorated soldier, was handcuffed in front of his young son and made to wait in a hot squad car while Oklahoma state troopers conducted a fruitless search. When Gerald complained that the officers had dismantled his car and scattered the contents of his luggage, one of the troopers replied, "We ain't good at repacking."[11] In 1995 a Liberian college student, Nelson Walker, pulled over for a seat-belt violation, stood by powerlessly as Maryland police dismantled his car in search of narcotics. According to Walker, finding none, they tossed him a screwdriver: "You're going to need this," they smirked, and left him to reassemble his car.[12] And the injuries inflicted by racial profiling aren't always limited to inconvenience and humiliation. In 1998 New Jersey troopers opened fire on three black men and one Latino man who were on their way to a basketball training clinic when their van slipped into reverse gear after they pulled over. Lawyer Johnnie Cochran obtained a $13 million judgment against the state. A civil rights lawyer suing the state police in another case said that racial profiling might have set the tragic events in motion: "A different choice might have spared . . . those kids in the van."[13]

Such anecdotes are backed up by statistics. The New York State attorney general reported that half the people the NYPD stopped and frisked in 1998 were black, although blacks were only 25 percent of the city's population. The U.S. Commission on Civil Rights found that 51 percent of people stopped by police in the Staten Island borough of New York were black, although blacks make up only 9 percent of Staten Islanders.[14] In California, Latinos stopped by the Highway Patrol were twice as likely as whites to have their cars searched; blacks were 1.5 times as likely.[15] In Montgomery County, Maryland, black drivers were three times as likely to be asked to submit to searches as white drivers.[16]

A stretch of the New Jersey Turnpike is known among black motorists as "white man's pass." In the late 1990s almost two-thirds of the motorists stopped by state police were racial minorities. In a 1999 interview, the police superintendent, Carl

Williams, offered the obligatory denunciation of racial profiling: "As far as racial profiling is concerned, that is absolutely not right. It has never been condoned in the State Police . . ." He went on to distinguish the racial generalization he *did* condone: "If you're looking at the methamphetamine market, that seems to be controlled by motorcycle gangs, which are basically white. If you are looking at heroin and stuff like that, your involvement there is more or less Jamaicans."[17] No one was surprised when Williams was promptly asked to resign, though many wondered whether it was because of the attitudes his comments reflected or his indiscretion in baldly stating what many in law enforcement believe.

Carl Williams's indelicate assessment of the drug trade was objectionable because it was so casual and flippant ("your involvement there is more or less Jamaicans"). It sounded like a crude, reflexive stereotype rather than a well-reasoned or researched observation. A lot of what is condemned as "racial profiling" probably doesn't involve a "profile" at all: it's just reflexive bigotry. But it's plausible that ethnically exclusive gangs do control certain criminal enterprises. Few would think it an outrageous stereotype to suggest, for instance, that Italian-Americans were disproportionately involved in sales of bootleg liquor in Prohibition-era Chicago or that people of Chinese ancestry were disproportionately represented among opium sellers in gold rush–era San Francisco. Is it so different to suggest that white biker gangs run most of the methamphetamine on the Jersey Turnpike or that Jamaican groups carry most of the heroin? Suppose Williams was right and had the evidence to back up his assertions. Wouldn't it make sense for police charged with stopping the free flow of heroin to target black drivers and subject those with West Indian accents to extra scrutiny? And if they did so and made more successful busts than random stops would have, wouldn't police be right to conclude that the targeting had been justified?

Of course, race is a very sloppy proxy for criminal behavior, but it's also a very convenient one. It's easy for police to identify members of particular racial groups on sight, whereas characteristics that correlate more closely with criminal behavior are either invisible (drug addiction) or too widely exhibited to serve as useful sorting criteria (male gender and adolescence). If race is even loosely correlated with criminal behavior, using race as part of a "profile" for traffic stops or customs searches might make sense from a law enforcement perspective. Racial profiles, based on reliable statistics that demonstrate that members of certain races are more likely to be involved in criminal activity, need not be motivated by animus or irrational prejudice.

Opponents of racial profiling insist that it is irrational and bigoted. According to Professor Banks, the critics regularly cite evidence that police stops and searches of minorities and of whites yield evidence of crime in roughly equal percentages. The opponents insist that these equal "hit rates" suggest equal rates of criminal behavior across racial groups. And if crimes rates are equal across races, then it makes no sense to use race as a factor in criminal profiling. As two leading opponents of racial profiling, David Cole and John Lamberth, argue, "If blacks are carrying drugs more often than whites, police should find drugs on the blacks they stop more often than on the whites they stop. But they don't."[18]

According to Banks, the opponents misunderstand the implications of equal "hit rates." Equal hit rates would suggest equal crime rates only if police *didn't* profile. Suppose police just stopped motorists at random. Police would search a representative sample of the general population, so we'd expect the hit rate to equal the crime rate, both generally and for each racial group. In this case, equal hit rates would suggest equal crime rates. But if police use a profile that actually *works* to identify criminals, then hits rates should exceed the crime rate. For instance, a study by the U.S. Customs Service found that targeted searches yielded from 1.5 to 15 times as many "hits" as random searches would have.[19]

If a profile works to identify more criminals than random stops would, the hit rate is a function of the crime rate *and* the accuracy of the profile: we can't infer anything about the underlying rate of crime from the number of "hits" alone. Suppose blacks are twice as likely as whites to be carrying drugs on a given freeway. If police stopped motorists at random, they'd find drugs twice as often on black motorists as on whites, because in this case the hit rate would equal the crime rate. But if police used an accurate profile that led them to stop black motorists disproportionately, hit rates might well be equal for the two groups, not because *crime* rates were equal but because the profile led police to target the people likely to be carrying drugs and a disproportionate number of those people were black. Here's another way to look at it: suppose police profiling was so good that the hit rate was 100 percent—every single stop yielded contraband. Hit rates would be equal for all racial groups—100 percent. But of course a perfect success rate wouldn't be evidence that police were using an *irrational* racial profile.

Equal hit rates don't necessarily mean that crime rates are equal or that racial profiling is irrational. But they do mean that police stop a disproportionate number of innocent minorities. Equal hit rates mean that, *of people stopped and searched,* equal percentages of all races are *innocent.* If a disproportionately large number of minorities are stopped because of racial profiling, a disproportionately large number of innocent minorities will be stopped. If police target blacks and hit rates are equal, innocent blacks bear a disproportionate share of the social cost of policing. So racial profiling imposes on innocent minorities what Harvard Law School professor Randall Kennedy has described as a "racial tax."[20] This is true even if the profiling is perfectly rational because a disproportionate number of blacks are involved in crime. Rational profiling in effect makes innocent blacks suffer for the sins of other people who share their race.

The real question is not whether racial profiling is rational or effective—it can be. The question is whether it is just. Is it okay to levy Professor Kennedy's racial tax? Is it acceptable to burden racial minorities with a disproportionate share of the cost of law enforcement? The answer depends on how large that share of the cost is and how important the law enforcement objectives are.

As to the cost: a lot of what riles people about racial profiling is the rough way police treat the innocent people they encounter. The most notorious cases of racial profiling involve harassment and abuse of authority. Innocent people who are handcuffed, thrown up against the hoods of cars, made to stand in inclement weather for hours, and then unapologetically left with their vehicles disassembled and their property strewn across the roadway make a strong case that the costs of racial profiling outweigh the benefits. But that's because a lot of the costs are unnecessary. Too often police add needless insult to the injury necessarily done by racial profiling. Police should treat everyone they stop as innocent until they have hard evidence of their guilt. They should recognize that they're imposing on a lot of innocent taxpayers and act accordingly. A little courtesy and respect could go a long way to quiet the outrage over racial profiling.

As to the importance of law enforcement priorities, until recently most racial profiling was used in connection with the war on drugs, and people who unequivocally opposed racial profiling were, not coincidentally, often also people who questioned the wisdom of drug interdiction efforts in general. If the war on drugs isn't worth fighting in the first place—if we'd be better served by a policy of decriminalization and regulation of many now illegal drugs than by the current policy of interdiction—then it's easy to conclude that the racial tax levied by profiling in service of interdiction is too high.

What if racial profiling were used to interdict not a nickel bag of weed being smuggled into Manhattan, but a bag of box cutters being smuggled onto an airplane? After terrorist hijackings of September 11, 2001, the racial profiling debate shifted focus from drug interdiction to antiterrorism, and the politics of racial profiling changed. Civil libertarians and left-wing liberals held firm to the orthodoxy that racial profiling was by its very nature abhorrent, but many mainstream commentators softened their opposition to the practice. In a PBS *NewsHour* interview shortly after the 9/11 attacks, two commentators—a columnist for *Newsweek* and a law professor—argued in favor of racial profiling in limited circumstances.[21] The intervening years have only emboldened the proponents of racial profiling: a 2004 opinion piece in *USA Today* described racial profiling as "a matter of survival" and insisted that "post 9/11, the belief that racial, religious and nationality profiling is never justified has become a dangerous bugaboo. It is unfortunate that loyal Muslims or Arabs might be burdened because of terrorists who share their race, nationality or religion. But *any* inconvenience is preferable to suffering a second mass terrorist attack . . ."[22]

Even as politicians continued loudly to condemn profiling, the officers in the field silently practiced it. Several months before the 9/11 attacks, President Bush said of racial profiling, "It's wrong and we will end it in America."[23] After 9/11, the Department of Justice directed the FBI and local police to question some five thousand legal immigrants based on their national origin. Norman Mineta, secretary of the Department of Transportation, which was charged with screening passengers for air travel shortly after 9/11, repeatedly condemned racial profiling: "Routinely pulling passengers out of line and subjecting them to searches need not, and should not, be done on the basis of race,"[24] he insisted. But he subtly hedged: "There are times when race and ethnicity are relevant . . . for instance, when we have information that a crime is being planned or has been committed and among the specifics we know about the suspects are their race . . . But there is a firm distinction," he insisted, "between that situation, and one where a law enforcement officer is willing to assume, *based on no reason other than race alone,* that a particular person is likely to be a criminal—or a terrorist." Although Mineta's rhetoric sounds like a wholehearted rejection of racial profiling, what he actually rejects is only the most narrow and crude type of racial profiling: the use of race and race alone—a practice no one defends. According to Amnesty International, "there has been a widely reported increase in racial profiling at airports, particularly applied to people who appear to be Muslim or of South Asian or Middle Eastern descent."[25]

Almost everyone claims to oppose racial profiling. New Jersey's Republican governor Christine Todd Whitman fired Carl Williams for suggesting that race and crime might be statistically correlated. Williams himself began his fateful comments by *repudiating* racial profiling. The Bush administration tempered its otherwise aggressive antiterrorism rhetoric with condemnations of racial profiling. But the consensus against racial profiling is a sham. It's easy for everyone from the ACLU and Amnesty International to Republican politicians and law enforcement agencies to condemn racial profiling, as long as no one insists on a precise definition of the term. Civil liberties groups play three-card monte by using the most narrow and extreme definition of profiling when describing it, but employing a more encompassing definition when seeking to prohibit it. Government and law enforcement play the same con game by heartily condemning racial profiling without defining it. Civil rights activists insist that racial profiling is always irrational, and police are happy to join them in rejecting *"irrational* racial profiling"—leaving the door open to racial profiling that is rational. The activists attack the odious practice of targeting people "because of race and race alone," and many states and police departments have seized on that rhetoric, prohibiting profiling based on race alone but tacitly exempting the type of profiling that police actually use, which is based on a combination of race and other factors.

We would be better served if we acknowledged that police sometimes have good reasons to consider race when carrying out investigations and if we made sure that they consider it only when they do have good reasons. Racial profiling—even when it is justified—does indeed impose the costs of law enforcement disproportionately on certain racial groups. Professor Kennedy is right to insist that it's a racial tax. The targets of profiling deserve the appreciation of their fellow citizens, courtesy from the officers charged to protect and serve them, and a bit less sanctimonious carping about "color blindness" in the handful of cases where rational discrimination favors, rather than injures, them.

"Reverse Racism" Isn't

Barbara Grutter was a forty-two-year-old single mother when she was denied admission to the University of Michigan Law School. She had good credentials: a 161 score on the LSAT, which put her in the 86th percentile nationally, and a 3.8 undergraduate grade point average. Good, but not good enough: plenty of applicants with as good or better numerical credentials were also rejected. But plenty of applicants with lower numbers than Grutter's were admitted. Grutter sued the university for race discrimination because most of these luckier applicants were racial minorities.

The predictable complaint of a rejected applicant captured the attention of the United States Supreme Court. As soon as the Court agreed to hear Grutter's case, the old adversaries from the last generation's affirmative action wars started honing their arguments and mustering their allies in preparation for another long and nasty fight. Almost twenty-five years earlier, Alan Bakke had applied and was denied admission to the University of California at Davis Medical School. Like Grutter, Bakke discovered that racial minorities with lower grades and lower test scores than his were admitted under an affirmative action program. The program Bakke challenged, unlike the one Grutter attacked, essentially established separate admission tracks for different racial groups—it was a quota system. Bakke sued the university, asserting that his Fourteenth Amendment rights to equal protection had been violated, and he prevailed. The Supreme Court split 4–1–4. The controlling opinion was the concurrence authored by Justice Lewis Powell. Powell invalidated the U.C. Davis affirmative action policy as an impermissible quota system, but he opined that a non–quota-based affirmative action plan might survive constitutional review if it was designed to promote "diversity." This was an effective stalemate: affirmative action would continue in a different form, and it would continue to be vulnerable to new legal attacks.

As a matter of principle, the affirmative action fight involves a simple conflict, familiar to everyone with even fleeting familiarity with the controversy. Affirmative action is unambiguous discrimination on the basis of race. Everyone acknowledges this, although its proponents prefer, for understandable reasons, to put it in different terms. *If* the evil of racism is race discrimination, then antiracists must oppose affirmative action. But no one really thinks that affirmative action is motivated by racism, the phrase "reverse racism" notwithstanding. No one seriously contends that proponents of affirmative action wish to injure or isolate the white and Asian students who don't enjoy racial preferences. A few crackpots and sophists press the implausible idea that affirmative action is "racist" because it reflects a racial stereotype—a demeaning lack of confidence in the talents of minority students. But affirmative action—unlike a racial stereotype—is not motivated by a "belief," but by hard facts about the numerical credentials of minority students as a group. And unlike a stereotype, it does not disparage their talents; if anything, it is optimistic that their talents will outstrip their high school grades and standardized test scores. If moral condemnation and legal sanction are to be reserved for actions that are motivated by racial animus or stereotypes, affirmative action gets a pass.

The legal debate on these points is somewhat rarefied, involving the intersection of constitutional and statutory law and some delicate yet flexible legal principles. Happily, the layperson has shown remarkable facility with the relevant doctrine. Less happily, he has also proved adept at the attendant legal posturing, sanctimonious bluster, and engorged rhetoric. Piety and self-righteousness are the obligatory tones on both sides.

Opponents of affirmative action insist that "racism is racism," whether its victim is "black, white, yellow, green or purple." The legal imperative, they insist, is equal treatment. They point out that the Constitution guarantees every person "equal protection of the laws" and does not make any particular downtrodden group the special ward of the law. The defenders of affirmative action retort that racism is not a matter of chromatherapy, it is a set of beliefs and practices that reduce some groups of people to second-class citizenship. The defenders insist that affirmative action does just the opposite. Having countenanced discrimination against minorities for decades, they say, society can undo the damage only by giving special consideration to those same groups: one can "only fight fire with fire"(at this point, the opponent, not do be outdone in the contest of hackneyed aphorisms, interrupts with "two wrongs don't make a right"). The proponents insist that legal principle cannot be understood in a vacuum and note that the historical circumstances that led to the ratification of the Fourteenth Amendment and federal antidiscrimination laws make it clear that their purpose was indeed to make historically subordinated racial groups effective wards of the law. They conclude that invalidation of affirmative action would return us to the "bad old days" of Jim Crow segregation.

And so it goes. These were the arguments advanced for and against "remedial race-conscious measures" before the ink was dry on the Civil Rights Act. The same sound bites accompanied the drumbeat of controversy echoing from Alan Bakke's lawsuit in 1978.[26] And in 2002, the same clichés, the same battle hymns, the same tone of righteous and wounded indignation from all concerned.

In theory, the debate involves two distinct inquiries. One is whether affirmative action is legally permissible under the Constitution of the United States and Title VI of the Civil Rights Act of 1964, which effectively applies the constitutional limitations to private schools that receive federal funding (that's almost all of them). The second is whether it's a good idea. Affirmative action could be legally permissible even if it's very bad policy, and it could be unlawful even if it's sound policy.

But many of the policy arguments are also legal arguments. This is because the relevant law does not strictly forbid discrimination—instead it allows it, but only if the university has a very good reason—what the Supreme Court has called a "compelling interest." This means that in practice, the legality of affirmative action depends on whether or not it's good policy. Over the years, defenders of affirmative action have offered several reasons to meet the legal test. Affirmative action corrects for possible bias in grades and test scores: bigoted teachers might unfairly give minority students lower grades, and some people have argued that standardized tests are culturally biased in favor of whites. Affirmative action helps to counteract societal discrimination that might artificially depress the performance of minority students. Affirmative action will reverse racial stratification by ensuring a place for minority groups in the nation's well-educated elite. Affirmative action ensures that some university and professional school graduates will be familiar with and serve underserved minority communities.

But only one policy goal got an unambiguous thumbs-up from the Supreme Court. According to the Court in both *Bakke* and *Grutter*, affirmative action furthers the compelling interest in a "diverse" student body. There is some ambiguity here. Some of the virtues of diversity are those once associated with the now apparently démodé goal of racial integration: diversity is said to promote "cross-racial understanding," "break down racial stereotypes," and "enable [students] to better understand persons of different races." These descriptions could have been taken directly from the defense of racial desegregation in *Brown v. Board of Education*. One could imagine a less convoluted and more compelling opinion that endorsed as a compelling interest not the ambiguous goal of "diversity," but the familiar and concrete one of integration. But unfortunately for the cause of clarity, Justice Powell in *Bakke* and the Court in *Grutter* both reject integration as "racial balancing." So the defense of diversity must refer to its pedagogical benefits. In *Bakke*, Justice Powell upheld the "the right [of a university] to select those students who will contribute the most to the 'robust exchange of ideas.'" And Justice O'Connor held in *Grutter* that the law school is entitled to "enroll a 'critical mass' of minority students" in order to achieve "the educational benefits that diversity is designed to produce."[27]

The diversity idea rests on a plausible but debatable empirical assertion: that racial diversity contributes to a more robust exchange of ideas. And because the Court insists that affirmative action must survive strict scrutiny, it is not enough that racial diversity contributes to better academic discussions; it must be "narrowly tailored" to do so. If there are other, less discriminatory means of achieving the same end, the university would be obliged to employ them instead of affirmative action.

Opponents have attacked "diversity" on both flanks. As to pedagogy, law schools provide one of the best exhibits for diversity proponents: classroom debate among students is an integral part of the learning experience, and the curriculum includes many subjects—constitutional law, employment discrimination, criminal law—to which race is relevant. But in many educational contexts the pedagogical value of racial diversity is obscure. Could a math department, a medical school, or a school of engineering, detractors asked rhetorically, defend affirmative action based on the *pedagogical* advantages of diversity? Is there a Native American perspective on advanced calculus, a distinctively black viewpoint on the relationship between built structure and load-bearing capacity, or a uniquely Latino approach to open-heart surgery? And even in those contexts where racial diversity does offer pedagogical advantages, they asked, can't those advantages be achieved in other, less discriminatory ways? Can't a law school assign appropriate texts or invite lecturers to expose students to racial perspectives underrepresented in the student body itself? Wouldn't the typical left-liberal elite university enjoy greater pedagogical benefits from ideological diversity or religious diversity? Why not admissions preferences for born-again Christians or libertarians?

Supporters of affirmative action needed to shore up the claim that racial diversity offered unique pedagogical benefits. To make the case for diversity, they had to emphasize racial difference. This was a sharp departure from the humanism of traditional civil rights, which emphasizes a common humanity that transcends racial difference. Whereas civil rights liberals had once insisted that we're all brothers under the skin, after *Bakke*, liberals were forced to embrace what had once been the fringe position of black nationalists (and white supremacists): the races are fundamentally—perhaps intrinsically—different.

Support for affirmative action was almost certainly motivated as much by the goals rejected by the Court—counteracting societal discrimination and training minorities who would serve underserved minority communities—as by the questionable pedagogy of diversity. But the emphasis on racial difference became an orthodoxy of necessity. After *Bakke*, diversity was, practically speaking, the only constitutionally acceptable rationale for affirmative action, so to question the importance of racial difference was to undermine the viability of affirmative action. Like many ideas first adopted of necessity, over time the diversity conception of deep and profound racial difference became a sincere commitment. Multiculturalism—an outgrowth of marginal and embattled ethnic studies departments of the 1970s—became in the 1980s a potent force that remade the core curriculum of many universities and, not incidentally, provided the intellectual justification for the pedagogical value of diversity.

Applicants to selective universities were not slow to figure out what was expected of them. As admissions literature and get-into-college handbooks harped on the importance of diversity, pretenders to the entering classes made sure to put their most diverse foot forward in the application process. But was all of this focus on diversity making the applicants more and more *alike*? Admissions officers noticed a minor literary genre of "cooking smells" essays, in which the applicant waxed nostalgic about the evocative aroma of a distant relative's ethnic cuisine.

Students of every color and hue described their diverse backgrounds and experiences. The bluntly titled *How to Get into Harvard Law School* offered examples of the personal statements of successful applicants. Here are some characteristic excerpts:

"My primary motivation for receiving a law degree surfaces from my personal experiences with the struggles of the Latin American immigrant . . ."

"My experience with other cultures gives me sensitivity to the voices of today's international America."

"When I supported funding for the Carolina Gay and Lesbian Association . . ."

"My curiosity about foreign cultures . . . began early."

"As the child of Paraguayan immigrants, I too occupy a borderland."

"I studied American Sign Language and was introduced to Deaf culture . . ."

"By the time I entered college, I had mastered the language of three communities: the Paraguayan Spanish spoken by my mother at home; the profanity-laden slang of our poor, all-Black Washington, D.C., neighborhood; and the textbook English enforced in the private schools I attended . . ."

"I am a fourth generation Mexican-American with Cajun ancestry . . ."

"As an expatriate I developed a keen awareness of cultural diversity by actually being a part of different cultures."

"I want to get involved with the law to preserve a state wealthy with culture and diversity."

"If accepted, I will bring to Harvard Law School a very rich and diverse background"[28]

The diversity rationale requires universities and their students to maintain a precarious balance. They must insist on the salience of racial difference: if race is only skin-deep, it is implausible that it will affect the educational experience. But some of the effects of racial difference are bad. Minorities *suffer* as a result of racism. They internalize negative stereotypes as a result of widespread bigotry, and they adopt dysfunctional behavior patterns as a result of the poverty and isolation of many minority communities. What we might call "black culture" includes these negative features as well as the many virtues multiculturalists are correct to extol. Education should correct and counteract the unfortunate legacies of racial injustice, not reinforce and encourage them. Liberal multiculturalists get tongue-tied when they have to confront this. When condemning bigotry, they want to insist on the deleterious effects of racism, but when describing the "culture" of the victims of that racism, they often deny that it has in fact had any deleterious effects. What looks like paranoia (understandable after years of deliberate persecution), they insist, is really an "alternative perspective"; what looks like belligerence (again, a predictable response to a sustained assault on one's dignity) is in fact a culturally unique mode of interaction.

The results are often tragicomic. Consider, for instance, a book titled *Black Children: Their Roots, Culture, and Learning Styles*, which admonishes educators to adapt to, rather than correct, the following allegedly black cultural traits:

> Afro-American people tend to prefer inferential reasoning to deductive or inductive reasoning . . .

> Afro-American people tend to approximate space, numbers, and time rather than stick to accuracy.

> Afro-American people in general tend not to be "word" dependent. They tend [instead?] to be very proficient in nonverbal communications.

> Black people think in terms of approximation of time, rather than punctuality. An "in house" expression is "C.P.T."— meaning "Colored People's Time"! . . . Meetings that begin on C.P. Time usually begin about twenty minutes after the appointed time.[29]

Is it bigoted or insensitive to point out that these traits are not distinctive to *black* children but are characteristic of children generally? Much of the point of primary education, after all, is to force immature humans—who, if left to their own devices, would choose to do something else—to learn inductive and deductive reasoning, to internalize the discipline of mathematical accuracy and punctuality, and to supplement the nonverbal communication common to all mammals with the "word-dependent" language unique to Homo sapiens. One can only hope that those charged with educating minority children reject the advice of this book and work to rid black children of the burden of these characteristics (and rid everyone of the stereotype that they are distinctively black) before graduation.

Diversity rhetoric is an admirable attempt to make a virtue of racial difference. In so doing, it has offered minority students a source of pride and self-esteem and has made all students rethink reflexive prejudices. But the resulting psychological investment in racial difference can be an impediment to the educational process. All education involves socialization as well as the acquisition of new knowledge. One of the practical virtues of an elite education is exposure to the mannerisms that mark one as cultured and "well educated" in our society. For the average occidental Brahmin, this process of socialization begins at home with the nanny and continues at Choate, Exeter, or Andover. If one isn't to the manner born, four years at Princeton might be just long enough to pick up some of the subtleties of the cultural elite. Like it or not, this socialization is as valuable a credential as any college degree. Of course, socialization is a two-way street. It's possible that the mannerisms of the elite will acquire a multicultural accent over time. But it's unrealistic to think that any such exchange of cultural affect will be strictly "equal." There are people who have jobs to offer and people who want those jobs, people who are members of the co-op and those who want to move in. Each may influence the other, but the relationship between them will not always be that of peers. The diversity idea reveals a touching naïveté about the world outside academia as well as a poignant irony: diversity emphasizes the value of cultural distinctiveness, yet many of the benefits of elite education flow from what it's fair to call cultural assimilation.

. . .

Barbara Grutter suffered race discrimination in the formal sense that because of her race, she was denied a preference that others enjoyed. But maybe she was also the victim of a racial stereotype: white people are dull milquetoasts whose virtues are limited to those easily measured by grades and test scores. Some of her public comments suggested such a complaint: she—a forty-two-year-old single mother—might have offered a more distinctive perspective than an upper-class black kid straight out of an elite college. Did Michigan fail to appreciate Grutter's uniqueness because of her race? Are white people victims of the demeaning "plain vanilla" racial stereotype?

The tragic young Caucasian who, eager to escape this racial stereotype, adopts another, mimicking the hip posture and cadence of the black rapper or professional athlete, is now so common as to be uninteresting. Jack Kerouac chronicled the anomie and racial envy of the Caucasian wannabe hipster in 1957:

> At lilac evening I walked with every muscle aching among the lights of 27th and Welton in the Denver colored section, wishing I were a Negro, feeling that the best the white world had offered was not enough life, joy, kicks, darkness, music, not enough nights. I passed the dark porches of Mexican and Negro homes; soft voices were there, occasionally the dusky knee of some mysterious sensual gal; and dark faces of the men behind rose arbors . . . I was only myself Sal Paradise, sad, strolling in this violent dark, this unbearably sweet night, wishing I could exchange worlds with the happy true-hearted ecstatic Negroes of America.[30]

Do we now confront a generation of Sal Paradises? Do the white applicants to selective universities wish they were black?

Hardly. Although many whites justifiably resent them, white racial stereotypes aren't really demeaning. They're backhanded insults, compliments in disguise. The stereotypical white person is a boring milquetoast: studious, conventional, deferential to authority. This is a description of many businesses' ideal employee. True, the stereotypical white isn't as hip, earthy, dangerous, or sexy as the stereotypical black or Latino, but that's precisely why whites are less likely to be targeted by police or shadowed by store detectives. As far as stereotypes go, Caspar Milquetoast's isn't all that bad.

What's really at stake in the "reverse racism" complaint isn't racism at all; it's class mobility. Higher education is one of the few sure paths to upward class mobility in contemporary society. Selective universities select aspiring members of the middle class for entry into the socially privileged and well-to-do. And they sort the next generation of precariously situated bourgeoisie into those who will retain their class position and those who will risk a downward slide. Naturally, this generates a lot of anxiety—on which a growth industry of testing-preparation services, private tutors, application consultants, and exclusive "feeder" prep schools capitalize.

Unfortunately, often higher education is valued as much or more for this status as for the knowledge and skills it offers. As a result, people don't think of selective universities—public or private—as institutions entitled to pursue their own social and pedagogical goals. They think of them as socioeconomic gatekeepers, as bouncers guarding the velvet rope between their kids and the lifestyles of the rich and famous. Universities aren't simply producing and passing on knowledge; they are also in control of the closest thing our society has to formal social status. As a result, people are as invested in their selection processes as medieval nobles were in royal prerogatives and papal favors.

The journalist Malcolm Gladwell wrote, "Elite schools, like any luxury brand, are an aesthetic experience—an exquisitely constructed fantasy of what it means to belong to an elite—and they have always been mindful of what must be done to maintain that experience."[31] A savvy observation, but I think Gladwell both exaggerates and understates. Those of us who pursue a life of the mind in universities —elite or not—like to think we do something a tiny bit more profound than offer a "luxury-brand experience." In fact, to the chagrin of many students who arrive with Ivy-covered wishes and blue-blooded dreams, the experience of elite university education is much more prosaic and matter-of-fact—much less "exquisitely constructed"—than Gladwell implies. More important, the advantages of an elite school education—especially for those who are not already privileged—are not a fantasy; they are quite real. A study by economists Alan Krueger and Stacey Dale, on which Gladwell relied in his article, emphasizes that an elite university education makes a big difference in the life chances of students from disadvantaged backgrounds. What that thick envelope from a selective university promises is not an experience, but a *status*.

Gladwell is right to suggest that the gloss of elitism is *part* of what makes admission to selective universities so coveted. And it's part of what makes rejection so personal. When Oprah Winfrey was turned away from Hermès, the most serious injury wasn't that she was denied a chance to overpay for a purse; it was that she was denied the prerogatives—practical and psychological—of elite status. When Barbara Grutter was turned away from the University of Michigan, perhaps the most grievous injury wasn't that she was denied the chance to study under that law school's excellent faculty; perhaps it was that she was denied the benefits of elite status—both the tangible opportunities and the intangible self-esteem that accompany it.

While the ancien régimes obsessed over the proprieties of aristocracy, today we pore over the norms of meritocracy. And like the aristocrats of the past, we believe our social hierarchy is not only expedient but also just: royalty held the orb and scepter by divine right; Ivy League graduates wear the tassel and mortarboard because they're the best and the brightest. To its opponents, affirmative action offends the morality of meritocracy. This is how it's "like racism." Few sincerely think that affirmative action is motivated by racial animosity or that it furthers racial inequality—one of which would seem to be an indispensable attribute of "racism." Rather they object that it, like racism, is offensive because it shortchanges those who deserve the laurels (or Ivy) of the elite in order to make preferences based on an accident of birth. Those who compare affirmative action to racism are motivated by the familiar intuition I discussed in Chapter Two: individuals deserve to be judged based only on their intrinsic individual merit. From this position, both kinds of racism—conventional and "reverse"— are equally suspect.

Is every racial distinction racist? Affirmative action isn't motivated by animosity against white or Asian students, and despite the diversity rhetoric imposed on universities by the Supreme Court, it is not by and large motivated by stereotypes—the belief that people of different races have different qualities and abilities—either. It is motivated by a simple desire to achieve meaningful racial integration (although universities can't say this openly, because the Supreme Court has disparaged this sensible goal as impermissible "racial balancing"). Affirmative action is designed to bring under-represented minorities in, not to keep whites and Asians out.

In principle, there's nothing more objectionable about considering race when making a decision than there is about considering any other morally arbitrary individual characteristic, such as weight or physical appearance. That's the insight that informed the racism-by-analogy claims in Chapter Two. I argued against those claims: racism is worse than weightism and looksism. It's worse not in principle, but in *context*, because of its widespread and severe social effects. These profound and stubborn social ills require the extraordinary medicine of civil rights law. Reverse racism—like weightism and looksism—isn't analogous to real racism in these critical respects.

While reverse racism may keep someone out of one or two colleges, real racism makes a host of jobs, neighborhoods, and ways of life unavailable. Racism is a social issue as well as an individual one, because racial hatred and irrational stereotypes keep socially and economically interdependent groups of people—families and communities—locked into unemployment, impoverished ghettos, or, worse yet, hellish prisons. And on a personal level, real racism—unlike reverse racism—isn't an isolated episode or two: it's an ongoing affliction, a regular feature of life, like migraines or herpes breakouts. Like those afflictions, racism is not an insurmountable obstacle to a good and happy life; it can be managed. But it is a real, pervasive, and ongoing social and personal problem.

"Reverse racism" isn't. Many universities prefer applicants from underrepresented states or regions of the country, or applicants with significant experiences in foreign countries. They do so because these characteristics often correspond to more ineffable virtues such as distinctive cultural perspectives or an unusually cosmopolitan outlook. Most private universities heavily prefer the children or relatives of alumni, in small part because they tend to be versed in certain university traditions and in large part because intergenerational connections to the alma mater dramatically increase alumni generosity. Most universities heavily prefer successful athletes because strong sports programs improve a school's image and increase alumni generosity.

Like many of the other factors universities consider in admissions, race is a rough but reasonable proxy for characteristics the university values in its students. Universities prefer black, Latino, and Native American applicants for several reasons. Such applicants would otherwise be grossly underrepresented. They will disproportionately (although not in every case) bring distinctive perspectives to the classroom. They will disproportionately go on to address issues of concern to their discrete racial communities. Elite universities aspire to train the next generation of elites. To the extent that each racial group has its own elites, universities must select applicants from each racial group. Many of these reasons for racial preference are debatable, but none of them are invidious.

Of course, some of the reasons universities practice affirmative action are not strictly self-serving. Many universities pride themselves on a commitment to civic virtue, and there is little doubt that many of its champions see affirmative action as a way for elite universities to advance social justice. Supreme Court doctrine notwithstanding, there's nothing wrong with helping to correct centuries of racial injustice by propelling some of the most promising members of the most despised racial groups into the elite. Only the tone deaf would suggest that such an attempt sounds in the register of "racism." Whites aren't in any danger of becoming a pariah caste. They aren't the targets of pervasive bigotry. Although affirmative action also typically denies preferences to Asians and Jews—two groups that *have* been the targets of widespread social animus—it's implausible that affirmative action is an instance of such animus. And both of these groups are relatively economically successful and well represented in selective universities; they have become quite well integrated into the mainstream of American life. Tragically, this isn't true of many blacks, Latinos, and Native Americans—the typical beneficiaries of affirmative action.

A grim irony of the Supreme Court's affirmative action jurisprudence is that it has effectively required colleges and universities—the very institutions that should encourage robust debate on controversial policy questions—to adopt a state-imposed orthodoxy on one of the most controversial issues of the day. In today's colleges and universities, supporters of affirmative action almost universally defend the diversity rationale *and only the diversity rationale* because the Supreme Court has made it clear that no other rationale will survive its scrutiny. The result has been a stilted and impoverished discussion of the virtues of affirmative action in which many of the strongest arguments have been ruled out by judicial fiat. This has, predictably, emboldened the opponents of affirmitive action and convinced many who began with open minds that it is indefensible.

Race matters when police are looking for a specific criminal suspect or a racially exclusive criminal gang. It matters when a specific racial group dominates a criminal enterprise. And race also matters for universities that want to correct for the effects of socially pervasive racial bias and ensure that people who have experienced that bias are part of the academic conversation. Like the targets of racial profiling, applicants like Barbara Grutter pay a sort of racial tax because of affirmative action. And like racial profiling, sometimes affirmative action is justified by the importance of the goals it furthers. It's understandable that some of those who must pay that tax will object to it, and we should be open to arguments that the policy has outlived its usefulness or is inappropriate in a particular context. But people who condemn affirmative action as "racism" are playing the race card. And because the Supreme Court has fallen for the bluff, colleges and universities must now advance a questionable and convoluted justification for affirmative action—diversity—when the more sensible one—integration—is a better fit.

A "MODEST" PROPOSAL

Supreme Court Justice Potter Stewart famously said of obscenity, "I shall not . . . attempt . . . to define the kinds of material I understand to be embraced within that shorthand description . . . But I know it when I see it." Most people think similarly about racism. But this only works for judges, who have the last word on the question: a Supreme Court justice doesn't *know* obscenity or racism when he sees it; he *defines* it as he sees it. For the rest of us, such regal confidence is counterproductive. Of course there are easy cases of blatant animus or obviously irrational stereotyping, but because the civil rights movement succeeded in making such overt bigotry dangerous and unpopular, today most racial conflicts involve ambiguous facts and inscrutable motivations. When racism is so well hidden that we must find its traces in offhand comments, aesthetic preferences, and the inadvertent effects of neutral policies, determining whether a conflict involves racism at all is half the battle.

As we've seen, even judges don't always know racism when they see it. The courts employ several methods to define discrimination, but these don't really identify a specific thing—a prohibited state of mind or distinct wrongful action. Instead they define a set of duties and obligations in an attempt to balance the goal of social justice against other considerations, such as privacy, productivity, and freedom of expression.

People who think they always know racism when they see it tend to expect more of the law—and of their fellow citizens—than either can deliver. The law can develop standards of care that employers and enterprises must follow to reduce the risk of irrational bias and to ameliorate its effects, but it can't eliminate all forms of bias without swearing in the thought police. It can't require color blindness without hampering law enforcement efforts and overturning important educational policies. Lawyers and judges don't typically advertise these limitations, and the consequence of this reticence has been a widespread and mistaken belief that there's always a simple yes or no answer to questions of bias.

A more modest attitude toward questions of bias is appropriate as we move into the fifth decade of modern civil rights law. When the Civil Rights Act was passed in 1964, few dared to hope for such rapid and comprehensive desegregation of restaurants, theaters, and retail stores, significant integration of elite universities, the growth of a sizable black middle class, or the rise of racial minorities to some of the most prestigious and important positions in government and business. But at the same time, many expected that by now we'd enjoy more integrated neighborhoods, suffer fewer impoverished racial ghettos, and see an improvement in the lot of the black poor. Just the opposite has been the case. In 2004, 72 percent of black male high school dropouts in their twenties were unemployed. And sociologists and criminologists still look with dismay at the bad and worsening rates of criminal arrest and conviction in many minority neighborhoods: in that same year, 21 percent of black men in their twenties who did not attend college were in jail or prison. And 60 percent of black men who had dropped out of school had been incarcerated by their mid-thirties.[32]

The typical response to this good news/bad news story is to demand that we redouble our efforts in eliminating racism and enforcing and expanding civil rights. Civil rights were spectacularly successful in those places where they succeeded, the reasoning goes: we just need to apply them more aggressively in those contexts where they have failed so far. But when a treatment works brilliantly for some ailments and fails miserably for others, good doctors don't just apply more of it in the tough cases and hope the patient recovers. Maybe it's time to consider the possibility that the civil rights approach to racial justice is doing just about all it can do. We should keep applying it where it works, but rather than search all the more stubbornly for hidden bigots and incognito racists, applying more rarefied and obscure definitions of racism with ever more shrill and anxious conviction, maybe we should look to new approaches to deal with racial injustices that don't fit well in the civil rights framework.

The race card is seductive because it lets us defer the question of substantive social goals. Rather than say definitively that we want integrated schools or more courtesy and respect from police officers or kudos for movies about same-sex romance, we can claim that we just want an end to bigotry. A new approach to the tough questions of social justice would force us to acknowledge our substantive commitments and convince others of their merit. And because these substantive commitments are often controversial, it would also force longtime civil rights allies to confront dissension and disagreement within their own ranks.

■ FOUR
THE CLASH OF ENDS: CONTESTED GOALS

I f academic multiculturalism was conceived during the long, hot summers of the 1960s and came of age in the canon wars of the 1980s, by 1996 it had reached an embarrassing midlife crisis. In the 1960s, racial justice struggles on college campuses focused on removing barriers to minority student enrollment and on counteracting subtle bias and social disadvantage through affirmative action. Student activists in the 1970s pressed reluctant universities to bring their intellectual and financial capital to segregated minority communities nearby. In the 1980s, students protested the racial apartheid of South Africa and pressed their universities to divest from corporations that did business there. As students attacked segregation abroad, they also sought an integration of the academic canon, resulting in "multicultural" curricular reforms that supplemented the traditional canon of European literature, history, and thought with at least the greatest hits from other continents and ethnicities.

By the 1990s, multiculturalists went the way of so many radicals before them and melted into the institutions they once attacked. Universities invited former sit-in leaders to join their faculties and boards of trustees. Rabble-rousers who once provoked administrators to call the sheriff's office now called the shots at the office of student affairs. Long-haired, scruffy twentysomethings protesting the canon grew to become balding, scruffy fortysomethings teaching it. This isn't to say that tenured multiculturalists abandoned all their youthful idealism. Instead, they found ways to introduce many of their long-held commitments—though to be sure a milder, domesticated breed—to the academy. The New Left had been institutionalized.

In response to the student activism of the 1970s and 1980s, many universities established ethnic studies departments and revised curricula to include minority authors and the study of racial justice issues. When student groups complained that minority students found campus life at elite universities alienating at best and menacing at worst, the universities sponsored ethnic students' organizations and established racially identified dormitories. These racial and ethnic "theme houses" are now almost as common as fraternities and sororities and at least as controversial. Like fraternities and sororities, ethnic theme houses offer a select group of students a close-knit, exclusive social cohort set off from the larger student body. They make day-to-day life at impersonal and intimidating universities more manageable and comfortable, but at the cost of making it less varied and less challenging. They allow students to immerse themselves in distinctive idioms and folkways but often leave them isolated from the cosmopolitan culture of university as a whole. As universities became more diverse, many began to question the need for these exclusive enclaves. Nurturing cohort or mind-numbing clique? This question dogged ethnic theme houses as it had dogged the "Greek" system to the end of the millennium.

Just as a midlife crisis can be hard on a marriage, so multiculturalism's seven-year itch made the 1990s tough years for race relations at Cornell University. Cornell's dorms included ten "program houses" with activities focused on a specific theme: music, environmentalism, African American culture, Hispanic culture. In theory the houses were open to all students, regardless of race. Predictably, the African American program house—Ujamaa—and the Latino Living Center attracted a disproportionate number of black and Latino students: Ujamaa was 79.2 percent black, and the Latino Living Center was 88 percent Latino in the 1995–96 academic year.

Conservatives mounted a sustained attack on ethnically identified dorms as shortsighted and hypocritical racial separatism. For instance, the conservative student paper, *The Cornell Review*, quipped, "Racial minorities on campus should demand not only their own houses, but also their own dining halls, their own public restrooms, their own water fountains!" But this time the conservatives were preempted by liberal civil rights activists. In 1995 the State of New York investigated Cornell for racial segregation in its student housing. The investigation was prompted by a complaint brought by New York City's Civil Rights Coalition, an organization originally formed in reaction to racial hate crimes in the Howard Beach district of Queens and the Bensonhurst district of Brooklyn.

The university was cleared of illegal discrimination in 1996, but the controversy over racial self-segregation in the program houses did not die with the official investigation. Convinced that the university could do better than narrowly avoiding a civil rights violation, Cornell's newly appointed president, Hunter Rawlings, proposed to limit residence in the program houses to upperclassmen. His goal was to ensure that Cornell's entering freshmen had exposure to an integrated experience before splitting off into self-selected groups: "New Students arriving at Cornell should have an experience that demonstrates that they are entering an academic community, first and foremost," Rawlings explained.

Rawlings may have thought that minority students and civil rights activists would praise his determination to exceed the minimal requirements of the law and actively promote racial integration. Instead, the proposal was met with student protests, rallies, hunger strikes, and sit-ins. Fifteen students vowed to refuse food until the university dropped the proposal. Two hundred students tied up traffic by marching and sitting down in intersections on campus. The Reverend Al Sharpton came all the way upstate to ridicule the proposal: "We want more blacks and Latinos on campus; we just want them to merge in with everyone else so we don't know they're here."[1] The events had all the hallmarks of the civil rights demonstrations of the 1960s, but the goal of the demonstrators was to *avoid* racial integration. All that was needed to complete this surreal scene was for President Rawlings, red-faced and sweating in the Ithaca sun, to stand on the steps of Ives Hall and, defiant to the end, declare his commitment to "integration now, integration tomorrow, integration forever!"

When did we step through the looking glass? Cornell couldn't be guilty of race discrimination both for establishing the programs houses *and* for trying to limit their segregative effects. Yet the claims were plausible enough to justify a governmental investigation on the one hand and, on the other, the type of social protest once deployed against the worst abuses of Jim Crow. How did the definition of racism become so malleable that passive acquiescence in minority self-segregation and well-meaning efforts at integration both qualified for the designation?

A HOUSE DIVIDED . . .

In the era of explicit policies imposing racial segregation and exclusion, it was easy for antiracists to agree on an immediate and pressing goal: reversing those policies. To most, it seemed logical that if segregation was the problem, its opposite— integration—was the practical solution. But as formal segregation waned, the antiracist agenda became less obvious. And as racial disadvantage and the psychological injuries of overt and subtle racism persisted, the commitment to integration wavered: *maybe integration isn't the magic bullet we were promised.* Law professor and former civil rights litigator Derrick Bell describes the initial optimism in the civil rights classic *And We Are Not Saved*:

> Flushed with the enthusiasm generated by the Supreme Court's 1954 holding that segregated public schools are unconstitutional, [civil rights leaders] pledged publicly that the progeny of American's slaves would at be "Free by 1963," the centennial of the Emancipation Proclamation. The pledge became the motto for the National Association for the Advancement

of Colored People's 1959 convention . . . where were gathered, in jubilant euphoria, veterans of racial bias and society's hostility who believed that they had finally, and permanently, achieved the reform of the laws that had been for a century vehicles for the oppression of black men, women and children.[2]

The mood had shifted by the time Bell wrote this in 1987. Black separatism and nationalism—currents in black social thought since the Back to Africa movements of the early twentieth century—reemerged in the 1960s and 1970s as powerful alternatives to a civil rights mainstream that championed integration. Even today, the Supreme Court's landmark opinion in *Brown v. Board of Education* is under attack from civil rights veterans—such as Bell—who argue that integration has failed to improve the education of black children *and* from multiculturalists who complain that minority cultural norms and practices are smothered in predominantly white integrated schools. This is puzzling, since so few American schools are in fact integrated: Harvard University's Civil Rights Project found that "one-fourth of black students in the Northeast and Midwest" attend schools that are "virtually all non-white."[3] Since *Brown* was decided in 1954, a growing number of scholars and activists have argued that the real evil of segregation was not the separation of the races, but instead the racially unequal distribution of education resources that it facilitated. "Green follows white" went one old integrationist slogan. Now a growing cadre of former civil rights stalwarts pondered giving up on whites and pursing the green directly. By 2004, the fiftieth anniversary of the *Brown* decision, Professor Bell argued that blacks might be better off if *Brown* had been decided in favor of continued segregation.

These ideas fit nicely with the hottest academic trend in the eighties: multiculturalism. The thing for a young star in a comp lit, history, or American studies department to do in the 1980s was to challenge the dominant paradigm and decenter the Eurocentric canon by insisting on the distinctive cultural contribution of subaltern cultures outside the hegemonic mainstream. Homer, Shakespeare, and Milton were all fine and well, but we also needed to study Latin American magical realism, Chinese folklore from the Qin Dynasty, Mong oral history, Zulu battle hymns, Native American tapestries, Maori cave paintings, Icelandic blood feud sagas. The worldviews of non-European civilizations offered a powerful critical perspective from which to judge and find deficient our own traditions.

A lot of divergent ideas were labeled "multiculturalism"—either by their authors or, more often, by later disciples and critics. Many sound ideas and reasonable prescriptions for reform were lumped together with quixotic schemes and dogmatic tirades under that title. Unfortunately, the nuances of the best "multicultural" thought traveled less well than the excesses of the worst, which always seemed to survive the trek across academic disciplines with undiminished vigor and resilience. The version of multiculturalism that made its way to popular culture, and to the law, was often not the best of breed, but rather an undisciplined mongrel.

The popular version of multiculturalism had its roots in the black power and ethnic pride movements of the 1970s (and deeper still in German Romantic nationalism—more on this below). Its basic premises, slightly simplified for economy, were: The world is made up of distinct racial, national, and ethnic groups, each of which has it own distinctive culture. Each of these distinctive cultures is equally valuable and precious—there are no mediocre, much less bad, cultures. And even if there were, we could never know it, because no one from outside a culture is competent to evaluate the norms, practices, and aesthetic artifacts that come from within a culture (this proposition came to travel and wreak havoc under the alias "standpoint epistemology"). One's own culture is a constitutive element of one's personality and deepest self (here are echoes of the Real Me). To pressure or force people to abandon or modify their culture, *or any part of it*, is a grave offense against their dignity and a violation of their human rights. Opposition to or distaste for any of the distinctive norms or practices of a cultural group (as defined by the group or, more precisely, by its self-appointed spokespersons) is tantamount to opposition to or distaste for the group itself—in other words, racist. These ideas, packed under the pop trademark of "multiculturalism," led directly to the condemnation of social integration and acculturation as "cultural genocide" and turned a significant and useful commitment of traditional antiracism on its head.

Many of the writings in this vein included what became an obligatory autobiographical passage, in which the author described and asserted his or her own racial or ethnic culture and described his or her personal experience with cultural discrimination. This was crucial, for under the rules of standpoint epistemology, only the members of a social group are competent to comment on the group's distinctive culture and experience. The authority of the author came from her status as a person who had personally suffered the discrimination she described and condemned. It was understood—and asserted explicitly—that multicultural critique was strictly an internal affair: only blacks could write about Afrocentric culture, only Latinos about *la raza,* only Asians about the customs of the Orient.

Standpoint epistemology was unintentionally ironic. If there was a time and place where the idea of distinctive racial culture was plausible, that time wasn't the 1980s and that place wasn't an American law school or university. Most of the people writing these articles were culturally assimilated professors at prestigious schools. They had attended fancy private prep schools or good suburban public schools. They had gone to predominantly white universities and colleges. They had worked at top-tier "white-shoe" law firms in New York, Washington, D.C., and Chicago. They were Latinos who spoke with a Peter Jennings accent. They were blacks dressed like models for a Brooks Brothers catalog. And their students, who eagerly edited and read their articles (in case you're wondering, I was one of those students) with a deep sense of righteousness, conviction, and personal investment, were, if anything, more assimilated than the professors. The call for multicultural rights was less a cri de coeur for genuine cultural preservation than a eulogy for an imagined authenticity.

This was nothing new: ethnic and national identity is often the product of nostalgic imagination, what historian Eric Hobsbawm has called the "invention of tradition." British historian Hugh Trevor-Roper, for instance, argues that the traditional Scottish kilt and ancient clan tartans were in fact made from whole cloth, as it were, in late-eighteenth-century London:

> The only way in which a highlander's loyalty could be discerned was not by his tartan but by the cockade in his bonnet. Tartans were a matter of private tastes . . . When the great rebellion of 1745 broke out, the kilt as we know it was a recent English invention and the "clan" tartan did not exist . . . The kilt . . . [was] invented by an English Quaker industrialist [as a ploy to sell off a surplus of plaid cloth].[4]

Or, more ominously, consider the similarities between late-twentieth-century American multiculturalism and the German Romantic nationalism of the late nineteenth and early twentieth centuries. As the philosopher Brian Barry asserts:

> The gist . . . was that different people developed their own unique ways of life . . . Culture was identified with the *Volksgeist*, or the spirit of the people, meaning their total way of life . . . Germans, for example, should sternly resist cultural imports, which can only contaminate the purity of their ancestral culture. French ideas are good for the French, and German ideas are good for the Germans, but neither will prosper if they borrow from the other. But why should the mere biological fact of German ancestry somehow make a human being incapable of living well except as a participant in German culture? The obvious answer is that Germans are a biologically distinct people, and that German culture is inherently suited to inborn German traits.[5]

If multiculturalism had a long (though not always admirable) pedigree, the demand that the state and a cosmopolitan civil society accommodate every "cultural" practice was new. A Scottish nationalist does not expect to wear a kilt to work at a London bank; a Basque separatist does not expect employers in Paris or Barcelona to translate Euskara. Conventional nationalist movements, including black nationalism in the United States, demand separation—not accommodation. Multiculturalism tried to combine the two great *opposing* ideologies of black liberation: the Romantic cultural nationalism of black separatism and the hopeful cosmopolitanism of integrationism. The result was not a synthesis, but a simple contradiction. Both the national-

ists and the integrationists were prepared to accept the compro-
mises that their respective visions necessarily entailed: nationalists
were willing to relinquish ongoing access to mainstream institutions in exchange for reparations and meaningful autonomy,
while integrationists understood that full and equal participation in the mainstream would require significant assimilation to
mainstream norms. By contrast, the multiculturalists insisted on
access without assimilation: they wanted to have their culture
and eat it too.

Multiculturalist quasi-separatism has influenced mainstream
public policy and bred new approaches to the educational mission. For instance, bilingual education and multicultural classes
championed by some minority activists and civil rights groups
have produced self-segregation, even in schools with integrated
student bodies. The preservation of group distinctiveness, the
need for "safe havens," and "cultural autonomy" have taken
precedence over the goal of integration. These programs are not
motivated by bigotry or animus, and they do not formally mandate the segregation of students by race. But they do effectively
and predictably segregate students. Multicultural programs designed to promote pluralism and bolster the self-esteem of minority students can effectively isolate those very students from
the social and educational opportunities of integrated institutions, thereby intensifying racial disadvantage, discontent, and
suspicion. And of course such effective segregation probably
also pleases bigots who favor segregation for conventionally bigoted reasons.

Integrationist policies, on the other hand, are pilloried as discriminatory attempts to whitewash minority culture. In a logic
that turns *Brown* on its head, multiculturalists insist that a *failure*

to develop distinctive curricula—and at times even separate classes, social clubs, and extracurricular organizations—for students of different cultural, ethnic, or racial groups is discriminatory. They argue that students who have distinctive racial and cultural backgrounds require educational environments tailored to their group. Taking the 1896 Supreme Court opinion in *Plessy v. Ferguson* one better, the claim here is not separate *but* equal; it is separate *therefore* equal.

Berkeley High is the only public high school in the city of Berkeley, home to the University of California's most prestigious branch and arguably the most elite public university in the United States. The Berkeley School District serves a diverse community. University professors and other very well educated and wealthy individuals live in the hilly areas near campus in north Berkeley, where stately homes and modern architectural masterpieces command panoramic views and prices to match. Low-income people, mainly African-Americans and Latinos, live in bungalows and battered multifamily apartments in the "flats" of southwest Berkeley.[6]

Unlike many American cities where segregated neighborhoods each have their own equally segregated schools, there is no institutional impediment to meaningful integration at Berkeley High School. Upper-income residents have not fled the district for another jurisdiction. They have not broken off and formed a separate school district. Berkeley parents who want to send their kids to public high school send them to Berkeley High School. In 1994, 38 percent of Berkeley High's student body was white, 35 percent African-American, 11 percent Asian and

Pacific Islander, 9 percent Hispanic, and 7 percent of mixed-racial parentage, making Berkeley High School a rainbow coalition—at least on paper.[7]

But in the classrooms, in extracurricular activities, and in social life Berkeley High School was as segregated as the typical suburban or inner-city high school. In a sense, it contained a microcosm of each—a wealthy suburban school filled with privileged high achievers and a poor inner-city school of struggling and at-risk students. Many students at Berkeley High had chosen segregation, and the administration facilitated that choice. Berkeley High had an African-American studies department—a rarity at the high school level. This, predictably, gave rise to pressure for a Chicano/Latino studies program, which the school duly established. There were rumblings in favor of Asian studies as well, but to no effect. "It is better to learn basic math, basic English," one father said in reaction to his son's newfound identity politics. "Culture is passed down from generation to generation, . . . not . . . at school." Some students and teachers saw the ethnic studies programs as necessary incubators for delicate ethnic pride. But others observed that the programs "contribute to segregation in the classroom by drawing black [and Latino] students away"[8] from other elective courses in the school. A PBS documentary about Berkeley High School showed class after class segregated along predictable lines: African American studies classes were almost exclusively black; Latino studies classes were almost exclusively Latino; and worst of all, advanced-placement classes were almost exclusively white and Asian.

Next door in Oakland, in December 1996, the school board declared that "Ebonics" was the native language of the district's twenty-eight-thousand black students. The resolution almost certainly began as an attempt to secure federal bilingual education funding for the district's underperforming children. But the Department of Education quickly parried this thrust: "The Administration's policy is that Ebonics is a nonstandard form of English and not a foreign language." That might have been that. But Ebonics was too good a sound-bite opportunity for righteous ideologues—left and right—to let die. The punditocracy sputtered into action. Racial activists and multiculturalists took up Ebonics as a cause. Stalwart guardians of traditional values and academic standards joined the fight, condemning Ebonics as the latest woolly-headed trend from the ghetto of liberalism. Soon a congressional subcommittee had scheduled hearings to address the pressing national question of Ebonics.

The Ebonics initiative got off to a bad start. The Oakland resolution implausibly insisted that Ebonics was a distinct *language* that had evolved from West African and Niger-Congo languages—not an English language dialect and indeed not an Indo-European language at all. It also claimed that Ebonics was "genetically based." Opinion leaders of all races balked: Ebonics looked like an embarrassing holdover from the extremes of the black power movement, akin to the street-corner theories that the melanin responsible for dark skin also contributed to sexual potency, proficiency in music, and a higher moral sensibility. A later revision of the resolution significantly toned down these claims, retreating to the position that Ebonics is "not *merely* a dialect of English." School board members also clarified (or revised) the claim that Ebonics is "genetically based." "Genetic," they explained, was meant to signify a sociolinguistic—not biological—relationship. These modifications brought the board closer to an account of black English embraced by some sociolinguists, such as William Labov of the University of Pennsylvania, who conducted some of the earliest studies of black vernacular, and Stanford University's John Rickford. Labov and Rickford vouched for the integrity of black English as a logical and coherent system of communication—not a distinct language, but also not merely "bad English."

Labov, Rickford, and other sociolinguists eventually testified before Congress, offering a nuanced account of the state of scientific findings on Ebonics. But Ebonics fell on deaf ears in Congress. As the congressional hearings opened, Senator Lauch Faircloth from North Carolina lambasted Ebonics as "absurd . . . political correctness gone out of control." This attack was ill informed and unfair, but claims that Ebonics was a distinct and "genetically" based language rather than a dialect made it easy to land this blow. With few exceptions, both sides of the Ebonics debate put ideological posturing first and pedagogy last.

Had pedagogy rather than politics been front and center, the debate might have taken a different form, as suggested by Professor Labov:

> There are two major points of view taken by educators. One is that any recognition of a nonstandard language . . . will only confuse children and reinforce their tendency to use it instead of standard English. The other is that children learn most rapidly in their home language, and they can benefit . . . by getting a head start in learning to read and write in this way. Both of these views are honestly held . . . but until now only the first has been tried . . . The essence of the Oakland school board resolution is that the first method has not succeeded and that the second deserves a trial.[9]

But there was more at stake than pedagogy. The Ebonics resolution was an attempt to redefine the disappointing academic performance of inner-city black children as a problem of language. This would not only make the school district eligible for federal bilingual education funding, it could also legally require the school district and the state to offer the children bilingual education classes as a matter of federal law. Indeed, the Oakland resolution claimed to "vindicate the rights [of students] under the 14th Amendment." Under the Supreme Court's 1974 decision in *Lau v. Nichols,* students may have a constitutional right to education in their native language if a language barrier prevents them from keeping up in English. In *Lau,* the plaintiffs were Chinese students in San Francisco. The students claimed that the schools, by refusing to offer Chinese-language instruction, were in essence denying them an education because of their national origin. By extension, refusing to offer Ebonics would be race discrimination.

And defining Ebonics as a language would give blacks access to the most coveted resource of all: respect. Just as the Spanish language is a source of pride for Latinos (even as poor English mastery confines many Latinos to segregated classes and low-wage jobs), so too Ebonics would bolster the self-esteem of black children currently told by teachers that they simply speak English poorly. As such, the Ebonics controversy had the same symbolic stakes as the long-standing controversy over bilingual education. The pedagogical stakes were similar too: Would bilingual education offer students a head start, or would it stymie their mastery of standard English?

In both cases critics worried that pedagogy might be beside the point. Did advocates of Ebonics and bilingual education really agree that the goal was English mastery, or did the ideology of ethnic pride and self-esteem loom so large as to obscure the practical need for English proficiency? Would some multiculturalists be happy simply training children in their "native" language indefinitely?

They had reasons to worry. In 1974 New York City settled a lawsuit by agreeing to offer some form of Spanish-language instruction to any "Hispanic children . . . who can more effectively participate in Spanish."[10] To fulfill their legal obligations, the schools automatically tested all children with Spanish surnames for English-language skills and tracked those with low scores into bilingual education programs. Roughly twenty years later, outraged Latino parents sued the school district over the practice. They alleged that "thousands of students are routinely kept in native-language classrooms for six years or longer, without even the pretense of individual progress reviews."[11] In the same year in Los Angeles, Latino parents boycotted a public school for two weeks, demanding that their children be removed from segregated bilingual education classes and integrated with other students in classes conducted in English.[12] In the year prior to the boycott, only six bilingual education students in that school were deemed sufficiently fluent to "graduate" to English-language classrooms in the next school year.

Bilingual education had become a mechanism of racial segregation in the hands of indifferent or ideologically rigid school administrators. Children of foreign parentage—largely Spanish-speaking Latinos, but a growing number of children of other ethnicities with other primary languages—were segregated into classes taught in their native languages for as many as six or seven years. As former bilingual education teacher and present-day bilingual education critic Rosalie Pedalino Porter puts it:

For thirty years the educational establishment has, perversely, acquiesced in a policy that segregates many children by language and ethnicity, while simultaneously proclaiming racial integration to be a major objective of our public schools. While promoting the importance of "inclusion" in regular classrooms for physically or mentally handicapped children, educators have agreed to the demands of ethnic activists that language minority students should be kept out of mainstream classes for years.[13]

Bilingual education was supposed to be a civil right. How did it become a new Jim Crow? Why did parents have to sue and boycott the schools to avoid segregation in bilingual education programs? Most public schools are large bureaucracies, governed by rules set at the district and state level. Bilingual education is especially susceptible to bureaucratic inertia and rigidity because failure to provide it can subject schools to legal liability under *Lau*. A formal procedure that tracks students into bilingual education is the surest way to avoid a lawsuit. By contrast, placing children in bilingual education classes—even those who could easily thrive in English-language classrooms—often poses little legal or political risk to the district.[14] Bureaucratic, legal, and political pressure leads schools to err on the side of segregation in bilingual education classes.

On June 2, 1998—a little over a year after the Oakland Ebonics controversy—California voters passed Proposition 227, which virtually eliminated bilingual education in the state. Predictably, bilingual education proponents accused the sponsors of the initiative and its backers of anti-Latino bias and xenophobia. But those backers included 61 percent of California's voters, 57 percent of Asian voters, and 37 percent of the Latino voters (as many as 84 percent of Latinos supported the measure at times during the campaign).[15]

Bilingual education was and is controversial, as it should be. There are sound pedagogical arguments for and against it—as there were for and against Ebonics—but in addition to the pedagogical stakes, the politics of bilingual education pitted ethnic pride and the psychological benefits of self-esteem against the ideal of integration and the practical benefits of acculturation. This conflict is not well described in terms of bigotry. Bilingual education segregated non-English-speaking students, and many voters were, with justification, suspicious that this segregation was not always in the interest of the children on whom it was imposed. Many Latino parents wanted an integrated educational environment for their children and did not expect the public schools to promote ethnic pride or preserve ethnic cultural difference. They expected the schools to provide the skills and socialization necessary for success in the mainstream of American society. They didn't trust the school districts that had resisted meaningful racial integration before the civil rights era when those districts again sought to isolate their children in classes effectively defined by race and ethnicity.

Too many activists and multiculturalists seemed happy to keep minority students segregated indefinitely in the name of ethnic pride and to coddle them in unchallenging academic ghettos. At the same time, many opponents of bilingual education and Ebonics came across as callous at best and bigoted at worst, committed to preserving the primacy of the Queen's English at the expense of educating the republic's citizenry.

At the very least, everyone should be able to agree that the primary goal of any bilingual education program in the United States should be the mastery of English and the full integration of foreign-language and nonstandard English speakers as quickly as possible. Then the problem would be merely one of technique. As Professor Labov suggested, given past failures in Oakland, Ebonics probably deserved a trial. By the same token, who could accuse opponents of bilingual education of bigotry after more than thirty years of lackluster results? There are plausible civil rights claims on both sides of the bilingual education controversy. In today's political and legal environment, where the goals of civil rights are contested and at times in conflict, it's not always easy to tell who is in the right.

RACIAL ARCHITECTURE AND SOCIAL ENGINEERING

As its name suggests, the Starrett City housing development in Brooklyn is more than an apartment building. Forty-six high-rises containing more than five thousand individual apartments, along with two public schools, a power plant, a cable television station, and a shopping center sit on its 153 acres. Starrett City—a community built from scratch—embodied the varied aspirations of sociological and architectural high modernism. Following in the tradition of the International style, Starrett City was stylistically neutral and aesthetically cosmopolitan. Its towers would not have looked out of place on a university campus, as part of a medical center, in an industrial park, or in an urban downtown. Its glass-and-brick buildings sported clean lines, elegant proportions, efficient use of space, and cost-effective materials. New York's concrete jungle yielded to an orderly geometry. Uniform residences offered modern conveniences and floor plans designed to maximize usable living space—no fifth-floor walk-ups with cold water and windowless chambers here.

The space-saving efficiency of vertically stacked residences left room for spacious plazas and greenways at ground level. Children would frolic in designated playgrounds with equipment engineered for safety and physical fitness while adults looked on from comfortable benches strategically placed near a canopy of foliage. Form followed function. La Ville Radieuse had leaped off the pages of Le Corbusier's notebook and landed just west of Canarsie.

Starrett City's high modernism didn't stop with its less-is-more aesthetic. The development also reflected the modernist ambition to remake the fraying social fabric through enlightened planning. A combination of progressive social science and architecture would guide interpersonal relations just as a dressmaker's pattern guides scissors, needle, and thread.

Architectural determinism—the belief that social behavior was a product of the built environment—was at least as old as the progressive anti-slum movement of the late nineteenth century. But Starrett City's social ambitions were unique to its time: here, carefully planned housing sought to reverse not only the effects of poverty but also those of racism. Its developers and architects sought the advice of some of the nation's most respected experts to help make sure the development was racially integrated and that it stayed racially integrated.

This was no short order. Four years after outlawing discrimination in employment and public accommodations, with the Civil Rights Act of 1968 Congress outlawed race discrimination in the sale and rental of most housing. In the context of public accommodations—restaurants, hotels, theaters—earlier civil rights laws quickly led to desegregation; the legislation was a rapid and unambiguous success. Thus, many people expected that if Congress outlawed overt housing discrimination, residential segregation would soon follow suit. But housing segregation was resilient. Almost forty years later, lawyers and social scientists still ask why our neighborhoods remain racially segregated. Some point out that discrimination in housing markets is much harder to identify than in public accommodations. The typical landlord discriminates among applicants for a host of legitimate reasons, making it easy for racism to hide in the crowd. But is racial discrimination in housing today as severe as it was in the 1960s? Probably not. Surveys and other social science evidence consistently suggest that racial intolerance has steadily and rather steeply declined since the 1960s. Racial bias still plays an important role in neighborhood segregation, but it's implausible that it's a solo performance.

Maybe differences in income and wealth can account for segregation. Blacks are disproportionately poor and hence overrepresented in poor neighborhoods. To some extent, racial segregation simply goes along with the income segregation that is characteristic of housing markets. But income and wealth can't explain all or even most racial segregation: blacks and whites of the same income and household wealth still typically live in separate neighborhoods.

These puzzles have led some to argue that segregation is no longer the result of discrimination at all, that it has become a matter of personal preference. They argue that people of all races may just prefer to keep to their own kind. Maybe segregation simply reflects the free market at work: innumerable individual choices combine to produce the neighborhoods in which people want to live. If even those blacks with the means to live in wealthier white suburbs prefer predominantly black upper-income enclaves, who can cry foul?

Still, questions remain: surveys consistently show that whites and blacks alike prefer integrated neighborhoods by wide margins. Yet very few integrated neighborhoods exist. This suggests the disquieting possibility that segregation might persist even when few people of any race want it. In fact, it seems that segregation can persist even in housing markets where most people— white and black—*prefer* integration.

The economist Thomas Schelling has offered an explanation. Even if blacks and whites prefer "integration," a relatively slight disagreement between whites and blacks about the ideal racial mix can lead to neighborhood segregation.[16] Surveys reveal that whites and blacks often mean different things by "integrated." In the 1970s, when Starrett City was developing its integrationist policies, most whites thought a neighborhood was "integrated" when it roughly reflected the demographics of the nation: 80 percent white, 20 percent black (sign of the times: surveys in the 1970s rarely asked about other races). By contrast, most blacks thought a neighborhood was "integrated" when the races were equally represented: 50 percent black, 50 percent white.

Blacks and whites didn't agree on the definition of the ideal integrated neighborhood, but neither group preferred the racial mix most commonly available—neighborhoods that were almost 100 percent white or almost 100 percent minority. Why didn't we see more integrated neighborhoods of *either* the proportions preferred by most whites or those preferred by most blacks? Schelling's answer: many whites and blacks would leave a neighborhood that had too few members of their own racial group, even when the alternative was a segregated neighborhood with *only* members of their own group. Of course each household has its own threshold. Some whites will leave or refuse to move to any neighborhood with less than 70 percent whites; for others, the minimum might be 50 percent; similarly, some blacks might be happy in a 10 percent black neighborhood while others might insist on 40 percent. The key point is that people who prefer "integration" won't settle for just any racially mixed neighborhood: they have some ideal in mind. And for most people, the deal breaker is some minimum number of people of their own race. Most people prefer integration to segregation. But they prefer segregation with people of their own race to integration in a milieu that they feel is dominated by people of another race.

The result is segregation. Schelling offered this example: imagine a modified game of checkers. To begin, you distribute the pieces at random. The rules of the game are: 1) a piece is "unhappy" in its location, and you must move it if all of the adjacent squares are occupied by pieces of the other color, and 2) you can move any piece to any empty square as long as one or more of the adjacent squares is occupied by a piece of the same color—in other words, as long as the moving piece won't be the only white or black in its new "neighborhood." If there is no location to which to move an unhappy piece, you must remove it from the board—it moves out of town. The result is that in surprisingly few moves, the board will be segregated. Schelling modeled this dynamic with varying "preferences" and found that even mild preferences for neighbors of the same color quickly led to a segregated board.

The reasons for the racial preferences underlying Schelling's dynamic are complex. Cultural difference and the desire for group solidarity play a role. So does anxiety about interracial hostility. And so does economics, especially for whites. It's often a tragic fact that property values tend to follow the racial composition of a neighborhood: they decline when neighborhoods transition from white to black and rise when formerly minority race neighborhoods "gentrify" and become attractive to whites. As a result, there's a financial reason to avoid a neighborhood with a sufficiently large minority population. In fact, for much of the twentieth century, unscrupulous real estate speculators exploited this fact in a grubby practice known as "blockbusting." The speculator would find a white neighborhood ripe for racial transition. He might even "prime" the target neighborhood by arranging for a black family to move in. He would then spread the word: the neighborhood is changing, and prudent homeowners had better sell now before it's "too late." This warning played on racism and on economics: for some, the threat of black neighbors was enough to encourage them to sell cheap; for others, the fear that property values would decline as a result of widespread racism among their neighbors provided the impetus. Either way, the speculator took advantage of "panic sales," snapping up properties for a fraction of their former value. And while whites could be convinced to sell their homes at a discount, blacks would often pay a premium for the promise of a welcoming, integrated neighborhood. So the speculator would sell those same properties at a steep markup to upwardly mobile blacks who were eager to find the rare integrated neighborhood with stable property values where they would be welcome. They were misled: the neighborhood wasn't stable or integrated. It was in transition from all white to all black.

Blockbusting exploited racism *and* fear of change. Some of the white homeowners who sold cheap were happy with the current racial composition of their neighborhoods, but they sold anyway because they feared that the neighborhood would change from predominantly white to overwhelmingly black. They sold, not because of their own reaction to racial integration, but because they feared the reactions of their neighbors. And many of their neighbors sold for precisely the same reasons. Blockbusting real estate speculators frightened white homeowners with the prospect of racial neighborhood change *and* declining property values. And the neighborhoods changed and values declined because people believed them. "There goes the neighborhood" was a self-fulfilling prophecy.

Blockbusting dramatizes Thomas Schelling's theory of neighborhood segregation: a relatively small change in the racial balance of an integrated neighborhood can trigger a vicious cycle of reaction, leading to rapid and dramatic segregation. University research and the school of practical experience in cities and housing developments across the nation taught the same lesson: when the nonwhite population reached a tipping point, the vicious cycle would begin and the community would rapidly and inexorably lose almost all of its white residents. The tipping point was hard to identify. It was different in every neighborhood. Usually, if you identified it, that was because you had already reached it, and by then it was too late.

If they were to create a racially integrated development, Starrett City's planners had to counteract this pattern of bigotry, fear, and reaction. They sought out some of the nation's most respected experts on housing patterns and race relations. Their solution was endorsed by notables such as the sociologist Kenneth Clark, whose testimony on the effect of segregation on the self-esteem of black children was central to the Supreme Court's milestone opinion in *Brown v. Board of Education*. Clark and other experts in architecture, urban planning, and housing believed that the tipping point was somewhere between 10 percent and 40 percent minority residents. So Starrett City implemented a tenant-selection policy designed to maintain a racial balance of 64 percent white, 22 percent black, and 8 percent Hispanic.

For their efforts to promote racial integration, Starrett City's management was sued for race discrimination. Starrett City's integration policy *was* blatantly and unapologetically discriminatory. Any vacancy had to be filled by an applicant of the same race as the previous tenant. Worse, this policy put minorities at a severe disadvantage: black applicants waited almost ten times as long as whites for a two- or three-bedroom apartment. It took almost ten years and several different lawsuits to put an end to Starrett City's policy. The NAACP and community civil rights groups, driven by conventional civil rights commitments, brought the first suit in 1978. The U.S. Justice Department, driven by a conservative opposition to all race-conscious policies, sued again in 1984. In 1988 a federal court found Starrett City in violation of the Fair Housing Act and ordered the management to end its integration-maintenance policy. *The New York Times* interviewed residents shortly after the ruling and discovered that Starrett City's management and residents were unlikely racists. They, like Cornell's President Rawlings, were defiant integrationists. "We want to live in an integrated community," said Ellie Mandell, the white president of the community school board. "That's what we're all about." The *Times* described Starrett City as "perhaps the most integrated area of the city." Spencer Holden, a black actor, said that Starrett City was "1,000 percent better than any other neighborhood . . . you've got blacks, Jews, Italians, all living together on the same floor . . . I'm not saying everybody loves everybody else, but everybody lives with everybody else in a comfortable, civilized manner. We want to give a model of how people can live to-gether." "The future of America should ideally look like this, a nation where the races live in authentic harmony," said Rabbi Avner German. "We don't think we should be reprimanded." Cathy Crispo, a Hispanic Starrett City resident, complained, "It's something too good to let go. Why do they have to kill this thing? Where else in the city are people living like this?"

The answer, of course, was, in very few other places. Several years earlier, just a few miles from Starrett City, a mob in over-whelmingly white Howard Beach attacked three black men and chased one into oncoming traffic, where he was struck by a car and killed. Howard Beach was so completely segregated that the mere presence of the black men—who were stranded with a disabled car—provoked suspicion, resentment, and violence. In terms of segregation, Howard Beach wasn't exceptional: in 1993's grimly titled *American Apartheid,* the urban sociologists Douglas Massey and Nancy Denton found "virtually no sign of progress in residential integration" since the 1960s. "In Boston, Chicago, Cleveland, Detroit, Gary, Philadelphia, Pittsburgh and St. Louis" the decline in segregation was almost negligible while "in . . . New York and Newark segregation actually *increased*" between 1970 and 1980. Sociologists agreed that black-white integrated neighborhoods were rare and often unstable or in transition. Some experts quipped that the definition of an inte-grated neighborhood was a neighborhood on its way to being either all white or all black.

Starrett City's integration plan tried to defy the iron logic of segregation. It was an experiment that may or may not have worked in the long run. Even if it did work, it may not have been possible to reproduce it outside the context of an intri-cately planned, federally subsidized housing development. And, like affirmative action and racial profiling, it would achieve its laudable goals by discriminating on the basis of race. But it was about as far from racist as it's possible to get.

In a nation where racial segregation seems about as certain as death and taxes, Starrett City's effort deserved a chance. But a combination of neoconservative cynicism, unrealistic civil rights idealism, and misguided racial pride killed one of the few successful attempts at racial integration in the United States outside of the military and professional sports. Knowing the long odds against stable integrated communities, civil rights groups still fought to stop a policy that had created such a community. And despite its repeated failures to achieve racial integration, the federal government was sufficiently confident in its own wisdom to end Starrett City's integration policy.

Starrett City's earnest commitment to integration had become unfashionable. In the 1980s, segregation came back into style. It was as if the period nostalgia that inspired fashion trends was now influencing public policy and political commitments: *while you're pulling those miniskirts and go-go boots out of your mother's cedar chest, why not complete the ensemble with the racial politics of 1960!* Of course, unlike mop-top haircuts and Nehru jackets, segregation had never gone away. But by the late 1980s you didn't need to feel bad about it anymore. Conservatives speculated that after two decades of fair-housing laws, any remaining segregation must be the result of individual free choice. Maybe blacks preferred to live with their own kind, just as the defenders of Jim Crow had always insisted. There was some evidence to support this hypothesis. Many upper-middle-class blacks who had the means to move into predominantly white neighborhoods preferred to create posh black communities in places such as Baldwin Hills in Los Angeles and Prince Georges County, Maryland, near Washington, D.C. Some black academics and intellectuals in the 1970s, in part out of a sense of racial pride and solidarity, actually sang the praises of segregated black ghettos. As the sociologist William Julius Wilson points out, "African-American scholars . . . reacted angrily . . . to . . . unflattering depictions of ghetto blacks . . . [They claimed] that blacks were developing a community power base that . . . reflected the strength and vitality of the black community . . . In fact, those elements of ghetto behavior described as pathological in the late-1960s . . . were seen as functional . . . it was argued inner city blacks . . . were resilient, able to survive and even flourish in a racist environment."[17] Wilson ruefully concludes, "For entirely different reasons, the devastating effects of the inner-city environment were either ignored, played down, or denied" by conservatives and liberals alike.

As Wilson insists, these sanguine accounts of segregation were misguided. Wealthy black neighborhoods and suburbs are relatively few and in any case have little in common with the isolated ghettos of the underclass. Ghetto neighborhoods did not come into being through free market forces or private choice—they emerged because discriminatory real estate agents and landlords, violent intimidation, and the force of law confined blacks to them. Today deliberate discrimination is less common (although audits continue to find it among landlords, real estate agents, and mortgage lenders), but the legally imposed segregation of the past is informally reinforced by local land-use planning and tax policy. As a result, a number of "ghetto cities" have emerged—entire municipalities dominated by poor racial minorities.

The modern American suburb emerged as a reaction against bloated and corrupt big-city political machines, urban crowds, noise, vice, and, not least of all, ethnic and racial diversity. In *Crabgrass Frontier: The Suburbanization of the United States*, the historian Kenneth Jackson notes:

> With the vast increase in immigration in the late nineteenth century, the core city became the home of penniless immigrants from Southern and Eastern Europe. And of course, in the early years of the twentieth century, increasing numbers of Southern blacks forsook their miserable tenant farms for [the city] . . . In the view of most middle class, white suburbanites, these newcomers were associated with and were often regarded as the cause of intemperance, vice, urban bossism, crime, and radicalism of all kinds . . . As the central city became the home of the disadvantaged . . . the [white middle class] . . . escapees from the central city were anxious to insulate their neighborhoods from . . . pernicious urban influences.[18]

The result was the rise of local "home rule"—a movement committed to suburban autonomy. It stopped central cities from annexing new developments on their periphery and encouraged independent municipal status for suburban towns and villages. Today the consequence of the home rule movement is that every metropolitan area in the United States is a crazy quilt of tens and in some cases hundreds of cities, towns, villages, and hamlets, each run by separate governments with independent taxing and land-use authority. True to their origins, many suburbs use their land-use planning to insulate their communities from the poor. They prohibit apartments and condominiums and require single-family homes to be of a minimum size on large lots. The result is an effective immigration policy: no one who cannot afford to purchase a large home and a large parcel of land can live in many American suburbs. It's not just the free market that makes this so; it is also the coercive power of the law.

The sunny notion that ghettos persist because their residents prefer to live in them and that ghetto subcultures are sources of strength and resilience is at best incomplete and at worst wishful thinking. In fact, residential segregation makes many other social problems—poverty, unemployment, crime, failing schools— harder to address. Ghetto residents are unable to establish the social networks that might alert them to better job opportunities. Studies such as the sociologist Mark Granovetter's landmark work *Getting a Job: A Study of Contacts and Careers* shows that most jobs are filled by word-of-mouth recommendations. But many people who live in impoverished ghettos know almost no one with a steady job. William Julius Wilson found that in many poor Chicago neighborhoods as few as one in three working-age adults held regular jobs. Ghetto residents remain unfamiliar with the social norms of the mainstream and hence have difficulty impressing favorably those few employers they may actually hear about—exacerbating employment discrimination.

A seemingly trivial example speaks volumes. Consider the difference between black ghetto slang and the English spoken in both middle-class white and black communities. Most people assume that distinctive black speech patterns are a result of the influence of African language patterns, just as, say, Italian-American accents reflect the cadence and inflection of the Italian peninsula. We would expect such ethnic accents to diminish over generations as the influence of the old country wanes. But sociolinguists have found that the distinctiveness of black English has *increased* over time. The sociolinguist William Labov found that many of the features of black English were not present in the late nineteenth century; instead, they developed in the twentieth century, *after* the end of the slave trade and of significant African in-migration. And although the distinctive idioms and inflections of middle-class blacks as a group are readily understood by whites, some ghetto blacks have developed a slang so unique it is almost incomprehensible to outsiders. As ghetto slang diverges more and more from mainstream English, it becomes a powerful symbol of socially undesirable behavior. As the sociologist Nathan Glazer notes, "A different style of English . . . particularly if it is associated with a historically lower caste, communicates something as to class, attitude, community, and a host of other factors, which add up to a sense of difference—the kind of difference that suggests the possibility of trouble to the dominant caste."[19]

Wilson's research among Chicago area employers confirms Glazer's hypothesis:

> An employer from a computer software firm in Chicago expressed the view "that in many businesses the ability to meet the public is paramount and you do not talk street talk to the buying public" . . . A suburban employer added "They [inner-city blacks] don't know how to dress when they come to an interview. They bring fourteen other people with them". . . A black employer in a Chicago insurance company argued that "there is a perception that most of your kids are black and . . . they don't know how to write. They don't know how to speak. They don't act in a business fashion or dress in a business manner . . . in a way the business community would like.

And they just don't feel that they're getting a quality employee." When asked whether he thought this was a false impression, the employer responded, "I think there's some truth to it."[20]

Many young ghetto residents have no role models who work in mainstream jobs. So many emulate the only economically successful people they encounter: drug dealers and gang members. Wilson's team of sociologists interviewed scores of people who sounded variations on this theme. One opined, "If you are raised in a neighborhood and all you see is . . . drug dealers on the corner and they see fancy cars and flashy money and they figure: 'Hey, if I get into drugs I can be like him.' [sic]" Another asked, rhetorically, "Who is their role model? They have none but the thugs. So that's what they wind up being, you know . . . They . . . deal with the only male role model that they can find and most of the time that be pimps, dope dealers." Another noted, "They see the street life. They see guys out here making big bucks with fancy cars, jewelry and stuff, and they try to emulate them." Ghetto residents become socialized to a ghetto subculture in which employment in the mainstream doesn't seem to be a viable option, and they become acculturated to norms that are functional *only* inside the ghetto environment. It's a vicious cycle: isolation leads to lack of access to job networks and "poor" socialization, which leads to greater isolation.

As if this weren't bad enough, the ghetto poor actually pay a premium to live in such noxious circumstances. The Brookings Institution conducted a systematic study of major American cities and discovered what ghetto residents already know all too well: you'll pay more for basic goods and services in the ghetto than in the posh part of town. Some call it the ghetto tax.[21]

For instance, while the typical middle-class family can choose between several full-service banks that offer free checking accounts in their neighborhood, those ghetto residents who overcome the odds and have a job or a legitimate source of income have to pay a premium—often as much 10 percent of face value—to cash their paychecks at check-cashing outlets.

What can they buy with what's left of their paycheck? Not as much as you might think. Middle-class neighborhoods enjoy large supermarkets stocked with a wide array of decent food at very competitive prices. (Some economists believe that Wal-Mart's low prices alone have done more for the working class than most public social programs.) The rich pay more for food at gourmet grocers such as Whole Foods, but they get what they pay for: organic Galia melons, grass-fed beef, wild Alaskan salmon, heirloom tomatoes. But there's no Whole Foods or Wal-Mart in the ghetto. Instead, residents must rely on small corner stores with limited selections of mainly prepackaged food sold at high markups.

And suppose a poor person in the ghetto needs to buy appliances to cook his overpriced food, or a table and chairs at which to sit down and eat it? Rich people can pay cash for such big-tickets items, and the middle class can save up—but they don't have to. People with good jobs and good credit can borrow at attractive interest rates. If you've maxed out your credit card, the store will usually offer you reasonably competitive credit on the spot. But stores in the ghetto don't offer consumer credit at market rates to their customers who have no choice other than to borrow. Instead, they offer "rent-to-own" arrangements, under which the customer pays what are in effect exorbitant interest rates in the form of "rent." For instance, Brookings reports that a two-hundred-dollar television set can actually cost seven hundred dollars in payments under a rent-to-own plan.

Why don't ghetto residents shop somewhere else? They might, if they could get there. Public transportation to and from poor neighborhoods is often unreliable, if it exists at all. Call a taxi? The fare would eat up most of the savings—assuming one would come at all. Drive? Not surprisingly, car insurance rates are higher in the ghetto too, and numerous studies have shown that low-income people—especially racial minorities—pay higher interest rates on their car loans.

And even if they do manage to get to another neighborhood, how will poor ghetto dwellers, who've internalized the norms, mannerisms, and speech patterns of the ghetto, impress the bank managers and sales people with whom they will have to interact? The real problem of "retail discrimination" doesn't involve wealthy black celebrities or even middle-class blacks seeking retail therapy. It involves poor people of all races, but especially minorities, whose demeanor, as Glazer puts it, "suggests the possibility of trouble" to the people who could offer them credit or bargain with them for goods. This isn't simple racism. Store clerks, car dealers, bankers, and employers alike inevitably consider grooming, poise, and demeanor as useful if rough proxies for traits like diligence, integrity, and commitment. As Wilson observes:

> Employers are looking for workers with a broad range of abilities: "hard" skills (literacy, numeracy, basic mechanical ability, and other testable attributes) and "soft" skills (personalities suitable to the work environment, good grooming, group-oriented work behaviors, etc.) . . . soft skills are strongly

> tied to culture, and are therefore shaped by the harsh envi-
> ronment of the inner-city ghetto . . . [Given this] it becomes
> increasingly difficult to discern the motives of employers: are
> they rejecting inner-city black applicants out of overt racial
> discrimination or on the basis of qualifications?

As I have noted, legal scholars and activists have published scores of law review articles suggesting that federal law should prohibit discrimination on the basis of "racial and ethnic traits" such as Ebonics. These arguments began with an important insight: the most severely disadvantaged people in our society suffer because their unconventional socialization suggests trouble to many employers; the capable and diligent ghetto residents suffer by association with the antisocial members of their impoverished communities. But, influenced by multiculturalism and politically correct idealism, the arguments unrealistically have demanded that employers do what no one would be expected to do in any other context—ignore appearances and first impressions entirely. It's not hard to guess why so many people embraced a civil rights approach to the problem: the real solution—help the ghetto poor to assimilate to mainstream norms—would be expensive and time-consuming. And for many, a policy of assimilation seemed to imply that the affectations and mannerisms of the ghetto poor (which had now, unfortunately, been defined as "*black* culture") were somehow intrinsically inferior. But it's enough to observe that ghetto traits have come to symbolize antisocial behavior—just as, say, a "redneck" accent has come to symbolize lack of refinement and low intelligence—and the law is incapable of changing that symbolic association.

No one chooses to live in an impoverished, crime-ridden ghetto with underperforming schools and overpriced basic goods and services. And if segregated black neighborhoods were once a source of strength, pride, and community, they aren't anymore. They've lost the middle class and most of the working poor who once brought in tangible resources, connections, and mainstream values. As Wilson points out in *The Truly Disadvantaged*, one of the grim ironies of the civil rights movement was that it may have inadvertently made the ghetto worse off. As fair-housing laws opened up new neighborhoods to blacks for the first time, the most successful blacks left segregated ghettos for leafy suburbs, leaving only the poorest and least well educated behind. This created a sort of "super ghetto" of concentrated poverty that enjoys only a fraction of the financial and social resources of the old, forcibly segregated ghetto.

There are no easy or cheap solutions to the problem of ghetto poverty. Even expensive answers have often been wrong. Government programs designed to "revitalize" ghettos by subsidizing private investment have by and large failed to change the vicious cycle of ghetto poverty. By contrast, the most successful job creation policy in American history involved public sector jobs. The Works Progress Administration initiated by Franklin Delano Roosevelt in 1935 was a deliberate job creation policy—what conservatives today deride as a "make-work" program. The journalist Mickey Kaus points out that this make-work program

> built or improved 651,000 miles of roads, 953 airports, 124,000 bridges and viaducts, 1,178,000 culverts, 8,000 parks, 18,000 playgrounds and athletic fields, and 2,000 swimming pools. It constructed 40,000 buildings . . . Much of New York City— including La Guardia airport, FDR Drive, plus hundreds of parks and libraries—was built by the WPA.

William Julius Wilson, like Kaus, endorses a new WPA as the policy most likely to improve the ghetto. He insists that the resulting jobs needn't and shouldn't be limited to ghetto residents, much less racially targeted. The improvements should also be broadly enjoyed: WPA-type programs could improve public services and repair crumbling infrastructure in the inner city and leafy suburb alike. At the same time, reducing unemployment and improving the public infrastructure would make a big difference for poor minorities. The resulting jobs would offer unemployed ghetto residents a dignified way out of poverty. And they would join people from different racial backgrounds together in a common enterprise, much as the military—and tragically few other institutions—do today.

In 1996 Wilson estimated that such a program would cost $12 billion for every million jobs created. Let's assume that's $15 billion in 2006 dollars. Can we afford it? Let's put it in perspective. Congressional appropriations for less than four years of occupation of Iraq were roughly $315 billion at the end of fiscal year 2006. For the roughly $80 billion a year we spent to occupy Iraq, we could help about 5,250,000 Americans escape poverty and unemployment and rebuild our aging public infrastructure, such as the levee systems that protect many American cities from catastrophic flooding. After hurricane Katrina, New Orleans residents complained that if we could rebuild Iraq, we should be able to rebuild New Orleans. Residents of impoverished ghettos nationwide, where everyday life can be a disaster on a less dramatic scale, might make a similar observation.

The most serious impediment to racial integration is a lack of political will. Integration will cost money and require sacrifices.

Integrated schools will require people of all races to embrace people they've learned to distrust. In order to have integrated classrooms, the more successful schools will have to relax or abandon academic tracking. Sometimes, school integration may require school districts to abandon neighborhood schools and accept busing—perhaps the most unpopular legacy of the historic *Brown v. Board of Education* decision. And we'll have to end or relax exclusionary local zoning policies and invest in job creation, training, and counseling to integrate our neighborhoods.

There's no political will do to any of these things, in part because there's no consensus that integration is worth the candle. For every argument that racial justice demands integration, there's now a counterargument that it requires separatism—in ethnic theme houses, ethnic studies classes, interminable bilingual education, multicultural organizations, and ethnic pride programs of every conceivable hue. Why should wealthy or middle-class whites agree to relax the zoning that guarantees the leafiness of their suburbs and the tracking that guarantees their children's academic and socioeconomic status and why should they agree to increased public expenditures and public policies, all to promote integration, when the people that will supposedly benefit from their efforts can't even agree that they want it? Isn't it a double standard to ask that some people agree to send their kids across town to a strange neighborhood for grade school when others demand separate classrooms as "safe havens" and bastions of fragile self-esteem? Supreme Court Justice Scalia pressed a similar point in a different but related context when he complained of

> universities that talk the talk of multiculturalism and racial diversity in the courts but walk the walk of tribalism and racial segregation on their campuses—through minority-only stu-

dent organizations, separate minority housing opportunities, separate minority student centers, even separate, minority only graduation ceremonies.[22]

The integrationist agenda of *Brown v. Board of Education* was premised on an older, now unfashionable ideal of race relations: the melting pot. When the court opined that a common public education was the "foundation of good citizenship . . . and a principal instrument in awakening the child to cultural values," it necessarily implied that public education is an instrument of public socialization to common values and a common national identity. The unmistakable premise of *Brown* was that primary education could and should coax children away from the racial and ethnic solidarities of their parents and supplement those affiliations with a sense of common citizenship that could, at least occasionally, transcend racial differences.

Today, multiculturalism, racial nationalism, and ethnic separatism challenge this commitment. Too many activists misunderstand and distort the implications of civil rights laws and press the counterproductive claim that ethnic and racial distinctiveness is not simply a matter of private choice, but a question of moral right. Basing their arguments on this unfortunate interpretation of our civil rights tradition, many insist that any attempt to create common institutions and encourage common norms is a form of unacceptable bigotry—an attempt to "whitewash" their cultural identity. When even liberals and civil rights activists can't agree that integration is a laudable goal, it's easy for conservatives—suspicious of governmental "social engineering" generally—and bigots, who are hostile to racial mixing in particular, to reject integration as anachronistic and quixotic.

Today's racial injustices are, in many ways, as severe as ever. But these injustices now stem from isolation, poverty, and lack of socialization as much as from intentional discrimination or racism. The integration of disadvantaged groups into the prosperous American mainstream is the only plausible long-term remedy for those injustices. The civil rights movement has lost momentum because of confusion and conflict over what was once—and should be still—its clear goal. And this has created more opportunities for accusation and finger-pointing: now integrationists and segregationists alike can play the race card.

■ FIVE
POST-RACISM: WHY THE
RACE CARD IS A CRISIS OF SUCCESS

Everyone remembers the car chase. The surreal, dreamy, low-speed chase down the freeway, as if someone had slowed down the film for insertion into a Hollywood blockbuster. We can bring to mind, even now, the white Ford Bronco making its leisurely way south, a squadron of patrol cars following at a wary, almost respectful distance. It was only later that we would know that this low-speed pursuit was the opening scene in the biggest murder story since Cain put a knife into Abel, the best courtroom melodrama since a Roman governor tried a Nazarene carpenter for heresy.

I should confess a profound personal connection to the controversy. I was born in Buffalo, New York, and although no one

in my family was a real football fan, my parents loved the Buffalo Bills, especially—no, *because of*—their charismatic and handsome star running back, the Juice, a.k.a. O. J. Simpson. We drove
a used Toyota station wagon without air-conditioning across fifteen sun-parched states in the summer of 1972 to our new
home in central California. Meanwhile, the Juice raced through
the airport to catch his flight—hurdling barriers, dodging
crowds—and picked up his Hertz rental on the other end,
where he drove it to a real estate agent to find a house in somewhat more glamorous West L.A. He seemed to settle in nicely
to a second career as a sports commentator and occasional actor.
Now and again he'd pop up in a cameo role or on reruns of the
great moments in sports. He wasn't a great sports commentator,
and he certainly wasn't a great actor; he was basically a professional celebrity. Nice work if you can get it. Eventually, he did
what a lot of wealthy single men do: he married a pretty blonde.

O.J. wasn't a major figure in civil rights or a powerful role
model for troubled youth or a tireless goodwill ambassador
bridging the chasm between the races. He was no Paul Robe-
son, Harry Belafonte, or Bill Cosby. But he was one of a handful of black athletes whom everyone liked. He was one of the
good blacks—upstanding, clean-cut, charming. For blacks—at
least for the aspiring black petite bourgeoisie of which my family was a part—O.J. set a good example: he wasn't a hero, but he
was a solid citizen, the public face we wanted to put forward.
For whites, he was the kind of black man you would enjoy having over for dinner. The kind of black man you wouldn't mind
if your daughter brought home.

The scene at Bundy Drive was straight out of a Raymond
Chandler novel: a chic condominium in the posh West Side of
Los Angeles—Brentwood, home to corporate executives, film

stars, political bigwigs, people with trust funds, professional athletes. Streets paved with fifty-dollar bills. Spanish Mediterranean
villas share the block with Tudor mansions and ranch-style
estates—a pastiche of architectural signals of prosperity. Two
corpses: Caucasian male, mid-twenties, medium height, medium
build; Caucasian female, early thirties, tall, athletic, blond.
Someone had hacked these two to ribbons. This wasn't a murder for hire or even a killing of expediency by some punk
caught robbing the place. This was done in a rage, frenzied, out
of control. This was personal.

When police fingered Simpson for the murder, his lawyers
convinced them to allow him to turn himself in. More than a
thousand reporters were waiting for him to show up at the
precinct. Instead, he fled, with a friend, a fake beard and mus-
tache, eight grand in cash, and, of course, a gun. When police
spotted the car, Simpson's friend told them that Simpson had
the gun to his head. So they just followed him. Onlookers gathered on overpasses to watch Simpson and the police cruise by at
about thirty-five miles an hour, like it was a parade or a caravan
of tricked-out hot rods cruising Colorado Boulevard on a Saturday night. All that was missing were floats or girls in bikinis.
Impromptu parties started on those overpasses—people held up
signs urging O.J. to turn himself in or advising him to run for
his life. Ninety-five million people tuned in nationwide. They
sat down with their popcorn and their beer and their bean dip
and settled in on the sofa or the Barcalounger to watch O.J run,
the police in hot pursuit but keeping a respectful distance, a
high-speed chase at 35 miles an hour, going north. *North*—not
south toward the Mexican border, but north toward . . . toward
what? Someone should have caught that in postproduction.

After that came the arrest and the trial. The largest district attorney's office in the United States had twenty-five lawyers working full-time to send O.J. to prison. O.J's defense team came straight from central casting: F. Lee Bailey, who defended the accused doctor Samuel Sheppard—the inspiration for the 1960s television series *The Fugitive*; Harvard Law professor Alan Dershowitz, whose defense of the aristocrat and accused murderer Claus von Bulow was made into the major motion picture *Reversal of Fortune*; and Barry Scheck, professor at Cardozo School of Law in Manhattan and an expert in evaluating DNA evidence in criminal trials. He later founded the Innocence Project, which uses DNA to prove the innocence of convicted criminals. And Johnnie Cochran, the flamboyant and brilliant attorney whose practice blended civil rights advocacy, high-stakes civil suits, and celebrity criminal defense. His clients included Black Panther Geronimo Pratt; NYPD victim Abner Louima; Reginald Denny, the white man dragged from his truck and beaten during the 1992 Los Angeles race riot; and soul legend James Brown. The "dream team," as they would quickly be dubbed, turned out to be a lineup of all quarterbacks, each hogging the ball. The legal lions scrabbled with one another for dominance until Cochran emerged as the alpha male.

The trial in the courtroom lasted several hours a day, five days a week, for nine months. But the real trial—the trial in the press—went on twenty-four hours a day, seven days a week, and ran simultaneously in every media outlet in the United States and in most of the rest of the world. Reporters, commentators, pundits, know-it-alls, hack writers, law professors, self-appointed experts, political activists, spiritual gurus, and publicists for hire descended on Los Angeles like wannabe miners to the Comstock Lode. The glare of the spotlight, always in search of new personalities, made minor celebrities of anyone remotely connected to the victims or the defendant. The mild-mannered trial judge, Lance Ito, became a household name, inspiring a dance troupe of look-alikes who performed in black robes and glasses. The Dancing Itos appeared on Jay Leno's talk show at the height of O.J. mania. Kato Kaelin, Simpson's confidant and sometime houseguest, an unemployed aspiring actor with shoulder-length blond hair and a surfer's drawl, become a minor celebrity and a walking stereotype of southern Californian vapidness. Court TV made its name with almost round-the-clock coverage of the trial: "All O.J., all the time" was almost its official trademark. Even global geopolitics took a backseat: when Russian president Boris Yeltsin arrived in Washington, D.C., to meet President Bill Clinton, reportedly the first question he asked of the leader of the free world was "Do you think O.J. did it?" More than 90 percent of people watching television were tuned to trial coverage when the verdict was announced.

Every detail of the predictably dull daily courtroom proceedings was presented, analyzed, critiqued, and dissected on television stations, newspapers, magazines, and radio shows. Scores of would-be judges ridiculed Ito's control (or lack thereof, according to the detractors) of the courtroom. Almost as soon as prosecutor Marcia Clark got out of bed and had coffee, some armchair D.A. somewhere would be on television taking a dig at her choice of French Roast. (*Starbucks? How's* that *going to play to the jury?*) The withering scrutiny would quickly focus on the prosecution's decision to file the case in downtown L.A. rather than in Santa Monica, the district where the crime occurred. Downtown would ensure a racially mixed jury pool, Santa Monica an almost all-white one. Many speculated that the prosecution wanted a racially diverse jury. Conviction by a lily-white jury would provoke accusations of racial bias and perhaps even provoke rioting. The jury ultimately impaneled consisted of nine black members—eight female; two whites—both female; and one Hispanic male. Some worried that a predominantly black jury would empathize with Simpson. To her credit but also to her regret, Clark tried to ignore both the glare of the 24-7 spotlight—and race. If you took away all the hype, this was simply a case of domestic violence that escalated into a murder. The female jurors would relate to Nicole and would convict. If identity politics was relevant, it was the politics of gender, not race.

But by the time the trial was over, it would be a case about race.

Race may have had nothing to do with the crime and little to do with the prosecution, but it had everything to do with the media coverage and the public fascination. *Time* magazine ran a doctored mug-shot photo on its cover in which Simpson's skin was darkened—had they hired the art director responsible for George Bush's Willie Horton advertisements? When attacked for the photo, *Time*'s illustrator copped a plea: "[I] wanted to make it more artful, more compelling." Civil rights groups were outraged—why, exactly, was it "more compelling" to make the face in a mug shot darker in complexion? If Willie Horton stood for the risks of soft policy for criminals, O.J. stood for the failure of integration and the perils of miscegenation. Here was a black man everyone liked—no rabble-rousing black nationalist but a charming, polite, clean-cut hero-athlete. And now, it seemed, a wife beater and a killer.

The O. J. Simpson trial was nonstop lurid voyeurism. Race and *sex*—not gender—accounted for the rapt attention lavished on the proceedings. Although cosmopolitan Americans at the end of the century would deny it, interracial relationships remained exotic and taboo. Few dared say so openly, but the subtext of the O.J. obsession was as obvious as the contrast between Simpson's artificially darkened mug shot and Nicole's golden blond tresses and creamy white skin. It was *Othello* without Iago, *Guess Who's Coming to Dinner* gone wrong.

For white racists, the murder confirmed what they had believed all along: this is what a white girl could expect if she got mixed up with a Negro, his violent passions as unrestrained as his carnal lusts. O.J. was King Kong, with the freeway substituting for the Empire State Building and Fay Wray crushed in the monster's grip rather than lovingly returned to terra firma. It had been decades since the law outlawed racial mixing, but the trial reawakened the old preoccupation with the dark menace to white female innocence and virtue. Emmett Till was murdered for *whistling* at a white woman. What was sufficient retribution for O.J., who presumably had regular intercourse with Nicole over the course of their five-year marriage and then killed her in a fit of jealous rage? Black separatists had a strikingly similar uptake—here was a black man who slept with the enemy and paid the price, driven crazy by the lure of forbidden fruit. It was Samson and Delilah: O.J. ruined by a foreign temptress, shorn of his God-given charisma.

Marcia Clark's confidence that feminist impulses would sway the female jurors severely underestimated the importance of racial politics. Not only did many black women not relate to Nicole; some resented her. Black-white marriages aren't common in the United States: in 2005, only about 9 percent of American blacks had a spouse of a different race; by contrast 59 percent of Asian-Americans did. But of those few, an overwhelming majority involve black men and white women—74 percent in 2005. This imbalance is a source of consternation for some black women, who complain that such racially adventurous fair maidens and blondes whom gentlemen prefer exploit racial privilege and racial stereotypes of femininity to snare some of the most eligible black men—like O. J. Simpson. These concerns shaped the attitudes of some black women—including perhaps some who sat on the jury—bringing them into line with the more extreme positions of black separatists and reducing any potential gender-based empathy with the leggy blond Nicole.

Racists, white and black, would agree on one point—the crime was proof that racial mixing could only end badly. Unnatural desire had led, inevitably, to a grim and tragic fate. Everyone else had to struggle with some uncomfortable issues. You and I might *think* race has little or nothing to do with romantic encounters, but there is social theory to contend with, which offers more provocative explanations. For instance, the sociologist Robert Merton proposed that interracial marriages involve "exchanges" of racial status for other advantages: successful black men who marry white women seek to "trade" their success for honorary white status through marriage; the women typically are compensated for the corresponding racial downgrade with improvement in class status or income.[1] Other starry-eyed social critics advance a "Mandingo" hypothesis: racial fetishes and sexual fantasies—strong black bucks and delicate white does—give extra fizz to black male/white female couplings. These analyses shared a punch line with the crude rants of white supremacists and black separatists: interracial intimacy is to be treated with caution and suspicion, if not derision and contempt.

Polite society has little place for such speculations, but the Simpson trial forced (or allowed) everyone to confront these uncomfortable issues. The politically correct position was the one that apparently informed Marcia Clark's trial strategy: this was a simple case of domestic violence, tragically all too common in our society, and had nothing to do with race. But the Simpson trial strained racial etiquette to the breaking point. Interracial relationships were (and are) still rare enough to be provocative, and this, combined with the subtle racism that still infuses American culture, was enough make race central to the popular perception of the crime, even if it was irrelevant to the crime itself. Simpson's successful integration into white society— precisely what made him so popular with whites—now took on a sinister cast. Was Simpson's rage somehow the result of his life of assimilation? If his relationship with Nicole symbolized racial tolerance and successful integration into white society (at one point he reportedly said, "I'm not black, I'm O.J."), did the demise of that relationship signify that integration was unworkable? If Simpson—a handsome, wealthy, and charming sports hero—couldn't find happiness and psychological well-being in a predominantly white social milieu, what hope was there in integration for the majority of blacks, who lacked his financial and cultural resources? Did the dramatic implosion of what seemed to be an integrationist success story prove the racial separatists right?

For some, interracial romance may be the object of contempt and repulsion; for others an exotic turn-on (and for still others, both). It is rarely the matter of bored indifference that politically correct etiquette requires us to feign. The Simpson trial gave the nation's Peeping Toms a chance to stroke this hidden fantasy under the trench coat of moral outrage and civic concern; the televised courtroom proceedings built to a climax four months in the making.

. . .

Police Detective Mark Fuhrman, the man who found the bloody glove at Simpson's estate, looked like a prosecutor's wet dream. He was no corrupt, overweight, gin-blossomed, doughnut-gorging big-city cop from the bad old days of film noir. Fuhrman was a product of the stem-to-stern overhaul of the LAPD—the type of reform that swept the nation in the mid century and turned big-city police from rowdy thugs juiced up on ward-boss patronage into disciplined, quasi-military professionals with strict chains of command and overseen by civilian commissions. Fuhrman was a well- and plainspoken veteran officer, an ex-marine. He was a clean-cut, trim, steely-eyed, no-nonsense, by-the-book, just-the-facts-ma'am professional—Joe Friday right out of *Dragnet*.

The defense introduced jurors to another side of Mark Fuhrman. Defense attorney F. Lee Bailey set the trap. He asked Fuhrman whether he had used the word "nigger" in the last ten years. Fuhrman answered, "Not that I recall, no." Bailey pressed the point: "You mean if you called someone a nigger, you have forgotten it." Fuhrman categorically denied using the word. Maybe the defense was fishing, hoping to get an admission or to plant the seed in the minds of the jury. But they hooked a Great White Whale. Fuhrman had given an interview in 1985 to a young writer, Laura Hart McKinny, who was working on a project about female police officers in the LAPD. She approached Fuhrman to get an insider's view of life on the force. Fuhrman spoke freely, and Ms. McKinny recorded his observations and opinions. He used the word "nigger" in those interviews. Forty-two times, if you're counting, and Simpson's defense team was. Fuhrman had also bragged about fabricating evidence to obtain convictions, beating suspects in order to extract confessions, framing innocent people, and lying to cover up his misconduct.[2] None of this was *directly* relevant to the Simpson case, but Fuhrman had opened to door to evidence that he used the word "nigger" by denying he had done so. Proof that he had used the word was now relevant to his credibility as a witness. Although most of the tapes were ruled inadmissible, the defense was allowed to introduce parts of the transcript as evidence that Fuhrman had in fact used the word "nigger." The defense had drawn their first ace.

Simpson's attorneys would use Fuhrman to suggest an alternative explanation for the evidence that linked Simpson to the crime: Simpson was framed by racist cops. To many, it seemed like a soap opera plot twist, and the racial chasm that the O.J. trial has come to symbolize was at its widest at this point. Most whites thought the idea that the police would frame a suspect was a paranoid fantasy. But most whites didn't closely follow the abuses of the LAPD in the past decade. Most blacks did. And there was plenty of evidence to confirm the suspicion that the LAPD was capable not only of framing innocent people but of much worse. In 1982, after a series of black men died in police custody after being held in choke holds, Police Chief Daryl Gates offered this explanation: "We may be finding that in some Blacks when [the choke hold] is applied the veins or arteries do not open up as fast as they do on *normal* people."[3] In 1987 Chief Gates launched Operation Hammer—a war on youth gangs, some would say on black youth generally. As part of Operation Hammer, police made thousands of arrests, raided private homes, and destroyed property in minority neighborhoods. In one infamous raid, police so severely damaged an apartment complex that the Red Cross offered displaced residents disaster relief; the raid uncovered less than one ounce of cocaine and six ounces of marijuana and resulted in one successful prosecution.[4] Community activists claimed that Operation Hammer was the most intensive police crackdown in black neighborhoods since the Watts riot of 1965.

And everyone, whites included, remembered Rodney King. Everyone had seen the videotape, taken by a civilian bystander with a new camcorder the night of March 3, 1991. The footage was grainy with the patina of authenticity, but the images were clear enough. King was crouched in a fetal position, writhing in pain, shielding his head with his arms as four police officers flailed away at him with billy clubs. It looked like footage from Selma during the Freedom Summers.

The video told the truth, but it didn't tell the whole truth. Unlike O.J., King—a felon on parole—led police on a *high*-speed chase through Northeast L.A. When King was finally pulled over, he resisted arrest. The arrest was bungled from the beginning. A California Highway Patrol officer approached the car with her weapon drawn: a dangerous tactic and for that reason not part of standard procedure. LAPD sergeant Stacey Koon asked the CHP officer to stand down and took over the arrest. According to police, King was belligerent and violent: he taunted the female CHP officer and, the officers claimed, lunged for one officer's gun. Koon ordered his men to subdue King, who threw the four men off his back. Officers shot King with electrified darts, which should have incapacitated him. They didn't, and King got up. The cops were now scared: they suspected that King was high on PCP or something that would allow him to withstand fifty thousand volts of electricity. In fact, King was just very tough and very drunk. Koon swung at King with his nightstick. It was a wild swing, not the controlled power stroke the department teaches officers to use, and King withstood it and stayed on his feet. Then the other officers piled on. One, Lawrence Powell, had failed a baton test against a *stationary* object two hour before. He flailed away at a very mobile King in a blind rage—or panic. Eventually King lay in a fetal position, futilely trying to shield his face from the torrent of baton blows. He ultimately suffered eleven skull fractures, several broken bones, shattered teeth, kidney injuries, and permanent brain damage.[5]

Less than two weeks later, a fifteen-year-old honor student, Latasha Harlins, walked into a corner grocery store in South Central L.A. and left in a body bag. She was shot dead by Soon Ja Du, the store's owner, after an altercation. It too was caught on videotape: Harlins took a bottle of orange juice and put it in her backpack. She walked toward the door. Du grabbed Harlins. Harlins slugged Du in the face, knocking her to the ground. Du threw a stool at Harlins. Harlins turned her back and walked away. Du shot Harlins in the back of the head.

What the tape didn't show: Du's family had received death threats from gang members, and she did not normally staff the store. She was inexperienced, she was angry, and she was scared. Another thing the tape missed: Latasha Harlins had money in her hand as she walked toward the door and the counter. She was about to pay for the juice when Du grabbed her and started the fatal altercation.

Both incidents resulted in high-profile trials. In October 1991 a jury found Du guilty of voluntary manslaughter. The trial judge suspended the sentence and gave Du probation and four hundred hours of community service. To many observers, Du had gotten away with murder. Meanwhile, the officers who beat Rodney King were put on trial for excessive use of force.

Defense counsel requested a change of venue, and the trial was moved to Simi Valley in nearby Ventura County, a largely white community, home to many conservatives and many police officers. The jury had no black members. The officers were acquitted the following April. And the largest race riot in American history erupted in Los Angeles.

The Rodney King riot of 1992 would rage for four days. More than 50 people died; 4,000 sustained injuries; 3,600 fires were deliberately set; 1,100 buildings were damaged or destroyed; and close to a billion dollars in damage was done. The National Guard, the army, and the Marine Corps were called in to restore order. This was not so much a typical race riot as a multiracial riot: rioters targeted Korean businesses in apparent "retaliation" for the Latasha Harlins shooting. Korean store owners took up guns and fired at rioters from rooftops. The riots began as a direct response to the Rodney King incident, but criminals and gangs made use of the ensuing chaos to loot, pillage, and settle old scores. Of the ten thousand people arrested, 42 percent were black and 44 percent were Hispanic: participation in the violence roughly reflected the racial composition of South Central Los Angeles, where it took place. It was an equal opportunity riot.[6]

Ironically, the notorious police abuses that culminated in the King riots were in a sense the result of the successful anticorruption reforms of the LAPD under Chief William Parker during the 1950s and '60s. Parker took cops off permanent beat assignments, where they could establish networks of graft and make regular shakedowns. He developed a statistical method of beat assignment whereby officers were dispatched according to the time and place of past crimes. He remade the LAPD as a paramilitary organization, recruiting heavily from ex-GIs after

World War Two and reorganizing the department to institute a strict chain of command and rigid discipline. His reforms gave birth to the spick-and-span image of the LAPD depicted in *Dragnet*. Later, Chief Gates would extend Parker's legacy—both in paramilitary reform and in media savvy—helping to create the nation's first Special Weapons and Tactics unit, or SWAT team, trained in hostage rescue and antiterrorism—the idea spread nationwide and, of course, inspired its own television series.

But reform had a dark side. Removing cops from a regular neighborhood "beat" reduced low-level corruption, but it also reduced the local knowledge that police relied on to evaluate ambiguous situations and defuse potential tensions. The cop on a regular beat knew who was a gang member and who was a good kid. He could tell whether the young man approaching an elderly woman was about to help her with her parcels or shake her down for cash. He knew who was sleeping with someone else's wife, whose business was failing and might be tempted to torch the joint, which gang controlled which neighborhood. He could tell the difference between a postgraduation celebration and a drunken brawl. The paramilitary officer, deprived of this local knowledge, had to treat everyone with suspicion. Without the context on which to base more nuanced judgments, the re-formed officer was like the test subject taking the Implicit Association Test—speeding up in his patrol car with split seconds in which to make a decision. Confronted with nothing more than a face, the officer often defaulted to racial stereotypes.

These abuses of authority by police and the explosive reaction of the city's poor minority communities informed the O.J. trial. They were common knowledge among the minority communities of Los Angeles and probably among the jurors who had to decide whether or not to trust the police officers who recovered key evidence against Simpson.

Three months after Mark Fuhrman was caught in a lie about his use of the word "nigger," assistant prosecutor Christopher Darden staged a dramatic courtroom demonstration. He produced the bloody glove found at the crime scene and insisted that Simpson put it on. It was a risky gambit: trial advocacy 101 instructs that a lawyer should never ask a hostile witness a question at trial unless the lawyer already knows the answer. By the same token, most trial lawyers wouldn't try such a stunt without already knowing that the glove would fit like, well, a glove. Darden hadn't gotten the rewrite: Simpson struggled to pull the glove over his hand and apparently could not. Johnnie Cochran would notoriously exploit the blunder, referring both to the glove and to the prosecution's theory of the crime: "If it doesn't fit, you must acquit," he admonished the jury. It didn't, and they did: after three hours of deliberation, on October 3, 1995, the jury returned a verdict of not guilty.

Many people of all races were shocked by the verdict. Despite police blunders and even despite the odious Fuhrman, this was as strong a circumstantial case as one gets. Simpson cut his hand on the night of the murders. Blood with DNA that matched Simpson's was found next to the footprints leaving the scene of the crime. Those footprints were size 12—Simpson's size and that of about only 9 percent of the population. Nicole's blood was found on a sock in Simpson's house. Ron Goldman's blood was found in Simpson's car. Nicole had given O.J. gloves for Christmas that were identical to the bloody glove found at the crime scene. The second glove was found at Simpson's home.

That glove had Goldman's hair and fiber from his shirt, Nicole's blood, Nicole's hair, Simpson's blood, and fibers from Simpson's car. Simpson had no alibi for the time the crime was committed. And Simpson, rather than cooperating with police so that they could find the "real killer," wrote what looked like a suicide note and fled with a gun, a disguise, and eight large in cash.

The New Yorker's Jeffrey Toobin, who followed the trial in its entirety, wrote shortly after the verdict:

> The core of the defense case was . . . that Fuhrman surreptitiously took that glove from the murder scene to the defendant's home. Not only would he have had to transport the glove . . . but he would also have had to find some of Simpson's blood (from sources unknown) to deposit upon it and then wipe the glove on the inside of Simpson's locked car (by means unknown)—all the while not knowing whether Simpson had an ironclad alibi for the time of the murders . . . Someone would have had to take some of Goldman's blood and put it in the Bronco . . . someone . . . would have had to take some of Nicole's blood and dab it on the sock . . . All of these illegal actions by the police would have had to take place at a time when everyone involved in the case was under the most relentless media scrutiny in American legal history.[7]

The most striking denunciation came from Simpson's own lawyer, Robert Shapiro, who in a CNN interview shortly after the trial lamented, "Not only did we play the race card, we dealt it from the bottom of the deck."

Simpson's defense team cobbled their winning hand together as any good lawyer does when faced with bad facts: they distracted the jury. They blew smoke about the "real killers"—

vengeful Columbian drug lords, anonymous mafiosi, mysterious hired assassins—*anything* to give the jury an alternative to the obvious. They exploited the complexity and inscrutability of DNA evidence, struggling to keep prosecutors from saying that DNA from the crime scene "matched" O.J.'s. They played up to O.J.'s celebrity and charisma: aside from Johnnie Cochran, the silent O.J. was the most charismatic person in the courtroom. Most of all, they played on justifiable fear of and anger over police racism.

Cochran played the race card. But he didn't pull it out of his sleeve. He didn't create the long, brutal history of American racism, where top on the list of hanging offenses was for a black man to even look sideways or whistle across the street at a white woman, much less marry one. Cochran didn't conjure up the history of police racism. And he didn't invent Mark Fuhrman: if he could have invented the ideal witness to discredit the police, he wouldn't have dared to hope that the officer who found the key piece of incriminating evidence had not only used racial epithets and bragged about framing suspects, but had done both *on tape*.

Cochran secured Simpson's acquittal by alluding to real and profound racial injustices that weren't relevant to the case at bar. Police *had* regularly hassled and manhandled poor blacks from South Central, but for the most part they handled rich blacks from Brentwood the same way they treated rich whites: with kid gloves. Even Fuhrman, who on the notorious tapes insisted that he would pull over any black person in a Porsche, qualified the statement with "unless he's wearing a $300 suit." Simpson wore expensive suits and, as we know, designer Italian shoes to match. Fuhrman was a racist, and therefore race was relevant. It went to his possible motivation to lie or plant evidence against

Simpson and, once Fuhrman denied using the "n-word," it went to his credibility as a witness. But he couldn't have planted or manufactured the evidence linking Simpson to the murders. Nevertheless, once racial issues were introduced, they couldn't be put back in Pandora's box. As prosecutor Christopher Darden warned Judge Ito when the defense sought to introduce the Fuhrman tapes, "[If race is an issue], the test will be whose side are you on: the side of the white prosecutors and the white policemen or the side of the black defendant? Either you are with the Man or you are with the Brothers."[8]

Cochran not only made an issue of race; he blustered on about it; he harped on it till he went hoarse. According to Toobin, when Darden asked a witness whether a voice he heard at the scene of the crime sounded like the voice of a black man—a description the witness had volunteered to police earlier—Cochran "nearly vaulted out of his chair: 'I resent that statement. You can't tell by somebody's voice whether they sound black . . . I resent that . . . racist statement . . . This statement about whether he sounds black or white is racist, and I resent it . . . I think it is totally improper that in America, at this time in 1995, we have to hear and endure this.'" As the Fuhrman debacle unwound, Cochran arranged for the defense team to wear African kente cloth ties. According to Toobin, the stunt "brought hoots from the reporters watching the trial." But Cochran's audience wasn't the press; it was the jury.

The stark contrast of black and white reactions—like the contrast between Simpson's artificially darkened mug shot and the white backdrop—made good copy. As the verdict was read, television cameras rolled not only at the trial itself but also in college dormitories, beauty parlors, barbershops, shopping malls, cafés, and bars across America. In its last seconds the trial had become a meta-spectacle: not only was the verdict news-worthy, so was the public reaction to the verdict or, more ac-curately, the reaction to the news coverage of the verdict. On cue, whites were almost unanimous in the conviction that the verdict was a travesty. In posh Pacific Palisades parlors, sunlit Middle American diners, and dimly lit Wall Street watering holes, white women wailed and moaned as if personally in-jured; white men buried faces in hands, punched walls, kicked over inanimate objects. Cut to the black reaction: in historically black colleges, neighborhood hair salons, community recreation centers, and Baptist church halls, young men pumped their fists in the air, an athletic victory gesture reminiscent of the black power salute. Young women hugged each other and bounced up and down in celebration. Older men and women let loose whoops of elation and praised God Almighty. How about the black women in battered-women's shelters? Didn't *they* relate to Nicole as another woman victimized by male brutality? Didn't they join their white feminist sisters in solidarity and outrage? No. They too let out big hip-hip-hoorays, slapped high fives, danced jigs.

And the television cameras reeled them in, ignoring the indi-vidual reactions and venues that didn't jibe with the predictable nation-divided-by-race angle. The usual gang of pundits and talking heads from the "black community" were obliged to of-fer the "black perspective" on an event that the media, as much as Johnnie Cochran, had insisted was a race relations inkblot test from day one. These talking heads dutifully defended the integrity of the predominantly black jury against the shrill ac-cusations of "nullification." And they were right to do so. Simpson's lawyers put on a skillful defense that could have con-vinced honest jurors—jurors who operated without the benefit of blow-by-blow professional analysis and were sequestered in stifling isolation—to acquit.

For those blacks who cheered the result, Simpson's acquittal was a symbolic conviction of LAPD and the criminal justice system. One Los Angeles businessman and activist, Kerman Maddox, acknowledged Simpson's guilt[9] but insisted that "the trial was more about a system that has treated us unfairly for years . . . you had this incredible divide . . . African-Americans on one side, white America on the other side . . . and we finally won one."[10] For the celebrants, the evidence that mattered wasn't introduced in court. It had been piling up over decades: the lethal choke holds and Chief Gates's use of crude biological racism to defend their abuse, Operation Hammer, Latasha Harlins, Rodney King, and the incidents that were never caught on film but which too many black Angelenos had experienced firsthand. If finally a black man—guilty or not—could take those years of abuse and contempt and throw them back in the white establishment's faces, then three cheers for him.

Whites were outraged. A rich man spent a fortune on lawyers and got away with murder. Tragically, that happens all the time, but this was different because they watched it happen—it was a film noir in slo-mo. Starting with the car chase opener, the fugitive driving *away* from the border, it was just like a movie, except everything happened backward, right down to the wrong verdict at the end. It wasn't just that a murderer got away scot-free. It wasn't just that he was black and his victims were white. The worst thing was that whites *trusted* O.J.—let him into their homes and their hearts. The verdict was bad enough for the bigots who knew all along that an interracial marriage would end badly. But it was worse for the liberals who had finally let go of that old prejudice—or thought they had, or tried to—and replaced it with a shiny new faith that we're really all brothers under the skin. It wasn't that Cochran skillfully outmaneuvered the prosecution and played his race card before they could play theirs. It was that the prosecution could have easily played the race card and chose not to. They took pains to make sure the trial *wasn't* about race—changing venue, accepting a predominantly black jury—and *then* Cochran moved into that breach and played the race card, like a duelist who, after selecting pistols rather than rapiers, turns around at nine paces and shoots his opponent in the back. The O.J. trial and its aftermath—the crowing, the high fives, the dancing in the streets—was a betrayal of racial chivalry and good faith.

For those whites who were free of or had conquered racial prejudice, or thought they had, the verdict was a disheartening reminder that good intentions would not undo centuries of racial injustice and also a frightening indication that many blacks would rejoice in retaliatory injustices. And for many, that must have let loose all of their latent, repressed, barely-below-the-surface subconscious racial prejudice—followed by guilt, recrimination, and then more anger that the blacks had put them through all this. O.J. Simpson's Los Angeles was a long way from the Mississippi of Emmett Till. A black man in L.A. wouldn't get lynched for whistling at a white girl. He could not only whistle at her, he could marry her. Not only would no mob come after him with a blindfold and rope but white folks would congratulate him on his good taste and come to the wedding with a toaster or a china setting. And then he could kill her and walk away scot-free. And as if to confirm the worst, black people cheered and broke out bottles of champagne and danced in the streets. Like Eldridge Cleaver, who wrote in *Soul on Ice* that he had raped white women as an "insurrectionary act," they saw Simpson's acquittal as some sort of civil rights victory. While the white prosecutors were bending over backward to make sure that no one could say the trial was tainted in the least by racism, the blacks were busy closing ranks and playing the race card.

For those blacks who thought they had finally "won one," the Simpson verdict was the most hollow of victories. The acquittal of a murderer did not send a message to the establishment about the injustices racial minorities regularly face at the hands and batons of police. Simpson suffered no such injustices. It did not expose police racism. What racism there was to expose—Fuhrman's bigoted rantings—had already been revealed on national television weeks before the verdict. Instead, the verdict *distracted* America from the real and continuing problem of police racism; it diverted outrage away from the racial injustices symbolized by Fuhrman and toward the injustice of the verdict itself. Least of all was it "payback" for police racism or prosecutorial misconduct. After all, whom did the verdict harm? Not Mark Fuhrman, the only obvious racist involved, who has gone on to a lucrative postretirement career as a conservative author and talk show guest in large part because the verdict allowed him to cast himself as a target of unjustified race-baiting. Instead, it harmed the families of the victims, who must live with the knowledge that the man who murdered their loved ones is free to enjoy a comfortable retirement.

Media stage management notwithstanding, most blacks, like most whites, knew this. Blacks were more likely to empathize with the jurors and defend their integrity, but many greeted the verdict itself with apprehension. There is no victory in injustice and nothing to celebrate in landing a wild punch that threatens to start a race brawl. God help us all if race relations are nothing more than the trading of injuries and the settling of old scores. Whites are as capable of retaliatory injustices as anyone, and we know who will suffer most in a state of unrestrained hostilities.

Amid its Hollywood film noir settings, its crime story archetypes, its central casting attorneys, its backstory told through grainy videotapes of police beatings and televised race riots, its slo-mo car chase and artfully edited trial drama, it was too easy to forget that this trial was supposed to be about a real killer—not someone who plays one on TV—and two real people who died under his knife. It is telling—and chilling—that the media's nonstop coverage of the Simpson trial rarely mentioned Ron Goldman, whose senseless death somehow didn't fit the script of racial lust, fallen heroes, and police conspiracies. Everyone, of every race, should feel frustration and dismay that this trial was turned into a tin-pot racial truth and reconciliation hearing. And everyone should hope that we can find a better vehicle for confronting racial injustice than the Simpson trial provided.

CONCLUSION: PLAYING OUR CARDS RIGHT IN A POST-RACIST SOCIETY

In 1892 Homer Plessy sat in a railroad car reserved for whites, violating Louisiana's Separate Car Act. Plessy was, in the parlance of the time, an octoroon—one-eighth black and seven-eighths white by ancestry. Unsurprisingly, he looked white. But Plessy wasn't trying to pass as white. He was persuaded by civil rights lawyers to violate the law and then sue to overturn it. Plessy's white skin made him an ideal plaintiff: a central element of Plessy's claim was that the Separate Car Act served no conceivable rational purpose, because it would exclude a man who in all outward appearances was identical to the people it admitted. Of course the larger ambition of the legal challenge was to demonstrate that racial distinctions generally were irrational. Plessy, famously, lost his lawsuit. He eventually paid a twenty-five-dollar fine for violating the Jim Crow law.

Plessy's suit underscored a defining feature of race and racism—its formal, monolithic nature. Jim Crow did not deal in nuance and subtlety. If one was black, he was always and everywhere unequivocally black. Though Homer Plessy was a white man in all outward appearances, his one black great-grandparent made him as black as the ace of spades, and the society he lived would never let him forget it.

O. J. Simpson, by contrast, could live a life that allowed him to believe, as he reportedly once said, "I'm not black; I'm O.J." A typical reaction to this statement is that Simpson was deluded: he lived in a fantasy world, walled up in his Rockingham estate, surrounded by sycophants like the grating Kato Kaelin, and out of touch with the grim realities of American racism. This may be true—by most accounts Simpson thought little about the plight of less fortunate blacks—but this reaction misses something important and true in Simpson's assessment of his social position. His celebrity and his wealth took much of the sting out of racism's ritualistic slaps in the face, and most of the time they spared him those slaps altogether. Times have changed: in today's America, racism is not monolithic. It often makes exceptions for VIPs. It applies a sliding scale according to income.

The Simpson courtroom was the birthing room for post-racism. Trial coverage was inescapable, and so were the questions of race that the attorneys and the media insisted were central to the case. But race in the Simpson trial was not a social fact, but a media simulacrum and a rhetorical device. Simpson's race didn't just affect the trial; it was an effect *of* the trial, of a thousand interpretative and expositional decisions such as *Time* magazine's decision to darken Simpson's skin on his mug shot and Johnnie Cochran's trial strategy that emphasized racism that Simpson didn't suffer. The Simpson trial forced Americans to think about race as no event had since the march on Washington, D.C., more than thirty years earlier. In 1963 the lessons to be learned were clear and inspiring. This time they were confused and disorienting. But they were learned nonetheless. Before the Simpson trial, most Americans—whether civil rights crusaders or Daughters of the Confederacy—thought of race and race relations as questions of sociological, if not biological, fact. After Simpson, a new, postmodern idea of race was unavoidable: race was a product of interpretation, a symptom of the gaze. Racism was in the eye of the beholder. And race and racism were something that could be gamed, a "card" that could be played to one's advantage.

Before the verdict was read, many people feared race riots if Simpson was convicted. But whites, some worried, could riot too. They would riot at the ballot box, passing punitive laws and withdrawing support for social programs that benefit minorities. A year after O.J.'s defense team secured his acquittal by playing the race card, California voters passed Proposition 209, which outlawed affirmative action in California government and public education. Its key proponent, the former University of California regent Ward Connerly, has dedicated himself to taking the race card out of as many decks as he can. Connerly, an avuncular, outspoken black entrepreneur, has gone on to press similar initiatives in other states, with mixed success: failure in Florida, victory in Washington and Michigan.

In 2003, Connerly returned to California's political arena to advance the Racial Privacy Initiative, which would prohibit government from "classifying" any person according to race. The Racial Privacy Initiative would have prohibited the state from gathering or using racial data, with a few curious exceptions: medical data, criminal suspect descriptions (remember Oneonta in Chapter Three), and prison assignments. Unlike Proposition 209, the Racial Privacy Initiative lost big, with almost 64 percent of voters opposed. Maybe Californians cooled down after the O.J. trial. Maybe they understood that outlawing any and all consideration of race in order to stop racism is a bit like outlawing umbrellas because you don't like rain.

We have to do better than the extremes of opportunistic charlatanism on display during the O.J. trial and the ostrichlike obliviousness of the Racial Privacy Initiative. We need a way of talking about race that captures its still often brutal salience and its nuances and complexities. We have to understand a society where blacks are both elites and the underclass, where black faces can sell both five-thousand-dollar Louis Vuitton bags and increased prison construction. The idea of an irredeemably "white supremacist" public culture doesn't jibe with a world where many of the most prominent and respected celebrities, politicians, and industry leaders are black. It doesn't reflect the dominant attitudes of many young adults who find racial difference a matter of casual interest, fluid role-playing, or relative indifference. It's wrong to dismiss the widespread admiration enjoyed by black musicians and athletes with the politically correct commonplace that blacks are "relegated" to the role of entertainers: celebrities are the closest we have to a visible American aristocracy, and the prominence of blacks in that symbolic elite suggests an inversion of the conventional equation of black skin and social contempt.

Does this mean that racism is a thing of past? Not at all. But today's race relations are more complex and contradictory than those of the unambiguously white supremacist past. In the beginning of this book, I introduced the idea of a post-racist society. But you'll recall that the "post" in post-racist doesn't signify "the end" of racism, or even necessarily the beginning of the end. It means the "next stage" of racism—in the same way postmodern doesn't mean the end of modernity but rather a later stage in which modern beliefs, institutions, and commitments are pervasive, but also superannuated and in crisis.

The comedian Sarah Silverman is an exemplary post-racist ("Everybody blames the Jews for killing Christ. And then the Jews try to pass it off on the Romans. I'm one of the few people who believe it was the blacks.") At her worst she's offensive and off-putting without being funny; at her best she's uproarious, Lenny Bruce with curves. Race is just one of the many taboos she gleefully violates: others include rape, famine victims, 9/11. What makes Silverman so funny and so disturbing is that her jokes couldn't work exclusively on the level of parody and critique. It's not just that she is making fun of bigots and anti-Semites when she quips that blacks killed Christ—although of course she is doing that. She's also having fun playing the bigot herself; her jokes evoke a spirit uncomfortably akin to nostalgia, as well as that of critique. To find her funny, somewhere, perhaps deep in your subconscious, you have to sort of enjoy hearing someone make fun of rape victims or 9/11 or Jews or black people. I suspect this is part of the point: Silverman mocks both bigotry and political correctness, but her work is also an implicit critique of the smug conviction that we're beyond racism: *if you weren't still a little racist, this wouldn't be so funny.* A Silverman monologue may be a better test for subconscious bias than the Implicit Association Test.

In 2004 Dairy Queen named its new milk shake the Moo-Latte. More than a few people noticed that this name bore an uncomfortable similarity to "mulatto," an archaic and derogatory term for a person of mixed race. In sardonic protest, a Houston newspaper called the company to suggest that it might also consider introducing the "High Yellow Butterscotch Sundae," the "Octoroonie" (an eight-flavored ice-cream treat), and a new dessert named "Sambo's Extra Dark Triple Chocolate Shake." The company representative deadpanned a polite interest. He insisted that no one at Dairy Queen noticed the similarity between "MooLatte" and "mulatto." But since that similarity is what makes the name clever, that seems unlikely. MooLatte isn't as offensive as the name of a German chocolate confection, the *Negerkuss* (even non–German speakers can probably guess that a rough translation is "nigger kiss"), which, according to a letter from a *Washington Post* reporter published in *Slate*, is advertised "with placards . . . showing an almost entirely naked African boy with an imbecilic grin, a huge bone jammed through his nose and every vicious stereotype of black facial characteristics ever used by the Nazis or any other hate group." No American marketer in possession of her faculties would deliberately use a racial epithet in a nationwide campaign. Unlike the overt racism of the *Negerkuss*, the MooLatte evokes race without quite naming it. This oblique, defanged, almost coy bigotry is another form of post-racism.

Post-racism is better than what preceded it—I'd much rather

have the MooLatte than the *Negerkuss*, Sarah Silverman than Father Coughlin. But post-racist is not the same as "not racist." Just as postmodernism is not just the withered hull of high modernism but also its apotheosis, so post-racism is, in an important sense, the continuation of racism by other means. If not itself a social justice problem, it is a symptom of one.

Post-racism aside, some racial issues remain firmly mired in the swamp of Jim Crow. Pollyanna herself couldn't put a sunny spin on the alarming rates of black poverty, unemployment, and imprisonment we see today. The ghetto subculture of violence and despair that multimillionaire rappers extol and exploit remains, in unvarnished fact, as grim as a bullet wound and as glamorous as a prison sentence. And old-school racism of the virulent and hateful variety, unafraid of its own shadow, rears its unwelcome head in posh uptown boulevards, leafy suburban lanes, and gritty ghetto alleyways alike more than occasionally. Post-racism couldn't exist without these stark examples of plain and unadulterated racism to refer to.

This makes the fight for social justice an exercise in discretion as well as valor. Post-racism is an inevitable and in some ways positive development. In a sense, it's a reaction to the stilted and dogmatic conventions of political correctness, one of the few ways most people can work through racial issues with some semblance of candor. It's not the same as old-school racism. It's not as destructive, not as mean-spirited, not as crude, and not as blameworthy. But it isn't exactly a great big hug and a kiss either. Sometimes it can look an awful lot like racism of the pre–civil rights era vintage. We need to continue to confront and resist old-school racism with as much resolve as ever. And we should exploit post-racism's potential to underscore issues that polite society would as soon ignore, but we must also be on guard against its tendency to echo old prejudices in deceptively ironic tones.

Post-racism is an inexact term. But it's a useful catchphrase for the ambiguous examples of bigotry that I've addressed in this book. Post-racism has emerged because legal rules and social norms against overt prejudice have succeeded. Black entertainers can afford to flirt with racial stereotypes because social activists, civil rights lawyers, and brave ordinary citizens have made it anathema to advance those stereotypes seriously. Because working people like Rosa Parks risked all to stand up to unabashed bigots who were backed by social convention and the force of law, celebrities such as Oprah Winfrey and Jay-Z have the luxury of complaining of minor and ambiguous slights from professional snobs. Because earlier generations had the guts to call racism by its name when the shape of society depended on their actions, professional intellectuals can now write books about playing the race card with the comfort of tenure and air-conditioned offices at elite universities. We all stand on the shoulders of, if not giants, then people who met admirably the challenges they faced at a moment in history that demanded much more of them that ours does of us.

We owe it to them and their legacy to at least meet the milder—if more subtle—challenges of our day. I think that debt requires more from us than simply to follow in their footsteps. We need to advance the civil rights agenda by tailoring it to fit the circumstances of today. The civil rights movement succeeded not only in the United States federal courts but also in the courts of public opinion. The reason I can typically expect courteous service and fair treatment, when my parents forty years ago often suffered deliberate rudeness and calculated injustice, is not only that I can sue for certain racial offenses but also that most people genuinely wish to avoid giving them.

People who "play the race card" opportunistically and with intentional deceit are the enemies of truth, social harmony, and social justice. All decent and honest people must join in condemning such people and their libelous claims. The race card can undermine popular support for racial justice. Every person who faces an undeserved accusation of racism is a potential future skeptic of all claims of racism. If too many people come to believe, as did the blogger I quoted in the Introduction, that the serious charge of racism has become a ploy used for undeserved advantage, the antiracist goodwill we currently enjoy may give way to a pervasive attitude of cynical indifference. It is obvious for this reason alone that no one who claims to be a friend of racial justice—to say nothing yet of justice generally—should deliberately play the race card. And those who know better should abandon the barracks mentality that keeps us silent or complicit with such opportunistic accusations of bias.

But most of the examples I have examined in this book—and most of the cases we'll encounter in the world—don't involve such intentional deception for gain. They involve disagreement over the interpretation of ambiguous facts and over contested goals. I'm sure that some of the conflicts I explored in this book involved plain and simple bigotry. But it is hard to be sure that any *specific* case did. Many of the conflicts I've examined involved clear instances of racial injustice, but they didn't necessarily involve blameworthy racists. When a black person can't get a cab, that's a racial injustice, even if the cabdrivers who pass her by are motivated by an understandable desire to avoid the inconveniently distant and crime-plagued neighborhoods that blacks disproportionately inhabit. When even the most success-ful and influential black woman must wonder whether a retail store is closed *to her* because of her race, that's a racial injus-tice, even if the store was really just closing for the day. When black motorists or Muslim air travelers are targeted to be stopped, searched, and questioned by law enforcement, that's a racial in-justice, even if the police have sound reasons to consider race when choosing whom to stop and question.

These more ambiguous cases call for close judgment calls and nuanced arguments that our sound-bite society doesn't easily accommodate. But we need to try. It would help to keep the necessary conversation civil and constructive if people weren't so quick to cry "bigot" under these circumstances. And it would also help if people weren't so quick to condemn controversial but plausible claims of bigotry as cases of playing the race card. Honest disagreement can lead to dialogue and reconciliation, but both the charge of bigotry and that of playing the race card leave no room for persuasion or holding one's peace—they are attacks on character and integrity and must either be pressed to a conclusion or recanted and apologized for. Or—most often of all—they remain, unresolved and unrelinquished, to rub and nee-dle and cut into goodwill and peace of mind, like a bullet lodged where surgeons dare not probe. This book, then, is an attempt to perform some risky but needed invasive surgery and a call for, if not bilateral disarmament, then greater caution and more careful aim.

Law professor Patricia Williams describes certain racial injus-tices as "spirit murder" in order to emphasize the severity of the psychological injury suffered by their victims. Others have taken Williams's evocative phrase further, and more literally, perhaps, than Williams intended, suggesting that we treat racial injuries as crimes and impose criminal penalties on putative racists (but I doubt that these zealous advocates would support extending the corresponding presumption of innocence and procedural protections that criminal defendants enjoy).

I propose just the opposite approach. We should begin by looking at racial injustice as a social problem to be solved collectively rather than as a series of discrete wrongs perpetrated by bad people. We should discuss the more ambiguous cases of bias in the cool tone of technical expertise rather than in the heated cadence of moral judgment. Suppose we reserved the moral condemnation that typically accompanies the word "racism" for clear cases of bigotry, and we thought of the more complex and nuanced problems in the way we think of, say, air pollution, rather than in the way we think of rape or murder. Air pollution, like racism, is a dire problem that demands immediate and sustained attention. And as is true with racism, there are people who are responsible for air pollution; in fact almost everyone is responsible for it to some extent (to cite the results of the Implicit Association Test and to quote from the Broadway musical *Avenue Q*, everyone's a little bit racist). We've inherited our bad habits, from casual stereotyping to segregated neighborhoods, and changing them will require ingenuity, effort, and personal sacrifice. Most people aren't really culpable, even if we all contribute to the problem. *I* didn't choose to design American cities around the private car rather than the streetcar. Given the cities we have, who can blame me for driving half an hour every day to and from work? *I didn't own slaves or discriminate against blacks* goes the typical disclaimer of responsibility for persisting racial injustice; *who can blame me for living in an all-white neighborhood?*

I've argued throughout this book that residential segregation is perhaps the most severe unaddressed legacy of America's two centuries of unapologetic racism. Almost every social problem—crime, unemployment, even the response to natural disaster—is magnified because of it. It's natural to speak of segregation and its related injustices in terms of racism, but because "racism" implies the active and ongoing efforts of "racists," it's also misleading. We need language for discussing the persistent and destructive legacy of overt racism of the past that doesn't lay undeserved blame in the present.

Of course, some people are bigger polluters than others. The worst offenders deserve moral condemnation, whether their acts are deliberate or the result of careless disregard. On the other end of the moral spectrum, the most responsible citizens, through extraordinary effort, stop being part of the problem and become part of the solution. Some people compost, install solar energy collectors on their roofs, drive electric hybrid cars or cars that run on vegetable oil, or ride bikes. And some people make it a personal project to violate the unspoken color line that still divides our society and proves W.E.B. Du Bois a prophet. They seek out integrated neighborhoods, integrated schools, they take pains to resist racial stereotypes in their own minds and contest them when expressed by others. Such people have my warmest thanks. But the problem isn't, by and large, the result of bad people intentionally doing harm, and the solution won't be extraordinary people taking special pains to do good. The problem is the result of decent (but not saintly) people inadvertently doing harm because they don't know what else to do, or because doing something else is too much trouble. And the solution will be in changing the conditions and incentives that currently lead decent people to contribute, in their own small and often unintentional ways, to the problem.

Shrill moral condemnation won't help to change such habitual behavior. But smart policy can. Some changes can simply be imposed by legislation. We can make employers think twice about policies that effectively screen racial minorities from the workforce, just as we make manufacturers install catalytic converters on new cars. When such laws are well considered and not overly burdensome, they tend to meet with widespread acceptance. A few crackpots still gripe about catalytic converters and unleaded gas, but most people accept them as reasonable attempts to reduce pollution. Perhaps the time has come for a similar unsentimental and pragmatic approach to the types of racial injustice I've called racism without racists.

This approach would suggest that in the effort to eliminate racism, we face clear trade-offs of costs and benefits, just as we do in reducing pollution. The most severe injustices should get the most immediate attention. No one should have to suffer blatant racism, even if his wealth and social status suggest that he can easily shrug it off. Here unequivocal moral condemnation is appropriate. But more ambiguous injuries demand a coolheaded pragmatism. Ghetto segregation should take precedence over "retail discrimination." Katrina victims searching for housing and jobs come first; Hollywood celebrities searching for designer bags and vintage champagne come later (if at all). Pragmatism not only directs scarce resources where they will do the most good; it also takes into account the need for public support and goodwill, which can be eroded by a flood of frivolous and trivial claims. Wealth and privilege are no inoculation against the injuries of overt bigotry, which deserves consistent condemnation. But the spectacle of pampered celebrities and privileged tycoons complaining that conditions most of us face every day can only be the result of "bias" when *they* encounter them is off-putting to average, struggling people of all races.

There's something unseemly about complaining that the red carpet wasn't rolled out quickly enough, when most people are stuck on the wrong side of the velvet rope. This doesn't mean that you should care about bias only when the victims are worse off than you are, but at some point the perks of wealth and power overwhelm any possible disadvantage suffered because of bigotry or chauvinism. And most of the bias that relatively privileged minorities face is indirectly caused by the dire conditions endured by the underclass: if we reduce racial segregation and poverty, many of the negative racial stereotypes and associations that lead to discrimination will shrink along with them.

The pragmatic approach to ambiguous claims of bias should extend to "racism-by-analogy" claims. Basic civil rights against discrimination in housing and employment on the basis of sexual orientation should be a no-brainer: they promise profound benefits in terms of human dignity and life opportunities and will require only the cost of enforcement and the rejection of irrational aversion. I personally hope that the same goodwill and good sense that are leading more and more businesses and local governments to endorse such rights will eventually lead to widespread acceptance of same-sex marriage. But same-sex marriage doesn't *inevitably* follow: it poses distinctive questions for deeply held religious beliefs and traditional sex roles that must be addressed in their own right. Employers should treat all of their employees with sensitivity and compassion: decisions based on unexamined prejudices, favoritism, and spite keep many qualified people from reaching their full potential and deprive us all of their contributions. But it's far from clear that "discrimination" on the basis of looks, weight, grooming, or culture is the cause of much of the injustice in today's tough labor markets. Because government is often ill equipped to distinguish between irrational prejudice and valid, if subjective, evaluation, controlling unfairness in the labor market requires a difficult trade-off between job security and legitimate employer prerogatives.

If, when simple bigotry is not to blame, we are to substitute a pragmatic approach for the heated moral absolutism of rights talk, we must set clear and objective policy goals. It's not helpful to say we wish to eliminate "racism" when much of the racism we would eliminate has already occurred and had its ill effects. We can't undo the wrongs of the past: trying to imagine what any given neighborhood, profession, or individual would have been like "but for" racism is idle speculation. But we can work to achieve the type of world we'd like to inhabit or leave to our children. The now unfashionable civil rights ideal of integration had the distinctive virtue of suggesting such a concrete and practical goal. Tragically, ideologues from both the right and left wing have conspired to attack this sensible approach to racial justice—the right with a simplistic assault on "quotas" and the left with a romantic attachment to cultural difference and racial solidarity. Because the ideologues have captured the conversation, defenses of integration are rare today. But tough-minded pragmatism has always been a distinctive American virtue: I suspect we could take the conversation back from the ideologues if sensible people of conscience were willing to demand a serious discussion of racial justice.

Against the right-wing obsession with "quotas," we should acknowledge that numerical goals and standards are often uncontroversial and cost-effective ways to measure progress and evaluate performance. Those who resist such probative—if imperfect—measures are usually those who wish to avoid having their progress measured and their performance evaluated.

The law currently allows plaintiffs in discrimination lawsuits to point to a disparity between the racial composition of the local labor pool and that of an employer's workforce as evidence of unlawful discrimination. It makes sense to use such demographic statistics as a rough benchmark, both to root out hidden or inadvertent discriminatory practices and to encourage integration. A more aggressive approach might bypass individual lawsuits and impose administrative fines for repeated failures to meet integration benchmarks—just as businesses are now fined for failure to meet pollution reduction targets. Unlike a judgment in a civil rights lawsuit, such fines wouldn't have to carry the moral stigma of racism; instead, we could see them as more mundane incentives, like those routinely used to encourage environmentally responsible behavior.

A pragmatic use of numerical benchmarks could help defendants as well as plaintiffs. For instance, consider the bottom-line defense to disparate impact liability that the Supreme Court rejected in *Connecticut v. Teal.* A pragmatic approach would allow this defense: A practice that produces a racially integrated workforce can't be a vehicle for discriminatory prejudice, and when prejudice isn't at work, the bottom line of integration is what's important. As long as an employer winds up with an integrated workforce, *how* it does so should be up to the employer—not the government. It's likely that many employers would prefer specific and verifiable requirements rather than what they perceive as a capricious system that constantly threatens embarrassing and costly discrimination lawsuits challenging innocent or defensible personnel decisions.

Against left-wing multiculturalists, we should insist that some degree of cultural assimilation is indispensable to any effective social and economic integration. Typically, when critics of integration complain that integration implies "coerced assimilation," its defenders, backs to the ideological wall, insist that it needn't. But it's a disingenuous defense. Integration *does* imply assimilation, and not simply as an unintended side effect: assimilation is a big part of the *point* of integration, as the Court in *Brown v. Board of Education* well understood. When one examines the cultural norms of segregated ghettos, whether through the caricatures of "gangsta rap" or through the careful study of such sociologists as William Julius Wilson, it seems clear that some degree of acculturation to mainstream cultural norms would be a welcome development. Assimilation has a dirty past, as the melodramatic alias "cultural genocide" would suggest, but it is an indispensable part of any broader project of national integration and solidarity. The radical multiculturalist insists that if assimilation will make greater demands on racial minorities than on whites, it must be summarily rejected as discriminatory. But the pragmatist would ask whether the unequal demands of assimilation are more or less severe than the likely alternatives. Racial minorities—especially the poor racial minorities most likely to display racially distinctive affectations and behavior—suffer *today* because society has abandoned any serious effort to integrate them into the prosperous mainstream. Will they suffer more or less if they are offered the chance to join the mainstream and offered incentives to conform to mainstream expectations?

Finally, a pragmatic approach would not only examine racial injustice as a discrete problem in and of itself, but also as, in part, a symptom of larger social evils. The proliferation of new claims of bias suggests a pervasive social unease and insecurity that affects millions of Americans. Improved job security and a social safety net (here I heartily endorse the usual proposals: better unemployment insurance, universal health care) could reduce the fear that the letters on a pink slip will spell "disaster."

While an attempt to expand the category of actionable discrimination treats these problems as discrete cases of exceptional bigotry, a pragmatic approach might address the economic conditions that underlie them. Just as a WPA program for the ghetto would advance racial justice and color-blind economic equity simultaneously, a renewed commitment to job security and universal health care would reduce unjustified terminations for all employees and take some of the sting out of those unfair firings that will inevitably occur.

My account of the racial conflicts I've discussed may strike some readers as overly optimistic. Given the long, sorry history of American racism, isn't it safer to assume that ambiguous cases involve hidden bigotry? I don't think so. Today racism is socially, as well as legally, unacceptable: for most businesses the biggest cost of a claim of racism isn't the legal liability—it's the bad publicity. This means that a lot of people sincerely abhor racism, and presumably those people would also seek to avoid it for their own part—not just because they're afraid of getting sued, but because they sincerely believe that racism is wrong. This reflects a profound change in social values. Given this change in attitudes, it's not overly optimistic to reserve judgment in the ambiguous cases. Unfortunately, in today's environment, reserving judgment usually means doing nothing. I suspect many people make accusations of racism because that seems to be the only way to draw attention to severe social injustices. But it shouldn't be. A pragmatic approach would address racial injustices and promote racial integration whether or not a culpable perpetrator was available to take the blame.

Optimism has always been a necessary part of the civil rights struggle. When black families willingly sent their children to some of the South's first integrated schools in the 1950s, they must have been optimistic enough to believe—against much of their immediate experience—that white racism would eventually yield to common human decency. Enough in our nation's subsequent history has proven those courageous families right to justify continued optimism.

No doubt some readers will wish to ask whether I really think playing the race card is now the biggest racial justice issue this society faces. No, I don't. I hope it's clear that I believe old-school bigotry remains a severe social problem and that subtler and systemic racial disadvantages—even when they can't be blamed on "racists"—are profound social evils that demand redress. These are bigger problems than playing the race card. But the race card is an impediment to dealing with these problems. It distracts attention from larger social injustices. It encourages vindictiveness and provokes defensiveness when open-mindedness and sympathy are needed. It leads to an adversarial, tit-for-tat mind-set ("You're a bigot!" "No, *you're* just playing the race card!") when a cooperative spirit of dialogue is required.

The race card is symptomatic of a real crisis in the way we currently think and talk about race: a crisis borne of our failure to keep up with a changing social world, a crisis of social change and of intellectual stasis. We need new intellectual tools and new language to deal with the new realities of American racism. Thus far we've failed to develop them, so we find ourselves increasingly unable to discuss issues of race intelligently and convincingly. We find ourselves listening to and repeating the slogans and catch-phrases of the past, whether or not they apply, like a catechism that's long since lost its power to evoke or inspire, or like a curse that damns guilty perpetrator and innocent bystander with indiscriminate contempt.

■ NOTES

INTRODUCTION: PLAYING THE RACE CARD

1. The following account is derived primarily from the grand jury report in *Pagones v. Maddox, Mason and Sharpton* (1988).
2. William Saletan, Ben Jacobs, and Avi Zenilman, "The Worst of Al Sharpton," *Slate*, September 8, 2003, www.slate.com/id/2087557; Patricia Williams, *The Alchemy of Race and Rights* (1991), 172.
3. Saletan et al., "The Worst of Al Sharpton."
4. "Brawley to Get Muslim Name," *New York Times*, October 11, 1998, B3.
5. Ibid.
6. Senate Judiciary Committee, *Hearing on the Nomination of Clarence Thomas to the Supreme Court*, September 17, 1991, morning session.
7. Williams, *Alchemy of Race*, 170.

8. "The O.J. Verdict," interview with Michael Eric Dyson, *Frontline*, March 21, 2005, www.pbs.org/wgbh/pages/frontline/oj/interviews/dyson.html.

9. Gideon Rachman, "Bubbles and Bling," *The Economist*, Summer 2006, www.economist.com/intelligentlife/luxury/displayStory.cfm?story_id=6905921.

10. PR Newswire, "Hip-Hip Community to Boycott Cristal," June 14, 2006.

11. Howard Schuman, Charlotte Steeh, Lawrence D. Bobo, and Maria Krysan, "Racial Attitudes in America: Trends and Interpretations" (1998).

ONE: RACISM WITHOUT RACISTS

1. This account is a summary of the *Hannity & Colmes* program of September 6, 2005, www.foxnews.com/story/0,2933,168684,00.html. Italicized phrases are my additions. Passages in quotations are verbatim.

2. Jacob Weisberg, "An Imperfect Storm: How Race Shaped Bush's Response to Katrina," www.slate.com/id/2125812.

3. Eric Lipton, Christopher Drew, Scott Shane, and David Rohde, "Storm and Crisis: Government Assistance; Breakdowns Marked Path from Hurricane to Anarchy," *New York Times,* September 11, 2005.

4. "Storm and Crisis," *New York Times*, September 11, 2005.

5. *Meet the Press*, NBC, September 4, 2005.

6. The Pew Research Center, "Two in Three Critical of Bush's Relief Efforts: Huge Racial Divide Over Katrina and Its Consequences," September 8, 2005, people-press.org/reports/display.php3?PageID=992.

7. Remi Kanazi, "Katrina Response Indicative of Racism," September, 8, 2005, www.aljazeera.com/me.asp?service_ID=9721.

8. Ibid.

9. Lara Jakes Jordan, "Katrina Victims Testify to Racism's Role," December 7, 2005, www.sfgate.com/cgi-bin/article.cgi?f=/n/a/2005/12/06/national/w141732S70.DTL.

10. Ibid.

11. Weisberg, "An Imperfect Storm."

12. Jack Shafer, "Don't Refloat: The Case Against Rebuilding the Sunken City of New Orleans," *Slate,* September 7, 2005, www.slate.com/id/2125810/#sb2125827 and www.slate.com/id/2125810/sidebar/2125827.

13. *New York Times Magazine,* February 5, 2006, 97.

14. "Houston, We May Have a Problem," Marketplace, American Public Radio, September 5, 2005; "Barbara Bush Calls Evacuees Better Off," *New York Times,* September 7, 2005 (emphasis mine).

15. Naomi Klein, "Let the People Rebuild New Orleans," *The Nation,* September 26, 2005, www.thenation.com/doc/20050926/klein.

16. "Nagin Apologizes for 'Chocolate' City Comments," CNN, January 18, 2006, www.cnn.com/2006/US/01/17/nagin.city.

17. Mike Davis, "Who Is Killing New Orleans?" *The Nation,* April 10, 2006, www.thenation.com/doc/20060410/davis.

18. Petula Dvorak, "Hurricane Victims Demand More Help," *Washington Post,* February 9, 2006, www.washingtonpost.com/wp-dyn/content/article/2006/02/08/AR2006020801826.html.

19. Kenneth T. Jackson, *Crabgrass Frontier: The Suburbanization of the United States* (1985), 278.

20. Henry Louis Gates, Jr., *Loose Canons* (1992) 147.

21. Cornel West, *Race Matters* (1993), x–xi.

22. George Kelling and Catherine Coles, *Fixing Broken Windows* (1998), 20.

23. Kit R. Roane, "Cabdrivers Punished Too Quickly in Crackdown, Lawyers Say," *New York Times,* November 15, 1999.

24. Schaller Consulting, "The Changing Face of Taxi and Limousine Drivers: U.S., Large States and Metro Areas and New York City," www.schallerconsult.com/taxi/taxidriversummary.htm.

25. Jack Trask, "Yellow Peril: Good Cabbies Are Being Punished by the TLC," *New York Press,* February 2001, vol. 14, issue 7.

26. Rudolph Giuliani, "Prohibiting Discrimination by Taxi Drivers," mayor's WINS address, November 14, 1999.

27. Richard Epstein, *Forbidden Grounds: The Case Against Employment Discrimination Laws* (1995).

28. Robin Givhan, "Oprah and the View from Outside Hermès' Paris Door," *Washington Post*, June 24, 2005.

29. Erin Texeira, "Minorities Empathize After Paris Boutique Clashes with Oprah," Associated Press, June 28, 2005.

30. Ibid.

31. Randall Kennedy, "Racial Equality in Public Accommodations," in *Legacies of the 1964 Civil Rights Act,* ed. B. Grofman (2000), 159, 161.

32. Patricia Williams, *The Alchemy of Race and Rights* (1991), 45–46.

33. Williams, *Alchemy*, 45.

34. Christopher Lasch, *The Culture of Narcissism* (1979), 125–26.

35. Tom Wolfe, *Radical Chic & Mau-Mauing the Flak Catchers* (1970), 119–20.

36. Ibid.

TWO: WILD CARD: RACISM BY ANALOGY

1. www.peta.org.

2. Brian Barry, *Culture and Equality: An Egalitarian Critique of Multiculturalism* (2002), 306.

3. Beth Landman, "Wagging the Dog, and a Finger," *New York Times*, May 14, 2006, Sec. 9, p. 6.

4. Combahee River Collective Statement, 1977, in *Black Men on Race, Gender and Sexuality*, ed. Devin Carbado (1999), 1 (emphasis mine).

5. Simone Sebastian and Tanya Schevitz, "Marriage Mania Grips S.F. As Gays Line Up for Licenses," *San Francisco Chronicle*, February 16, 2004.

6. Rachel Gordon, "S.F. Defies Law, Marries Gays," *San Francisco Chronicle*, February 13, 2004.

7. Jonathan Rauch, "Gay Marriage: Why It Is Good For Gays, Good for Straights, and Good for America," *New York Times Magazine*, March 3, 2004.

8. Andrew Sullivan, *Virtually Normal* (1996).

9. Gabriel Rotello, *Sexual Ecology* (1998).

10. Joe Garofoli, "Acceptance of Gay Marriage Growing in State: Many Blast Same-sex Unions—But Traffic a Bigger Problem They Say," *San Francisco Chronicle*, February 26, 2004.

11. Rachel Gordon, "S.F. Defies Law."

12. "Crushed Flyer Wins Obesity Payout," BBC News World Edition, October 21, 2002 (news.bbc.co.uk/2/hi/uk_news/wales/2346319.stm).

13. www.southwest.com/travel_center/cos_guidelines.html.

14 *Trina Blake v. Southwest Airlines* (E.D. Washington), Order Denying in Part and Granting in Part Southwest's Motion for Summary Judgment in CV-04-0118-EFS (2005). Litigation was ongoing as of this writing.

15. A jury found that Southwest Airlines did not discriminate on the basis of race. Kathy McCormack, "Jury Finds No Discrimination in Southwest Lawsuit," *New Hampshire Union Leader*, February 11, 2006, A1.

16. Dan Fitzpatrick, "Airline Making Heavy-set Flyers Buy Extra Seat," March 13, 2005, www.post-gazette.com/pg/05072/470035.stm.

17. Council on Size and Weight Discrimination, www.cswd.org.

18. Howard Gensler, "CORE, Fat People Have Issues with 'Idol' Too," *Philadelphia Daily News*, January 25, 2006.

19. Susan Flockhart, "The Big Issue," *Sunday Herald*, September 15, 2002.

20. Ibid.

21. Andrew Dannenberg, Deron C. Burton, and Richard J. Jackson, "Economic and Environmental Costs of Obesity: The Impact on Airlines," *American Journal of Preventative Medicine*, 27, no. 3.

22. Elizabeth Fernandez, "Teacher Says Fat, Fitness Can Mix," *San Francisco Chronicle*, February 24, 2002.

23. Jazzercise agreed to change its policy after mediation with the San Francisco Human Rights Commission under a San Francisco ordinance outlawing discrimination on the basis of height and weight. Elizabeth Fernandez, "Exercising Her Right to Work: Fitness Instructor Wins Weight-Bias Fight," May 7, 2002, www.sfgate.com/

cgi-bin/article.cgi?f=/c/a/2002/05/07/MN223501.DTL&hw= portnick+jazzercise&sn=002&sc=713).

24. "Sizing Up Weight Discrimination, Tolerance in the News," Southern Poverty Law Center website, www.tolerance.org/news/ article_tol.jsp?id=505.

25. Tom Wolfe, *The Purple Decades* (1987), 280.

26. Martha Grove, "Looks Won't Mean a Lot if Anti-Bias Law Is Approved," *Los Angeles Times*, January 24, 1992, 3.

27. Jane Adams, "California City Faces Raging Dress Code War," *Chicago Tribune*, February 16, 1992, C4.

28. Richard Paddock, "California Album: Santa Cruz Grants Anti-Bias Protection to the Ugly," *Los Angeles Times*, May 25, 1992, A3.

29. Adams, "California City."

30. Katheryn Bold, "Corporate Cleanup: That Well Groomed and Manicured Look at Many Orange County Tourist Spots Is No Accident: Dress Codes Make Sure Workers' Appearances Suit the Image," *Los Angeles Times*, May 9, 1996, E1.

31. Sources for this discussion: "Librarian Accused Harvard of Discrimination," Associated Press, March 21, 2005, www.msnbc.msn.com/ id/7259979; Robin Perguero, "Harvard Cleared of Discrimination," *The Harvard Crimson*, April 5, 2005.

32. Joseph Farah, "Job Bias Law Takes a Walk in Purple Zone," *Los Angeles Times*, February 7, 1992, B7.

33. Dipboye, Arvey, and Terpstra, "Sex and Physical Attractiveness of Raters and Applicants as Determinants of Resume Evaluations," 62 J. *Applied Psychology* (1977), 288, 293.

34. G. Patzer, *The Physical Attractiveness Phenomena* (1985), 109.

35. Jeff Biddle and David Hammermesh, "Lawyers, Looks and Lucre," National Bureau of Economic Research Working Paper 5366 (1995).

36. "Facial Discrimination: Extending Handicap Law to Employment Discrimination on the Basis of Physical Appearance," 100 *Harvard Law Review* Note 2035 (1987).

37. Grove, "Looks Won't Mean a Lot"; Paddock, "California Album."

38. *Renee Rogers et al. v. American Airlines, Inc.*, 527 F. Supp. 229 (1981).

39. Johanna Omelia and Michael Waddock, *Come Fly With Us: A Global History of the Airline Hostess* (2003), 90.

40. Elizabeth Rich, *Flying High: What It's Like to Be an Airline Stewardess* (1972), 76.

41. *Donohue v. Shoe Corp.*, 337 F. Supp. 1357 (C.D. Cal. 1972) (emphasis mine.)

42. Stephen G. Hirsch, "Santa Cruz Law Could Be Attacked for Vagueness," *American Lawyer*, January 17, 1992, 1.

43. Paul Sniderman, Thomas Piazza, Phillip Tetlock, and Ann Kendrick, "The New Racism," *American Journal of Political Science*, 35 (2): 423–47

44. Kurt Vonnegut, "Harrison Bergeron" (1961).

45. Kingsley Amis, *Lucky Jim* (1958).

46. *Hazen Paper Company v. Biggins*, 507 U.S. 604 (1993).

47. Thomas Peele, "Judge to Rule on Contempt Charges," *Contra Costa Times*, October 26, 2004.

48. The account that follows is a summary derived from the published opinion of the California Supreme Court in *Miller v. Department of Corrections*, 36 Cal. 4th 446 (2005).

49. "Rumors circulated among prison employees that Yamamoto and Brown were engaged in a relationship that was 'more than platonic.'" Ibid.

50. *Harris v. Forklift Systems*, 510 U.S. 17 (1993).

51. *DeCinto v. Westchester County Medical Center*, 807 F.2d 304 (2d Cir. 1986).

THREE: CALLING A SPADE A SPADE: DEFINING DISCRIMINATION

1. *Palmer v. Thompson*, 403 U.S. 217 (1971).

2. Thomas Barlett, "Irresistible Force," *Salon*, May 2004, dir.salon.com/story/ent/feature/2004/05/01/magnetic/index.html?pn=1.

3. www.sashafrerejones.com/2004/05/ gerrymandering_on_ice.html.

4. John Cook, "Blacklisted: Is Stephin Merritt a Racist Because He Doesn't Like Hip-hop?" *Slate*, May 9, 2006, www.slate.com/id/2141421.

5. Kenneth Turan, "Breaking No Ground," *Los Angeles Times*, March 5,

2006, theenvelope.latimes.com/awards/oscars/env-turan5mar05,0, 5359042.story.

6. Nikki Finke, "How Gay Will Oscar Go?" *L.A. Weekly*, February 1, 2006, www.laweekly.com/general/deadline-hollywood/how-gay-will-oscar-go/12564.

7. The theory of discriminatory effects or "disparate impact" endorsed by the Supreme Court in *Griggs* was first developed by the federal agency charged with enforcing Title VII: the Equal Employment Opportunities Commission (EEOC). The EEOC developed the disparate impact doctrine as an interpretation of Section 703 (h) of the Civil Rights Act, which authorizes "any professionally developed ability test . . . not designed, intended or used to discriminate because of race . . ." Section 703 (h) was the result of a delicate compromise designed to mollify conservative senators who worried that Title VII would require employers to hire unqualified minorities while also ensuring that employers could not use facially race-neutral criteria as proxies for race discrimination. But as the lower courts hearing the *Griggs* controversy demonstrated, the exact meaning of "designed, intended or used to discriminate" was obscure. The lower courts read this language to define a discrete state of mind: someone had to intentionally "design" or "use" the test to discriminate—a plausible reading since "discrimination" denotes an intentional mental process. But the EEOC and the Supreme Court read the language to encompass tests that were unintentionally "designed" or "used" to discriminate as well as those that were "intended" to do so. This was also a plausible reading, since otherwise the terms "designed" and "used" would be superfluous—the entire proscription would be described by the term "intended."

8. *Brown v. City of Oneonta*, 221 F.3d 329 (2d Cir. 2000).

9. See R. Richard Banks, "Race-Based Suspect Selection and Color-blind Equal Protection Doctrine and Discourse," 48 *UCLA L. Rev* 1075 (2001).

10. *Wilkins v. Maryland State Police*, Civil Action No. CCB93483, Maryland Federal District Court (1993).

11. *Gerald v. Oklahoma Department of Pub. Safety*, CIV-99-676-R, First Amended Complaint and Jury Demand, www.aclufl.org/legislature _courts/legal_department/briefs_complaints/geraldcomplaint.cfm; Ziva Credit, "Two Hour Search Yielded Nothing, ACLU Suit Says," *Tulsa World*, May 13, 2001, 8.; *Gerald v. Oklahoma Department of Pub. Safety*, CIV-99-676-R slip op. at 6 (W.D. Okla. Dec. 21, 1999) (the Department settled the case out of court for $75,000), www .racialprofilinganalysis.neu.edu/legislation/litigation.php?state =10.

12. *Maryland State Conference of NAACP Branches et al. v. Maryland State Police et al.*, CCB-98-1098, First Amended Complaint and Jury Demand; Debra Dickerson, "Racial Profiling: Are We All Really Equal in the Eyes of the Law?" *Los Angeles Times*, July 14, 2000. Litigation was ongoing as of this writing.

13. David Barstow and David Kocieniewski, "Records Show New Jersey Police Withheld Data on Race Profiling," *New York Times*, October 12, 2000.

14. *Police Practices and Civil Rights in New York City*, www.usccr.gov/ pubs/nypolice/ch5.htm; New York State Attorney General, "Stop and Frisk" Report, www.oag.state.ny.us/press/reports/stop_frisk/ ch5_part1.html.

15. "Racial Bias in CHP Searches," *San Francisco Chronicle*, July 15, 2001.

16. "Montgomery Traffic Data Show Race Disparity," *Washington Post*, November 2, 2001.

17. Robert D. McFadden, "Whitman Dismisses State Police Chief for Race Remarks," *New York Times*, March 1, 1999.

18. David Cole and John Lamberth, "The Fallacy of Racial Profiling," *New York Times*, May 13, 2001, A13.

19. U.S. General Accounting Office, "U.S. Customs Service: Better Targeting of Airline Passengers for Personal Searches Could Yield Better Results" (2000).

20. Randall Kennedy, *Race, Crime and the Law* (1998), 159.

21. *NewsHour*, PBS, September 26, 2001.

22. Michelle Malkin, "Racial Profiling: A Matter of Survival," *USA*

Today, August, 16, 2004, www.usatoday.com/news/opinion/editorials/2004-08-16-racial-profiling_x.htm.

23. Address of the President to the Joint Session of Congress, February 27, 2001, www.whitehouse.gov/news/releases/2001/02/20010228.html.

24. Norman Y. Mineta, Remarks for Arab Community Center for Economic and Social Services Gala Dinner, April 20, 2002, www.dot.gov/affairs/042002sp.htm.

25. Amnesty International, "Threat and Humiliation: Racial Profiling, Domestic Security and Human Rights in the United States," U.S. Domestic Human Rights Program, *Amnesty International Newsletter* 8 (2004).

26. *University of California Regents v. Bakke*, 438 U.S. 265 (1978).

27. *Grutter v. Bollinger*, 539 U.S. 306 (2003), 16–18.

28. Willie J. Epps Jr., *How to Get into Harvard Law School* (1996), 273.

29. Janice E. Hale-Benson, *Black Children, Their Roots, Culture, and Learning Styles* (1982), 42.

30. Jack Kerouac, *On the Road* (1957), 148–49.

31. Malcolm Gladwell, "Getting In: The Social Logic of Ivy League Admissions," *The New Yorker*, October 10, 2005.

32. Erik Eckholm, "Plight Deepens for Black Men, Studies Warn," *New York Times*, March 20, 2006.

FOUR: THE CLASH OF ENDS: CONTESTED GOALS

1. Nick Goldin, "Cornell Battles Anew Over Ethnic Dormitories," *New York Times*, May 1996, B5.

2. Derrick Bell, *And We Are Not Saved* (1987), 3.

3. *A Multiracial Society with Segregated Schools: Are We Losing the Dream?*, Civil Rights Project, Harvard University, January 2003.

4. Hugh Trevor-Roper, "The Highland Tradition of Scotland," in *The Invention of Tradition*, eds. Eric Hobsbawm and Terrence Ranger (1993), 23, 26.

5. Brian Barry, *Culture and Equality: An Egalitarian Critique of Multiculturalism* (2002), 260.

6. "School Colors," *Frontline*, PBS, first aired October 18, 1994.

7. Ibid., press kit, WGBH.

8. Ibid.

9. William Labov, testimony before the United States Senate Sub-committee on Labor, Health and Human Services and Education, January 23, 1997, www.ling.upenn.edu/~wlabov/L102/Ebonics_test.html.

10. *Aspria et al. v. Board of Education of the City of New York*, No. 72 Civ. 4002 (1975).

11. Rosalie Pedalino Porter, "The Case Against Bilingual Education," *The Atlantic Monthly*, May 1998.

12. Amy Pyle, "Latino Parents to Boycott School Bilingual Plan," *Los Angeles Times*, February 13, 1996.

13. Rosalie Pedalino Porter, "Twisted Tongues: The Failure of Bilingual Education," the Communitarian Network, 128.164.127.251/~ccps/pop_billing.htm (January 5, 2004).

14. Glenn Garvin, "Loco Completamente Loco: The Many Failures of 'Bilingual Education'" *Reason*, reason.com/9801/fe.garvin.shtml (January 5, 2004).

15. *Los Angeles Times*–CNN exit poll, "Profile of the Electorate," June 4, 1998.

16. Thomas Schelling, "Dynamic Models of Segregation," *Journal of Mathematical Sociology* 1 (July 1971); Schelling, "Models of Segregation," *American Economic Review* 59 (May 1969); Schelling, *Micromotives and Macrobehavior* (1978).

17. William Julius Wilson, *When Work Disappears* (1996), xvii.

18. Kenneth Jackson, *Crabgrass Frontier: The Suburbanization of the United States* (1985).

19. Nathan Glazer, *Impediments to Integration: The African American Predicament*, ed. Christopher H. Foreman, Jr. (1999).

20. William Julius Wilson, *When Work Disappears* (1997), 117, 120, 121.

21. The Brookings Institution, Metropolitan Policy Program, "From Poverty, Opportunity: Putting the Market to Work for Lower Income Families" (2006).

22. *Grutter v. Bollinger*, 539 U.S 306 (2003), 3.

FIVE: POST-RACISM: WHY THE RACE CARD
IS A CRISIS OF SUCCESS

1. Robert Merton, "Intermarriage and the Social Structure: Fact and Theory," *Psychiatry*, 1941, 4:361–74.

2. Defense Amended Offer of Proof re: Fuhrman Tapes, *People of the State of California v. Orenthal James Simpson*, August 22, 1995.

3. Alex Prud'homme, "Police Brutality!" *Time*, March 25, 1991; *Los Angeles Times*, March 28, 1988.

4. Mike Davis, *City of Quartz* (1991).

5. Lou Cannon, *Official Negligence: How Rodney King and the Riots Changed Los Angeles and the LAPD* (1998); Lori Leibovich, "Rethinking Rodney King," *Salon*, March 13, 1998, www.salon.com/news/1998/03/13news.html; Online NewsHour Forum: Author's Corner with Lou Cannon, April 7, 1998, www.pbs.org/newshour/authors_corner/jan-june98/cannon_4-7.html.

6. See Special Senate Task Force on a New Los Angeles, "New Initiatives for a New Los Angeles: Final Report and Recommendations" (1992); Melvin L. Oliver, James H. Johnson Jr., and David M. Grant, "Race, Urban Inequality and the Los Angeles Rebellion," in Craig Calhoun and George Ritzer, *Introduction to Social Problems* (1993), 727–753.

7. Jeffrey Toobin, "A Horrible Human Event," *The New Yorker*, October 23, 1995.

8. Ibid.

9. "The O.J. Verdict: How the Black Community Viewed O.J. and the Verdict," interview with Kerman Maddox, *Frontline*, October 4, 2005.

10. "The O.J Verdict," interview with Michael Eric Dyson, *Frontline*, March 21, 2005.

▪ BIBLIOGRAPHY

Adams, Jane. "California City Faces Raging Dress Code War." *Chicago Tribune*, February 16, 1992.

Address of the President to the Joint Session of Congress, February 27, 2001.

Amis, Kingsley. *Lucky Jim* (1958). Reprint. New York: Penguin, 1992.

Banks, Richard. "Race Based Suspect Selection and Colorblind Equal Protection Doctrine and Discourse." *UCLA Law Review* 48 (2001): 1075.

"Barbara Bush Calls Evacuees Better Off," *New York Times*, September 7, 2005.

Barlett, Thomas. "Irresistible Force," *Salon*, May 2004 (dir.salon.com/story/ent/feature/2004/05/01/magnetic/index.html?pn=1).

Barry, Brian. *Culture and Equality: An Egalitarian Critique of Multiculturalism*. Cambridge, Mass.: Harvard University Press, 2001.

Barstow, David, and David Kocieniewski. "Records Show New Jersey Police Withheld Data on Race Profiling," *New York Times*, October 12, 2000.

Bell, Derrick. *And We Are Not Saved*. New York: Basic Books, 1987.

———. *Silent Covenants: Brown v. Board of Education and the Unfulfilled Hopes for Racial Reform*. New York: Oxford University Press, 2004.

Biddle, Jeff, and David Hammermesh. "Lawyers, Looks and Lucre." NBER Working Paper 5366, 1995.

Bold, Katheryn. "Corporate Cleanup: That Well Groomed and Manicured Look at Many Orange County Tourist Spots Is No Accident: Dress Codes Make Sure Workers' Appearances Suit the Image." *Los Angeles Times*, May 9, 1996, pt. E.

Brown v. Board of Education of Topeka, 347 U.S. 483 (1954).

Brown v. City of Oneonta, 221 F.3d. 329 (2d Cir. 2000).

Cannon, Lou. *Official Negligence: How Rodney King and the Riots Changed Los Angeles and the LAPD*. New York: Times Books, 1997.

Cole, David, and John Lamberth. "The Fallacy of Racial Profiling." *New York Times*, May 13, 2001, A13.

Combahee River Collective Statement, 1977. In *Black Men on Race, Gender and Sexuality*, edited by Devin Carbado. New York: NYU Press, 1999.

Connecticut v. Teal, 457 U.S. 440 (1992).

Cook, John. "Blacklisted: Is Stephin Merrit a Racist Because He Doesn't Like Hip-hop?" *Slate*, May 9, 2006 (www. slate.com/id/ 2141421).

Credit, Ziva. "Two Hour Search Yielded Nothing, ACLU Suit Says." *Tulsa World*, May 13, 2001.

"Crushed Flyer Wins Obesity Payout." BBC News World Edition, October 21, 2002 (news.bbc.co.uk/2/hi/uk_news/wales/ 2346319.stm).

Dannenberg, Andrew, Deron C. Burton, and Richard J. Jackson. "Economic and Environmental Costs of Obesity: The Impact on Airlines." *American Journal of Preventative Medicine* 27:264.

Davis, Mike. *City of Quartz*. London: Verso, 1991.

————. "Who Is Killing New Orleans?" *The Nation*, April 10, 2006 (www.thenation.com/doc/20060410/davis).

Defense Amended Offer of Proof re: Fuhrman Tapes. *People of the State of California v. Orenthal James Simpson*, August 22, 1995.

Dickerson, Debra. "Racial Profiling: Are We All Really Equal in the Eyes of the Law?" *Los Angeles Times*, July 14, 2000.

Dipboye, R., R. Arvey, and D. Terpstra. "Sex and Physical Attractiveness of Raters and Applicants as Determinants of Resume Evaluations." *Journal of Applied Psychology* 62 (1997): 288, 293.

Dvorak, Petula. "Hurricane Victims Demand More Help." *Washington Post*, February 9, 2006 (www.washingtonpost.com/wp-dyn/content/article/2006/02/08/AR2006020801826.html).

Eckholm, Erik. "Plight Deepens for Black Men, Studies Warn." *New York Times*, March 20, 2006.

Epps, Willie J. Jr. *How to Get into Harvard Law School*. New York: McGraw-Hill, 1996.

Epstein, Richard. *Forbidden Grounds: The Case Against Employment Discrimination Laws*. Reprint. Cambridge, Mass.: Harvard University Press, 1995.

Farah, Joseph. "Job Bias Law Takes a Walk in Purple Zone." *Los Angeles Times*, February 7, 1992.

Fellowes, Matt. "From Poverty, Opportunity: Putting the Market to Work for Lower Income Families." Metropolitan Policy Program, Brookings Institution, July 2006.

Fernandez, Elizabeth. "Exercising Her Right to Work: Fitness Instructor Wins Weight-Bias Fight." *San Francisco Chronicle*, May 7, 2002.

————. "Teacher Says Fat, Fitness Can Mix." *San Francisco Chronicle*, February 24, 2002.

Finke, Nikki. "How Gay Will Oscar Go?" *L.A. Weekly*, February 1, 2006 (www.laweekly.com/general/deadline-hollywood/how-gay-will-oscar-go/12564).

Fitzpatrick, Dan. "Airline Making Heavy-set Flyers Buy Extra Seat." *Pittsburgh Post-Gazette*, March 13, 2005 (www.post-gazette.com/pg/05072/470035.stm).

Flockhart, Susan. "The Big Issue," *Sunday Herald*, September 15, 2002.

Frankenberg, Erica, Chungmei Lee, and Gary Orfield. "A Multiracial Society with Segregated Schools: Are We Losing the Dream?" Civil Rights Project, Harvard University, January 2003.

Garofoli, Joe. "Acceptance of Gay Marriage Growing in State: Many Blast Same-Sex Unions—But Traffic a Bigger Problem, They Say." *San Francisco Chronicle*, February 26, 2004.

Garvin, Glenn. "Loco, Completamente Loco: The Many Failures of 'Bilingual Education.'" *Reason*, January 1998 (reason.com/9801/fe.garvin.shtml).

Gates, Henry Louis Jr. *Loose Canons*. New York: Oxford University Press, 1992.

Gensler, Howard. "CORE, Fat People Have Issues With 'Idol' Too." *Philadelphia Daily News*, January 25, 2006.

Gerald v. Oklahoma Department of Public Safety, CIV-99-676-R, First Amended Complaint and Jury Demand.

Gerald v. Oklahoma Department of Public Safety, CIV-99-676-R, Slip Op. at 6 (W.D. Okla., Dec. 21, 1999).

Giuliani, Rudolph. "Prohibiting Discrimination by Taxi Drivers." Mayor's WINS address, November 14, 1999 (www.nyc.gov/html/records/rwg/html/99b/me991114.html).

Givhan, Robin. "Oprah and the View From Outside Hermès' Paris Door." *Washington Post*, June 24, 2005.

Gladwell, Malcolm. "Getting In: The Social Logic of Ivy League Admissions." *The New Yorker*, October 10, 2005.

Glazer, N. "Impediments to Integration." In *The African American Predicament*, edited by Christopher H. Foreman, Jr. Washington, D.C.: Brookings Institution Press, 1999.

Goldin, Nick. "Cornell Battles Anew Over Ethnic Dormitories." *New York Times*, May 6, 1996, B5.

Gordon, Rachel. "S.F. Defies Law, Marries Gays." *San Francisco Chronicle*, February 13, 2004.

Granovetter, Mark. *Getting a Job: A Study of Contacts and Careers*. Chicago: University of Chicago Press, 1995.

Griggs v. Duke Power Co., 401 U.S. 424 (1971).

Grove, Martha. "Looks Won't Mean a Lot if Anti-Bias Law Is Approved." *Los Angeles Times*, January 24, 1992, 3.

Grutter v. Bollinger, 539 U.S. 306 (2003).

Hale-Benson, Janice E. *Black Children, Their Roots, Culture and Learning Styles*. Provo, Utah: Brigham Young University Press, 1982.

Hannity & Colmes, September 6, 2005 (www.foxnews.com/story/ 0,2933,168684,00.html).

Hearing of the Senate Judiciary Committee. Subject: The Nomination of Clarence Thomas to the Supreme Court, September 17, 1991, morning session.

"Hip-Hip Community to Boycott Cristal," PR Newswire, June 14, 2006.

Hirsch, Stephen G. "Santa Cruz Law Could be Attacked for Vagueness." *American Lawyer*, January 17, 1992.

"Houston, We May Have a Problem," *Marketplace*, American Public Media, September 5, 2005.

Jackson, Kenneth T. *Crabgrass Frontier: The Suburbanization of the United States*. New York: Oxford University Press, 1985.

Jordan, Lara Jakes. "Katrina Victims Testify to Racism's Role." *San Francisco Chronicle*, December 7, 2005 (www.sfgate.com/cgi-bin/ article.cgi?f=/n/a/2005/12/06/national/w141732S70.DTL).

Kanazi, Remi. "Katrina Response Indicative of Racism." *Aljazeera Magazine*, September 8, 2005 (www.aljazeera.com/me.asp?service_ID =9721).

Kelling, George, and Catherine Coles. *Fixing Broken Windows*. Reprint. New York: Free Press, 1998.

Kennedy, Randall. *Race, Crime and the Law*. Reprint. New York: Vintage, 1998.

———. "Racial Equality in Public Accommodations." In *Legacies of the 1964 Civil Rights Act*, edited by Bernard Grofman. Charlottesville: University of Virginia Press, 2000.

Kerouac, Jack. *On the Road* (1957). Reprint. New York: Penguin, 1976.

Klein, Naomi. "Let the People Rebuild New Orleans." *The Nation*, September 26, 2005 (www.thenation.com/doc/20050926/klein).

Labov, William. Testimony before the United States Senate Subcommittee on Labor, Health and Human Services and

Education, January 23, 1997 (www.ling.upenn.edu/~wlabov/
L102/Ebonics_test.html).

Landman, Beth. "Wagging the Dog, and a Finger." *New York Times*,
May 14, 2006, sec. 9.

Lasch, Christopher. *The Culture of Narcissism*. Reprint. New York:
Warner Books, 1979.

Leibovich, Lori. "Rethinking Rodney King." *Salon*, March 13, 1998
(www.salon.com/news/1998/03/13news.html).

"Librarian Accused Harvard of Discrimination." Associated Press,
March 21, 2005 (www.msnbc.msn.com/id/7259979).

Lipton, Eric, Christopher Drew, Scott Shane, and David Rohde.
"Storm and Crisis: Government Assistance; Breakdowns Marked
Path from Hurricane to Anarchy," *New York Times*, September 11,
2005.

Los Angeles Times–CNN Poll. "Exit Poll: Profile of the Electorate,"
June 4, 1998.

Malkin, Michelle. "Racial Profiling: A Matter of Survival." *USA Today*,
August 16, 2004 (www.usatoday.com/news/opinion/editorials/
2004-08-16-racial-profiling_x.htm)

McDonnell Douglas v. Green, 411 U.S. 792 (1973).

McFadden, Robert D. "Whitman Dismisses State Police Chief for
Race Remarks." *New York Times*, March 1, 1999.

Merton, Robert. "Intermarriage and the Social Structure: Fact and
Theory." *Psychiatry* 4:361 (1941).

Mineta, Norman Y. Remarks for Arab Community Center for
Economic and Social Services Gala Dinner, April 20, 2002
(www.dot.gov/affairs/042002sp.htm).

"Montgomery Traffic Data Show Race Disparity." *Washington Post*,
November 2, 2001.

"Nagin Apologizes for 'Chocolate' City Comments." *CNN*,
January 18, 2006 (www.cnn.com/2006/US/01/17/nagin.city).

New York State Attorney General. "Stop and Frisk: Report"
(www.oag.state.ny.us/press/reports/stop_frisk/ch5_part1.html).

"Official Negligence: Lou Cannon Dissects the Rodney King Case and the L.A. Riots." Online News Hour Forum, April 7, 1998, (www.pbs.org/newshour/authors_corner/jan–june98/cannon_4–7.html).

"The O.J. Verdict." Interview with Michael Eric Dyson, *Frontline*, March 21, 2005 (www.pbs.org/wgbh/pages/frontline/oj/interviews/dyson.html).

Omelia, Johanna, and Michael Waddock. *Come Fly with Us! A Global History of the Airline Hostess*. Portland, Ore.: Collectors Press, 2003.

Paddock, Richard. "California Album: Santa Cruz Grants Anti-Bias Protection to the Ugly." *Los Angeles Times*, May 25, 1992, A3.

Palmer v. Thompson, 403 U.S. 2167 (1971).

Patzer, G. *The Physical Attractiveness Phenomena*. New York: Plenum Press, 1985.

Peele, Thomas. "Judge to Rule on Contempt Charges." *Contra Costa Times*, October 26, 2004.

Peguero, Robin M. "Harvard Cleared of Discrimination." *Harvard Crimson*, April 5, 2005.

"Police Practices and Civil Rights in New York City," chapter 5 (www.usccr.gov/pubs/nypolice/ch5.htm).

Porter, Rosalie Pedalino. "The Case Against Bilingual Education," *Atlantic Monthly*, May 1998.

———. "Twisted Tongues: The Failure of Bilingual Education." Communitarian Network, January 5, 2004 (128.164.127.251/~ccps/pop_billing.htm).

Price Waterhouse v. Hopkins, 490 U.S. 228 (1989)

"Profile of a Terrorist," *NewsHour with Jim Lehrer*, Newshour, September 26, 2001.

Prud'homme, Alex. "Police Brutality!" *Time*, March 25, 1991.

Pyle, Amy. "Latino Parents to Boycott School Bilingual Plan." *Los Angeles Times*, February 13, 1996.

Rachman, Gideon. "Bubbles and Bling." *The Economist*, Summer 2006 (www.economist.com/intelligentlife/luxury/displayStory.cfm?story_id=6905921).

"Racial Bias in CHP Searches," *San Francisco Chronicle*, July 15, 2001.

Rauch, Jonathan. "Gay Marriage: Why It Is Good for Gays, Good for Straights, and Good for America." *New York Times Magazine*, March 3, 2004.

Regents of the University of California v. Bakke, 438 U.S. 265 (1978).

Rich, Elizabeth. *Flying High: What It's Like to Be an Airline Stewardess.* Rev. ed. New York: Stein & Day, 1972.

Roane, Kit R. "Cabdrivers Punished Too Quickly in Crackdown, Lawyers Say." *New York Times*, November 15, 1999.

Rotello, Gabriel. *Sexual Ecology*. Reprint. New York: Plume, 1998.

Saletan, William, Ben Jacobs, and Avi Zenilman. "The Worst of Al Sharpton." *Slate*, September 8, 2003 (www.slate.com/id/2087557).

Schaller Consulting, "The Changing Face of Taxi and Limousine Drivers: U.S., Large States and Metro Areas and New York City" (www.schallerconsult.com/taxi/taxidriversummary.htm).

Schelling, Thomas. "Dynamic Models of Segregation." *Journal of Mathematical Sociology* 1 (July 1971).

———. *Micromotives and Macrobehavior* (1978). Revised. New York: Norton, 2006.

———. "Models of Segregation." *American Economic Review* 59 (May 1969): 488.

Schuman, Howard, Charlotte Steeh, Lawrence Bobo, and Maria Kysan. *Racial Attitudes in America: Trends and Interpretations*. Revised. Cambridge, Mass.: Harvard University Press, 1998.

"School Colors." *Frontline*, October 18, 1994.

Sebastian, Simone, and Tanya Schevitz, "Marriage Mania Grips S.F. as Gays Line Up for Licenses." *San Francisco Chronicle*, February 16, 2004.

Shafer, Jack. "Don't Refloat: The Case Against Rebuilding the Sunken City of New Orleans." *Slate*, September 7, 2005 (www.slate.com/id/2125810/#sb2125827 and www.slate.com/id/2125810/sidebar/2125827/).

"Sizing Up Weight-Based Discrimination." Southern Poverty Law Center (www.tolerance.org/news/article_tol.jsp?id=505).

Sniderman, Paul, Thomas Piazza, Phillip Tetlock, and Ann Kendrick.

"The New Racism" *American Journal of Political Science* 35(2):423–47.

St. Mary's Honor Center v. Hicks, 509 U.S. 502 (1993).

Sullivan, Andrew. *Virtually Normal*. Reprint. New York: Vintage, 1996.

Texeira, Erin. "Minorities Empathize After Paris Boutique Clashes with Oprah." Associated Press, June 28, 2005.

"Threat and Humiliation: Racial Profiling, Domestic Security and Human Rights in the United States." Amnesty International, U.S. Domestic Human Rights Program Report, September 2004.

Toobin, Jeffrey. "A Horrible Human Event." *The New Yorker*, October 23, 1995.

Trask, Jack. "Yellow Peril: Good Cabbies Are Being Punished by the TLC." *New York Press* 14 (February 14, 2001): 7.

Trevor-Roper, Hugh. "The Highland Tradition of Scotland." In *The Invention of Tradition*, edited by Eric Hobsbawm and Terrence Ranger. Reprint. Cambridge: Canto/Cambridge University Press, 1993.

Trina Blake v. Southwest Airlines (E.D. Washington), Order Denying in Part and Granting in Part Southwest's Motion for Summary Judgment in CV-04-0118-EFS (2005).

Turan, Kenneth. "Breaking No Ground." *Los Angeles Times*, March 5, 2006 (theenvelope.latimes.com/awards/oscars/env-turan5mar05,0,5359042.story).

"Two in Three Critical of Bush's Relief Efforts: Huge Racial Divide over Katrina and Its Consequences." Pew Research Center, September 8, 2005 (people-press.org/reports/display.php3?PageID=992).

U.S. General Accounting Office. "U.S. Customs Service: Better Targeting of Airline Passengers for Personal Searches Could Yield Better Results." Report to the Honorable Richard J. Durbin, U.S. Senate, March 17, 2000.

Vonnegut, Kurt. "Harrison Bergeron" (1961). In *Welcome to the Monkey House*. Reprint. New York: Bantam, 1991.

Weisberg, Jacob, "An Imperfect Storm: How Race Shaped Bush's Response to Katrina." (www.slate.com/id/2125812).

West, Cornel. *Race Matters*. Boston: Beacon Press, 1993.

Williams, Patricia. *The Alchemy of Race and Rights*. Cambridge, Mass.: Harvard University Press: 1991.

Wilson, William Julius. *The Truly Disadvantaged*. Reprint. Chicago, University of Chicago Press, 1987.

Wolfe, Tom, *Radical Chic & Mau-Mauing the Flak Catchers*. New York: Farrar, Straus and Giroux, 1970.

————. *The Purple Decades: A Reader*. Reprint. New York: Berkley, 1987.

■ ACKNOWLEDGMENTS

People often say that writing is a solitary effort—hours spent alone, quill in fist, parchment on the writing blotter (or fingers poised over the keyboard, eyes fixed on the screen). But this is only half true. Successful books are group efforts: conversations inspire ideas; discussions while the work is in progress improve them; editors temper polemical excesses and correct potentially embarrassing errors. *The Race Card* has benefited from the very best of all of these helpful influences: its virtues are much to their credit and its flaws are probably entirely the result of my failure to exploit them.

Here are some of those influences, in no particular order.

I gave lectures based on chapters of this book at the Stanford Law School, the Harvard Law School, and the American University's Washington College of Law. I received extremely useful feedback each time.

My thinking about discrimination and bias has profited from the lectures and written scholarship of, and countless private conversations with, my colleagues at Stanford Law School. I should simply list the entire faculty, but even in such an outstanding group a few stand out. Mark Kelman has been a mentor and friend since I joined the faculty in 1994—his work analyzing federal antidiscrimination law—especially his book *Jumping the Queue,* coauthored with Gillian Lester—has formed the backbone of my thinking. Rick Banks has been a friend and collaborator, consistently challenging me with thoughtful, counterintuitive, and utterly convincing work. Barbara Fried—one of the most rigorous and serious humanists in the legal academy—has been a profound intellectual influence, a role model, a mentor, and a generous and charming friend.

Kathleen Sullivan was a supportive dean during her tenure; she encouraged both intellectual excellence and public relevance and thus helped inspire me to write a book for a popular audience. Larry Kramer has been a wonderful dean—thoughtful, intellectually engaged, patient, and generous with every resource a scholar might need.

I first began to think hard about the relationship between race and the law after taking a course from Randall Kennedy as a student at the Harvard Law School. His intellectual influence and guidance have continued ever since—he is a role model of intellectual curiosity, integrity, and courage. I've been engaged by many conversations and constructive disagreements about the nature of bias and the limits of the law with Kenji Yoshino of the Yale Law School. My thinking about race and the law owes a great deal to Reva Siegel and Robert Post of the Yale Law School; my discussion of appearance discrimination in particular was heavily influenced by Post's excellent book *Prejudicial Appearances.*

My fusion of social criticism, political philosophy, and legal analysis reflects the profound influence of two of Harvard Law School's most challenging and charismatic professors: Duncan Kennedy, a true polymath whose mastery of a wide range of intellectual traditions is matched only by his professional generosity and joie de vivre—I owe my career in academia to his help and encouragement, and a better mentor, friend, and occasional martini drinking companion I cannot not imagine; and Gerald Frug, whose wit, passion, and agile intellect transform any legal conflict into an urgent social drama—I owe my first and greatest intellectual interest, the intersection of law and urban studies, to his influence.

One influence deserves a paragraph of her own. I owe whatever ability I have to think clearly about the relationship between law and culture to my dear friend and former colleague Janet Halley, now, much to my personal regret, of the Harvard Law School. Janet has raised lucid thinking and intellectual courage to the level of what can only be called moral virtue (though she would resist such terms). She has a downright eerie instinct for the intellectually challenging and counterintuitive insight, a philosopher's sense of the profound, a comic playwright's sense of the absurd, and a poet's sense of the sublime. My analysis of racism by analogy owes its genesis to Halley's courageous and lucid article "Like Race Arguments," and my analysis of the connection between feminism and gay rights owes a great deal to her scholarship—especially her brilliant book *Split Decisions*—and to our many private conservations.

Farrar, Straus and Giroux has been exactly what a scholar needs from a publisher. From the beginning, FSG has believed in this project—not just in its potential to sell books but also in its potential to contribute to public discourse about race. Eric Chinski has been a sensitive and engaged editor: he's helped correct my excesses and obscurities while amplifying—but never distorting—my voice. Our many conversations have improved the book's substantive content as well as its exposition. My agent, Wendy Strothman, has done more than I imagined an agent could or would be willing to do—she took an interest in the project when it was just a few vague ideas expressed in a ten-minute conversation; she make sure it found, not just *a* publisher, but *the* right publisher; and she has continued to discuss it and help improve it as it has developed.

Finally, Marlene Williams Ford has given me her support, insight, enthusiasm, patience, and most of all, her love, and Cole Ford has offered his toddler's energy and love, and given me a healthy sense of perspective.

■ INDEX